# Applying International Financial Reporting Standards: Financial Instruments

by

**Ian PN Hague**
*Principal, Accounting Standards Board – Canada*

LexisNexis™ UK

## Members of the LexisNexis Group worldwide

| | |
|---|---|
| United Kingdom | LexisNexis UK, a Division of Reed Elsevier (UK) Ltd, Halsbury House, 35 Chancery Lane, London, WC2A 1EL, and 4 Hill Street, Edinburgh EH2 3JZ |
| Argentina | LexisNexis Argentina, BUENOS AIRES |
| Australia | LexisNexis Butterworths, CHATSWOOD, New South Wales |
| Austria | LexisNexis Verlag ARD Orac GmbH & Co KG, VIENNA |
| Canada | LexisNexis Butterworths, MARKHAM, Ontario |
| Chile | LexisNexis Chile Ltda, SANTIAGO DE CHILE |
| Czech Republic | Nakladatelství Orac sro, PRAGUE |
| France | Editions du Juris-Classeur SA, PARIS |
| Germany | LexisNexis Deutschland GmbH, FRANKFURT and MUNSTER |
| Hong Kong | LexisNexis Butterworths, HONG KONG |
| Hungary | HVG-Orac, BUDAPEST |
| India | LexisNexis Butterworths, NEW DELHI |
| Ireland | LexisNexis, DUBLIN |
| Italy | Giuffrè Editore, MILAN |
| Malaysia | Malayan Law Journal Sdn Bhd, KUALA LUMPUR |
| New Zealand | LexisNexis Butterworths, WELLINGTON |
| Poland | Wydawnictwo Prawnicze LexisNexis, WARSAW |
| Singapore | LexisNexis Butterworths, SINGAPORE |
| South Africa | LexisNexis Butterworths, Durban |
| Switzerland | Stämpfli Verlag AG, BERNE |
| USA | LexisNexis, DAYTON, Ohio |

© Reed Elsevier (UK) Ltd 2004
Published by LexisNexis UK

A CIP Catalogue record for this book is available from the British Library.

ISBN 0 7545 2257 1

Typeset by Kerrypress Ltd, Luton, Beds (www.kerrypress.co.uk)
Printed and bound in Great Britain by Hobbs the Printers Ltd, Totton, Hampshire
Visit LexisNexis UK at www.lexisnexis.co.uk

# Acknowledgements

I have often wondered why authors feel compelled to include acknowledgements and dedications in the front of their books. Now I know. It is not possible to write a publication like this without significant support from others. In this case I want to thank three individuals. First, I would like to thank Alex Milburn, who without the opportunity to learn from his vast experience during previous projects, such as those leading to the March 1997 Discussion Paper, 'Accounting for Financial Assets and Financial Liabilities', and the Financial Instruments Joint Working Group of Standard-setters' December 2002 Draft Standard and Basis for Conclusions, 'Financial Instruments and Similar Items', I would never have had the confidence to approach a task such as this. Secondly, I must thank my wife Donna and son Bryan, for putting up with my absence in my office as I worked on this book. Their support is very much appreciated.

I have also learned much from my colleagues – those at the Canadian Accounting Standards Board, those at the International Accounting Standards Board, and those with whom I have had the pleasure to work on various working groups and through numerous presentations on financial instruments. This book attempts to draw on all of those experiences, and to put the results in one place so that others may also benefit. Thank you to all who are dedicated to the cause of a single, high quality set of global accounting standards for financial instruments.

# Contents

Chapter 1

# Introduction

> 'A standard on financial instruments is an essential element of any complete set of accounting standards. Implementing IAS 39 certainly poses challenges, but this reflects the fact that derivatives today are complex instruments, and IAS 39 bridges the world of traditional cost accounting and a model that relies more on market values.'
>
> [Sir David Tweedie, IASB Chairman, 21 August 2003 (press release on introducing proposals to modify IAS 39 to enable fair value hedge accounting for a portfolio hedge of interest rate risk).]

## OBJECTIVE

**1.1**  The market for financial instruments has experienced tremendous growth over the past 20 years. Companies have moved from using only straightforward financial instruments, such as cash, trade accounts receivable and payable, long-term debt and investments in bonds or stocks and shares, to the adoption of sophisticated risk management strategies using derivatives and complex combinations of financial instruments. It is now possible to manage virtually any financial risk or speculate on key rates and prices in the increasingly global economy. However, while the types and availability of financial instruments have advanced considerably, traditional accounting recognition, measurement and disclosure principles have struggled to keep pace.

**1.2**  To address this inadequacy, the International Accounting Standards Board (IASB) has developed accounting standards dealing comprehensively with financial instruments. These are contained in two main standards: International Accounting Standard No 32, 'Financial Instruments: Disclosure and Presentation' (IAS 32) and International Accounting Standard No 39, 'Financial Instruments: Recognition and Measurement' (IAS 39). IAS 32 and IAS 39 are amongst the most complex of accounting standards but must be applied by most public companies in Europe, as well as many companies elsewhere, by 2005. The standards apply not only to complex financial instruments, such as derivatives, but also to more straightforward instruments, such as trade debtors, trade creditors and long-term debt.

**1.3**  The objective of this book is to provide a practical guide to the application of International Financial Reporting Standards (IFRS) for financial instruments –

1

primarily IAS 32 and IAS 39. Not only does it explain what the requirements are, but it also provides background on why the IASB reached the conclusions it did, and how to apply the requirements. The book seeks to explain the standards in user-friendly terms, in a manner that will enable the reader to understand the rationale behind the requirements, as well as what he/she needs to do to apply them. While it does not deal explicitly with issues for specialised industries, such as sophisticated banks and financial institutions, the principles and approaches discussed should be equally relevant to people seeking to understand the accounting for the first time and to those seeking to better understand the accounting, or to understand the improvements made to IAS 32 and IAS 39.

**1.4** IAS 32 and IAS 39 continue to be under development in some respects. However, the vast majority of the improved versions of the standards issued in December 2003 will be the standards implemented in 2005. This book takes into account developments to March 2004, including anticipating some clarifications that had been decided upon, but not yet issued, at that time. A company may need to check whether additional clarifications or amendments to the standards have been made since March 2004.

**1.5** The book commences with an overview of the standards, developed primarily for those unfamiliar with them. It also provides a brief introduction to the main types of financial instruments addressed by the standards. The remaining chapters then examine in some detail when to recognise a financial instrument in the financial statements, when to remove it from the financial statements, how to measure it once recognised, what to do with the gains and losses arising on the instrument while it is recognised, and when and how to apply hedge accounting, illustrating application of the standards and providing tips to be considered in applying them. The book also considers basic measurement techniques and disclosure requirements, as well as identifying significant differences from US and UK generally accepted accounting principles (GAAP). However, these differences are not comprehensive – there will inevitably be additional differences arising from the details of how standards are expressed and applied. The book concludes with a brief look at the future development of accounting for financial instruments.

**1.6** The book should be used in conjunction with the standards themselves. It does not purport to address every aspect of the standards. Neither does it deal with every aspect of implementation that may be discussed elsewhere in the standards. Ultimately, a company must apply the standards. While due care has gone into preparing the material in this book, if a company concludes that application of the standards results in a different conclusion from that illustrated in this book, it is the standards that must be adhered to.

**1.7** This chapter provides an outline of the development of IAS 32 and IAS 39, as well as a consideration of the principles underlying the standards – something that it is easy to lose sight of when considering the detailed requirements, but which can be valuable in understanding their intent.

THE DEVELOPMENT OF IAS 32 AND IAS 39

**1.8**  In 1988 the International Accounting Standards Committee (IASC) (the predecessor body to the IASB) commenced work to develop comprehensive standards to address the accounting for all financial instruments. The first phase of the IASC's financial instruments project culminated in 1995 with the publication of IAS 32, 'Financial Instruments: Disclosure and Presentation'. The Canadian Accounting Standards Board (AcSB), which had worked jointly with the IASC on the project, released an equivalent standard and since then other standard-setters have followed suit.

**1.9**  At the same time, the IASC had sought to develop standards for recognition and measurement of financial instruments. However, after two unsuccessful exposure drafts proposing to introduce a mixed cost/fair value model, the IASC and AcSB turned their attention to the development of a discussion paper. This discussion paper, 'Accounting for Financial Assets and Financial Liabilities' was issued in March 1997 and proposed a comprehensive fair value model for accounting for financial instruments, as well as making recommendations regarding hedge accounting, and recognition and derecognition of financial instruments. Respondents to the discussion paper proposals were almost unanimous in their support for comprehensive international standards on accounting for financial instruments. However, many respondents believed that further study was needed on the relevance of fair value measurement for all financial instruments, as well as the practical implementation of some of the proposals.

**1.10**  The IASC continued to explore a full fair value measurement model for financial instruments, in collaboration with representatives of standard-setting bodies from nine countries through the Financial Instruments Joint Working Group of Standard-Setters (JWG). In December 2000, the JWG published a draft standard and basis for conclusions, 'Financial Instruments and Similar Items'. That draft standard proposed far-reaching changes to accounting for financial instruments and similar items, including the measurement of virtually all financial instruments at fair value. In light of the comments received on the proposals of the JWG, and consultations with parties that would have been affected by the proposals, it is evident that significant further work is needed before a comprehensive fair value accounting model could be introduced. In particular, many commentators questioned the reliability of fair value measurement for some financial instruments and some questioned the relevance of measuring certain financial instruments at fair value. Commentators were also concerned that the proposed preclusion of hedge accounting would not reflect risk management practices and could result in income statement volatility that would be difficult to explain to users of financial statements.

**1.11**  In the meantime, the Financial Accounting Standards Board (FASB) in the US had introduced several standards in this area, including FASB Statement of Financial Accounting Standards No 107, 'Disclosures About Fair Value of Financial Instruments', FASB Statement of Financial Accounting Standards No 114, 'Accounting by Creditors for Impairment of a Loan', FASB Statement of Financial Accounting Standards No 115, 'Accounting for Certain Investments in Debt and Equity Securities' (FASB Statement 115) and FASB Statement of Financial Accounting Standards No 133 (as amended by FASB Statement of Financial Accounting Standards No 138), 'Accounting for Derivative Instruments and Hedging Activities' (FASB Statement 133), as well as related Emerging Issues Task Force (EITF) abstracts and guidance from its Derivatives Implementation Group (DIG). These standards are complex. However, some of the complexity is inevitable in a mixed-measurement model based in part on management's intentions for holding financial instruments and given the complexity of finance concepts.

**1.12** The IASC had agreed with the International Organization of Securities Commissions (IOSCO) that a standard on recognition and measurement of financial instruments was an essential part of a core set of standards that might be considered suitable for use in cross-border securities offerings. Towards the end of 1997 it became clear that a comprehensive fair value measurement model was going to be some time in development, and even longer in general acceptance. Therefore, the IASC concluded that it should develop recognition and measurement standards that reflected best international practice at that time – such best practice being, largely, the standards developed by the FASB in the US (as the only standard-setter to have issued final standards in this area).

**1.13** In early 1999, the IASC issued IAS 39. IAS 39 was developed based on guidance in US generally accepted accounting principles (US GAAP). It reflected a mixed-measurement model where some financial assets and financial liabilities are measured at fair value and others at cost or amortised cost depending in part on an entity's intent for holding an instrument. It also addressed recognition and derecognition of financial instruments and hedge accounting. Like FASB Statement 133, it too was supported by a body of implementation guidance in the form of questions and answers.

**1.14** In July 2001, the IASB announced that, as part of its initial agenda of technical projects, it would undertake a project to improve IAS 32 and IAS 39. The objective of the proposed amendments was to improve the existing requirements on the accounting and disclosure for financial instruments in IAS 32 and IAS 39. The improvements dealt with practice issues identified by audit firms, national standard-setters, regulators or others, and other issues identified in the IAS 39 implementation guidance process or by IASB staff. The improvements also eliminated or mitigated some differences between International Accounting Standards and US GAAP.

**1.15** The project provided a valuable opportunity for the IASB to step back and consider the overall package of standards on financial instruments, as well as world-wide experience in implementing the previous versions of IAS 32 and IAS 39. While fundamental reconsideration of the approach was not within the scope of the project, some significant improvements have been made to the standards which should assist their implementation. In some respects the standards may not appear to provide an 'ideal' solution, or may appear very complex to apply. However, as long as financial instrument contracts themselves are complex, and accounting continues to apply a mixed recognition and measurement model, some imperfections and complexity is inevitable. This book seeks to throw some light onto the reasons for necessary imperfections and to make some of the complexity clearer.

**1.16** The improvements were developed with a process of consultation and debate perhaps like no other in international standard-setting. Building on the experiences and consultations undertaken in developing the US standards on which IAS 39 was based, as well as numerous consultations undertaken in developing the previous two exposure drafts for recognition and measurement of financial instruments, and the 1997 discussion paper and December 2000 JWG draft standard and basis for conclusions, the IASB deliberated the improved standards over almost two-and-a-half years. The process involved public round-table discussions involving constituents from a wide variety of backgrounds, geographic locations and industry groups, and numerous private consultations with experts and with those who would be affected by the proposals. It also involved a full exposure process. The result was issued in improved versions of IAS 32 and IAS 39 in December 2003 (with modifications to some aspects of hedge accounting issued in March 2004), effective for years commencing on or after 1 January 2005.

**1.17** The resulting standards are likely to result in significant changes to existing practice, requiring complex implementation processes for many companies. However, the standards will significantly enhance the transparency of the use of financial instruments by companies. Although financial statement preparers and users alike may need to get used to greater volatility in profit or loss and equity, any such volatility should reflect that which arises from the financial risks to which a company is exposed, and users of financial statements will be able to better understand the manner in which a company manages its financial risks.

**1.18** Many choices will need to be made in implementing the standards. This book seeks to guide the reader through many of these choices and establish an informed basis for effectively applying the standards to a company's individual circumstances.

BASIC PRINCIPLES

**1.19** It is easy to get lost in the detailed requirements of IAS 32 and IAS 39 and to forget that they are built upon several key underlying principles. These principles are set out here as a reference point to which aspects of the remainder of the book will return to explain the reasons for particular approaches adopted in the standards. They may also assist in understanding the rationale for the standards, thus helping clarify the underpinning for the requirements in the reader's mind. Similar principles also underpin FASB Statement 133.

---

**PRINCIPLE 1**

Financial instruments and non-financial derivatives create rights and obligations that meet the definitions of assets or liabilities and, as a result, should be recognised in financial statements.

---

5

**1.20** Not only are derivatives assets or liabilities because they create rights and obligations, but all financial instruments falling within the scope of the proposals are also assets and liabilities. The IASB 'Framework for Preparation and Presentation of Financial Statements' defines 'assets' and 'liabilities' as:

> *'An asset* is a resource controlled by an enterprise as a result of past events and from which future economic benefits are expected to flow to the enterprise.'

[IASB Framework, paragraph 49(a)]

> *'A liability* is a present obligation of the enterprise arising from past events, the settlement of which is expected to result in an outflow from the enterprise of resources embodying economic benefits.'

[IASB Framework, paragraph 49(b)]

**1.21** In the case of a financial asset, it is the contractual right that gives rise to the resource (ie the expected future inflow of economic benefits) and an enterprise's control over that resource is usually specified by the financial instrument contract. When control is specified by the contract, the past event will be when the enterprise becomes a party to the underlying contract, because it is that event that establishes the rights that make up the asset. Similarly, in the case of a financial liability, the expected outflow of resources is defined by the contract, and the past event is becoming a party to a contract that allows the enterprise little, if any, discretion to avoid the outflow of resources it specifies.

**1.22** The ability to settle a financial instrument in a gain position by receiving cash, another financial asset or a non-financial asset is evidence of a right to a future inflow of economic benefits and is compelling evidence that the instrument is an asset. Similarly, the payment of cash, a financial asset or a non-financial asset that is required to settle a financial instrument in a loss position is evidence of an obligation to deliver economic benefits and indicates that the instrument is a liability.

**1.23** In accordance with this principle, all financial instruments and non-financial derivatives falling within the scope of IAS 32 and IAS 39 are recognised on the balance sheet – none are retained 'off-balance-sheet'.

---

**PRINCIPLE 2**

Fair value is the most relevant measure for financial instruments and the only relevant measure for derivatives.

---

**1.24** Fair values for financial assets and financial liabilities provide more relevant and understandable information than cost or cost-based measures. In particular, fair value reflects the current cash equivalent of a company's financial instruments rather than the price of a past transaction; it is the same no matter which company holds the financial instrument and it does not depend on the future use of the financial asset or financial liability. Consider, for example, an investment in shares as part of a retirement savings plan. In assessing how that investment is performing relative to other potential investments, one needs to know the current fair value of the investment. With that information, one can assess whether the change in fair value of that investment has yielded returns better or worse than alternative investments.

**1.25** Fair values are also the only relevant measure for derivative financial instruments. The cost of a derivative is often zero, yet a derivative generally can be settled or sold at any time for its fair value. Without measuring derivatives at fair value they are invisible on the balance sheet and gains and losses, which may change disproportionately in response to market movements, would be reported only when the derivative is settled or sold rather than in the period in which the change in fair value occurred. This information is essential for users of financial statements to understand the nature of the risk exposures associated with derivatives as well as the success, or otherwise, of the company in managing financial risks.

**1.26** Fair value measurement is also practical for most financial assets and financial liabilities. It can be observed in markets or estimated by reference to markets for similar financial instruments, or, if market information is not available, it can be estimated using other measurement techniques. Many companies have provided fair value disclosures for most financial instruments for several years.

**1.27** In accordance with this principle, derivatives falling within the scope of IAS 32 and IAS 39 are always measured at fair value, even when other exceptions are made – for example for hedge accounting. For other financial instruments fair value is used when reliable and most relevant.

---

**PRINCIPLE 3**

Only items that meet the definitions of assets and liabilities should be recognised as such in the balance sheet.

---

**1.28** If financial instruments are measured at fair value, then the losses or gains that result from changes in their fair values must be reported in the financial statements. Those losses or gains do not have the essential characteristics of assets or liabilities (see paragraph **1.20**). There is no future economic benefit associated with a loss. Neither can it be exchanged for cash, a financial asset or a non-financial asset to produce something of value, or used to settle liabilities. Similarly, there is no obligation resulting in an outflow of economic benefits in the future that results from a gain. There is nothing that has to be given up to settle a gain. Accordingly, losses or gains on re-measuring financial instruments do not constitute assets or liabilities that should be reported in the balance sheet.

**1.29** In accordance with this principle, gains and losses on changes in fair value are not deferred on the balance sheet. Such gains and losses are recognised either in profit or loss or in equity.

---

**PRINCIPLE 4**

Special accounting for items designated as being part of a hedging relationship should be provided only for qualifying items.

---

**1.30** When financial instruments are used together with other assets, liabilities or anticipated transactions, and those items are measured on different bases or recognised at different times, there is a demand for modifications to the basic method of accounting to adjust for these differences. This creates a demand for hedge accounting. Hedge accounting is an exception to the basic principles underlying the recognition and measurement requirements. Accordingly, it is applied only for certain qualifying items.

**1.31** This principle, therefore, results in the standards being very specific about the circumstances in which special accounting (hedge accounting) may be applied. A hedging relationship qualifies for hedge accounting only when the hedging relationship is:

(a)    clearly defined by designation and documentation;
(b)    reliably measurable; and
(c)    actually effective.

**1.32** There are a further two principles that underlie hedge accounting:

(a)    Since the objective of hedge accounting is to reflect gains and losses on exposures managed together in profit or loss at the same time, to the extent that a hedging relationship is effective, the offsetting gains and losses on the hedging instrument and the hedged item should be recognised in profit or loss at the same time.
(b)    To the extent that a hedging relationship is not effective, the profit or loss effects of that ineffectiveness should be recognised in profit or loss immediately.

**1.33** In accordance with these principles, hedge accounting matches recognition of gains and losses in profit or loss when, and only to the extent that, a hedging relationship is effective.

**1.34** Other principles underlie more detailed aspects of the standards. For example, the principles underlying the distinction between liabilities and equity are discussed in **Chapter 15**. Principles underlying derecognition of a financial asset are discussed in **Chapter 13**.

Chapter 2

# Overview of the requirements

INTRODUCTION

**2.1** All companies applying IFRS will be affected, to some degree, by the accounting requirements for financial instruments. In many cases there will be little change from current accounting treatments. However, for some companies, substantial accounting and system changes will be necessary to apply the requirements to many commonly occurring contracts.

**2.2** Many companies may already have been providing some information about financial instruments in their financial statements, in accordance with standards such as FRS 13, 'Derivatives and Other Financial Instruments: Disclosures', or IAS 32, 'Financial Instruments: Disclosure and Presentation'. However, unless a company previously adopted IAS 39, 'Financial Instruments: Recognition and Measurement', any recognition, measurement or hedge accounting policies previously adopted are likely to have been based on practice rather than the requirements of standards and might require modification or substantial change as a result of applying IFRS. Requirements to separately present financial liabilities and equity are also likely to be new and requirements for derecognition of financial instruments differ from those in current UK GAAP.

**2.3** A company with no financial instruments other than cash, trade debtors, trade creditors and debt will find little difference in accounting for these instruments. A company that invests in equity instruments, such as common shares, that holds or issues derivatives, or that actively trades other types of financial instruments, will probably be significantly affected by the requirements of IAS 32 and IAS 39.

**2.4** This chapter provides an overview of the requirements for accounting for financial instruments in IFRS and outlines an approach to help companies tackle implementation.

OVERVIEW OF FINANCIAL INSTRUMENTS
ACCOUNTING REQUIREMENTS

**2.5** The two main IFRS addressing financial instruments are IAS 32 and IAS 39. However, other IFRS, including International Accounting Standard No 21, 'The Effects of Changes in Foreign Exchange Rates' (IAS 21) and International Accounting Standard No 1, 'Presentation of Financial Statements' (IAS 1), also contain requirements that affect the accounting for financial instruments. For banks and similar financial institutions, International Accounting Standard No 30, 'Disclosures in the Financial Statements of Banks and Similar Financial Institutions' (IAS 30) specifies additional disclosure requirements.

**2.6** The objective of IAS 32 and IAS 39 is to enhance financial statement users' understanding of the significance of financial instruments to a company's financial position, performance and cash flows. IAS 32 specifies information required to be disclosed about a company's use of financial instruments, as well as how financial instruments should be presented in financial statements. IAS 39 specifies when a financial instrument is to be recognised on the balance sheet and at what amount. It also specifies when to remove a financial instrument from the balance sheet, and what to do with gains and losses arising while the financial instrument is recognised and when it is removed from the balance sheet. IAS 39 also deals with the circumstances in which hedge accounting may be applied and, if it is applied, how hedge accounting alters the normal accounting. The hedge accounting aspects of the standard need only be applied when a company chooses to apply hedge accounting.

**2.7** There are no exclusions from the scope of IAS 32 or IAS 39 for any type of company. Therefore, the requirements apply to all companies adopting IFRS.

**2.8** The improved versions of IAS 32 and IAS 39 become effective for annual periods beginning on or after 1 January 2005. Therefore, planning for their implementation should already have started or, if not, should be started very soon. Even though there continues to be some 'fine-tuning' of the standards, the basic requirements are unlikely to be changed and represent today's best practice in accounting for financial instruments. Any delay in planning for implementation is likely to be costly in the loss of time available to effectively make decisions about the many choices that are available as to how to account for certain financial instruments, as well as the time needed to gather information and implement systems in more complex situations.

APPLYING THE STANDARDS

**Step 1: Identify all financial instruments**

**2.9** The first step in applying the standards is to identify all of the financial instruments that the company has. Therefore, a company needs to understand the basic definitions of a financial instrument, financial asset, financial liability and derivative instrument, in order to ensure that all of the items that will be affected by the standards are identified. These are explained in **Chapter 3**.

**2.10** Financial instruments include cash, trade debtors and creditors, loans and notes receivable and payable, investments in stocks and bonds (including investments in common shares, bank term deposits, treasury bills, etc), as well as derivative contracts such as forwards, swaps and options. Therefore, even though a company may not actively enter into derivative contracts, it is likely to be affected by the standards to some degree. The standards also apply to some contracts to buy or sell non-financial items.

**2.11**   Even companies with no direct involvement with derivatives might have a derivative embedded in another type of instrument. Examples include investments in convertible debt and loans where the interest payments, or possibly the final principal amount, are linked to changes in the price of a commodity, equity or currency other than that in which the debt or loan is denominated. An embedded derivative appears as a feature in a conventional contract that changes key elements of the contract in response to changes in a specified rate, price, index, etc. Since the general requirement is to measure all derivatives at fair value, a company may need to separate derivatives embedded in any instrument classified as held-to-maturity investments, loans and receivables, available-for-sale financial assets or non-trading financial liabilities or in a non-financial instrument contract, and account for them at fair value through profit or loss (if they meet certain conditions). Companies also need to be aware of these requirements as they negotiate new loans, leases, insurance and other contracts. **Chapter 6** considers the requirements in detail.

**2.12**   A company will also need to understand which financial instruments are excluded from the scope. A number of financial instruments, whose accounting is addressed in other IFRS, are excluded from IAS 32 and IAS 39. These include interests in subsidiaries and joint ventures, employee benefit plan rights and obligations, insurance contracts, etc. **Chapter 4** considers scope exclusions, as well as the inclusion of certain commodity-based contracts within the scope.

**2.13**   Identifying all financial instruments will almost certainly involve a process of consulting with individuals outside the accounting department to ensure that all such instruments come to the attention of those responsible for the accounting. A company will, therefore, need to understand the types of instruments that it is searching for and explain in straightforward terms to others, who might not be familiar with accounting terminology, what those instruments are – particularly for more complex instruments such as derivatives and embedded derivatives.

### Step 2: Classify all financial instruments

**2.14**   The classification of financial instruments is a vital step in the accounting process, since it is this classification that will determine how the financial instrument is measured or presented on the balance sheet and when gains and losses are recognised in profit or loss. In many cases, the initial classification decision cannot be changed after the financial instrument is first recognised.

**2.15**   All financial instruments are classified as being in one of the following categories:

(a)   Financial assets and financial liabilities at fair value through profit or loss – all derivatives are in this category, as are any instruments that the company is actively trading. In addition, a company may choose to designate financial instruments when first recognised to be included within this category when that may assist with having a financial instrument accounted for on the same basis as other financial statement items that it is managing.

(b)   Held-to-maturity investments – this category is for fixed maturity financial assets with fixed or determinable payments that the company has the positive intention and ability to hold to maturity. A company uses this category only if it is virtually certain that it will hold the financial asset to its maturity. If there are significant sales of assets within this category before maturity it is necessary to reclassify all financial assets in this category to the available-for-sale category, unless the reason for the sales is outside the company's control.

(c)   Loans and receivables – this category is for non-derivative financial assets with fixed or determinable payments that are not quoted in an active market. There is no need for a fixed maturity. Trade debtors, as well as longer-term loans receivable, would generally be included in this category. Alternatively, loans and receivables may be designated as at fair value through profit or loss or available for sale.

(d)   Available-for-sale financial assets – this category includes all financial assets that are not classified as at fair value through profit or loss, held-to-maturity investments, or loans and receivables. It will generally include investments in equity instruments, since these may only be classified as at fair value through profit or loss or available for sale, but might also include debt instruments that an entity does not wish to classify as held to maturity.

These classifications are discussed in more detail in **Chapter 5**.

**2.16**   It is also necessary for an issuer of a financial instrument to classify financial liabilities and equity separately for presentation purposes. This might involve separating parts of an instrument that contains both liability and equity components. This classification will also have an effect on the resultant profit or loss effects and may result in companies having to reconsider debt covenants if the amount classified as financial liabilities or equity changes significantly. **Chapter 15** addresses this classification more comprehensively.

**Step 3: Record the financial instrument on the balance sheet**

**2.17**   All financial assets and liabilities are recognised on the balance sheet. They are initially measured at their fair value when the company becomes a party to the contract creating the item. Most of the time this will be the cash paid or received. However, if the instrument is constructed in a way which confers an apparent benefit on one of the parties (usually by incorporating 'off-market' rates, such as in the case of an interest-free loan), fair value must be determined with reference to fair value prices for the risks involved. In many cases this will require discounting future cash flows at a fair market rate with the resultant premium or discount recognised in a manner consistent with the substance of the transaction. **Chapter 7** addresses recognition and **Chapter 8** considers initial measurement.

### Step 4: Measure the financial instrument subsequently

**2.18** Subsequent measurement depends on the manner in which the financial instrument was classified in Step 2. Therefore, that classification decision has an important effect on the subsequent accounting for the financial instrument.

(a) All financial assets and financial liabilities classified as at fair value through profit or loss, including all derivatives and all available-for-sale financial assets, are measured at fair value.

(b) Held-to-maturity investments, loans and receivables and financial liabilities other than those classified as at fair value through profit or loss are measured at amortised cost. This will probably be little different from the manner in which such instruments are accounted for today.

(c) Investments in equity instruments for which fair value cannot be reliably measured[1] are measured at cost.

**Chapter 8** discusses subsequent measurement.

[1]    And derivatives with an underlying based on such instruments.

**2.19** For many financial instruments, calculation of fair value will require locating a reliable current price or rate. When a current price in an active market is not available, future cash flows are discounted using appropriate discount rates for the term of each cash flow. For more complex derivatives and other financial instruments it may be necessary to use valuation models. Some are relatively straightforward, such as certain option pricing models. However, others may require development of more complex instrument-specific models. Consistency in approach and, ideally, price sources is necessary for all. **Chapter 9** discusses fair value determination in more detail.

**2.20** Amortised cost is required to be determined using the effective interest method. This is illustrated in **Chapter 8.**

### Step 5: Recognise gains and losses

**2.21** Like the measurement requirements, the method of recognising gains and losses in profit or loss depends on the classification of the financial instrument.

(a) Instruments classified as at fair value through profit or loss, including all derivatives – all gains and losses are included in profit or loss in the period in which they arise.

(b) Held-to-maturity investments, loans and receivables, and other financial liabilities – amortisation of premiums or discounts using the effective interest method, and losses due to impairment, are included in current period profit or loss, as are most foreign exchange gains and losses in accordance with IAS 21. Other gains and losses are recognised only on removal of the instrument from the balance sheet.

(c) Available-for-sale financial assets – gains and losses, other than impair ment losses and foreign exchange gains and losses, are included in equity until the asset is removed from the balance sheet[1]. The premium or discount recognised on acquisition of a fixed income security is amortised to profit or loss as interest income or expense using the effective interest method. Losses due to impairment and foreign exchange gains and losses are included directly in profit or loss.

(d) Gains and losses on financial instruments classified as financial liabilities are recognised in profit or loss, whereas those classified as equity are recognised in equity.

Chapters **10** and **15** discuss these aspects in more detail.

**Figure 2.1: Summary of requirements for measurement and recognising gains and losses**

| | Categories | Initial measure-ment | Subsequent measure-ment | Gains and losses |
|---|---|---|---|---|
| Assets | Loans and receivables Held-to-maturity investments | Fair value | Amortised cost using the effective interest method | Recognised in profit and loss (P&L) during the year in which the asset is derecognised or impaired (foreign exchange and impairment recognised in P&L immediately) |
| | Available for sale | Fair value | Fair value[2] | Recognised directly in equity (foreign exchange and impairment recognised in P&L immediately)[3] |
| | Fair value through P&L | Fair value | Fair value | Recognised in P&L for the year |

| Categories | | Initial measure-ment | Subsequent measure-ment | Gains and losses |
|---|---|---|---|---|
| Liabilities | Fair value through P&L | Fair value | Fair value | Recognised in P&L for the year |
| | Other | Fair value | Amortised cost using the effective interest method | Recognised in P&L during the year in which the liability is derecognised or impaired (foreign exchange recognised in P&L immediately) |

[1] At the time of writing, the IASB was considering the possibility of introducing an option for gains and losses on available for sale financial assets, except for loans and receivables that are in this category by election, to be recognised in profit or loss in the period in which they arise, to allow those companies, such as investment funds, that wish to account for financial instruments in this manner to do so even though they might be unable to classify the financial asset as at fair value through profit or loss in accordance with paragraph **2.15**(a) above.

[2] Equity instruments for which fair value cannot be reliably measured are measured at cost even if the instruments are classified as financial assets available for sale.

[3] With possible option for gains and losses in profit or loss. See footnote 1.

## Step 6: Remove the financial instrument from the balance sheet

**2.22**   In many cases, the removal of a financial asset or financial liability from the balance sheet is straightforward. If the company no longer has any contractual rights or obligations associated with the financial asset or financial liability – if it has been sold outright, expired or otherwise disposed of in a manner that leaves the company with no further interest in the instrument – it is removed from the balance sheet at the time the sale, expiration or other event occurs.

**2.23**   However, in other circumstances a company may relinquish contractual rights or obligations to only part of a financial instrument, or assume other rights and obligations in exchange for those relinquished. In these situations the decision as to when to remove the financial instrument is more complicated. **Chapter 13** explains the process to be followed in determining when to remove the financial asset or financial liability in these circumstances.

## Step 7: Provide disclosures

**2.24**   Once a company has determined how to account for its financial instruments, it needs to consider how to provide information about those instruments in the financial statements that will enable a user to understand their use. Disclosure requirements are discussed in **Chapter 16**. These include not only information about the financial instruments themselves, but also the manner in which a company uses financial instruments in financial risk management. In some cases, a company will need to develop systems to gather the necessary information to provide the required disclosures.

## HEDGE ACCOUNTING

### Step 1: Understand risk exposures and their effect on financial statements

**2.25**  Hedge accounting is always optional. Therefore, it is considered separately in this overview. There is no requirement to adopt hedge accounting. However, many companies may wish to do so to some extent to reflect the effects of certain financial risk management strategies in profit or loss.

**2.26**  Hedging involves entering into one or more contracts designed to offset exposure to one or more risks. This is distinct from hedge accounting, which is special optional treatment available to ensure that the timing of the profit or loss recognition on the hedging item matches that of the hedged item. Accordingly, a company needs to evaluate the risks to which it is exposed and the manner in which it is managing those risks, and then consider whether it wishes to apply hedge accounting to reflect the effects of the risk management in profit or loss. Having made this evaluation, a company may decide not to adopt hedge accounting, or to adopt it only in limited circumstances. However, if it does choose to adopt hedge accounting, it must do so within the parameters laid out in IAS 39.

### Step 2: Designate and document the hedge relationship

**2.27**  Having decided to adopt hedge accounting, a hedging relationship must be designated and documented. This is because hedge accounting is optional. It is necessary to know whether a particular financial instrument is to be accounted for in accordance with hedge accounting or otherwise. Documentation includes the risk management objective and strategy for the relationship as well as the method for assessing the effectiveness of the hedge (the correlation of changes in fair values or cash flows of the hedged and hedging items) on an ongoing basis. Documentation and designation must be in place before entering into the hedging relationship. If it is not in place, hedge accounting is precluded. Advance planning is, therefore, essential.

### Step 3: Account for the hedging relationship

**2.28**  There are two primary types of hedging relationship. The accounting differs for each. Accordingly, a company needs to clearly identify the exposures to which it is applying hedge accounting.

**2.29**   A fair value hedge is a hedge of the exposure to changes in fair value of all or a portion of a recognised asset or liability or an unrecognised firm commitment attributable to a specified risk. In this case, all gains and losses from both the hedged item and the hedging item attributable to the hedged risk are recognised in current period profit or loss. This is accomplished by making an additional adjustment to the carrying amount of the hedged item for the gain or loss attributable to the hedged risk, and reflecting that adjustment in profit or loss in the same period as the corresponding gain or loss on the hedging item.

**2.30**   A cash flow hedge is a hedge of the exposure to variability in cash flows of a recognised asset or liability or a highly probable forecast transaction, attributable to a specified risk. In this case, the portion of the gain or loss on the hedging item determined to be effective is recognised in equity. Any ineffective portion is accounted for in the same manner as the instrument would be treated without hedge accounting. The accumulated gains or losses in equity are recognised in profit or loss in the same period that the resultant asset, liability or forecast transaction affects profit or loss. A hedge of a net investment in a self-sustaining foreign operation is treated in a similar manner.

**2.31**   Throughout the hedging relationship, a company is required to consider whether the hedge remains effective. Gains and losses resulting from any ineffectiveness are reflected in profit or loss. If the hedge relationship as a whole becomes ineffective, hedge accounting is discontinued.

## Step 4: Discontinue hedge accounting

**2.32**   When a hedging relationship becomes ineffective or is otherwise terminated – perhaps because the hedged or hedging item no longer exists or merely because the company chooses to no longer apply hedge accounting to that relationship – hedge accounting ceases. Hedge accounting generally ceases on a prospective basis, so that the accounting up to the date of discontinuance does not change. However, after that date, the hedging instrument and hedged item are accounted for in accordance with the normal requirements for those items, and the effects of the previous hedge accounting unwind in the manner in which they had originally been intended.

## Step 5: Provide disclosures

**2.33**   Because hedge accounting is optional, disclosure is required of the company's objectives and strategies employed as well as sufficient information to understand the effect of the hedge accounting.

**2.34**   **Chapter 12** provides more detailed consideration of the requirements for hedge accounting.

Chapter 3

# Financial instruments explained

---

Principal IFRS references:

- IAS 32, paragraphs 11, 13, AG3–AG24.
- IAS 39, paragraphs 5–7, 9, AG9–AG12.

---

## INTRODUCTION

**3.1**   Often, the first reaction when someone mentions financial instruments is to think of instruments such as derivatives. However, the term has a much more wide-ranging meaning. It includes not only derivatives, but also more straight-forward, everyday instruments such as cash, accounts receivable and payable, investments in bonds, stocks and shares, and loans payable and receivable. For the most part, application of IAS 32 and IAS 39 may not change present-day accounting for many of these more straightforward financial instruments; but more of that later.

**3.2**   A basic understanding of what is a financial instrument and what is a derivative is vital to determining the application of IAS 32 and IAS 39 to any company's circumstances. All companies will have some financial instruments. Many companies may have derivatives. Understanding what these are is the starting point for understanding the effect of the accounting requirements.

**3.3**   This chapter considers the definitions of a financial instrument, financial asset, financial liability and equity instrument in IAS 32, and their application to common situations. It then considers the definition of a derivative, and its application, as well as briefly commenting on commodity contracts.

## DEFINITIONS

**3.4**   A financial instrument is defined, in IAS 32, as:

'any contract that gives rise to a financial asset of one entity and a financial liability or equity instrument of another entity.'

[IAS 32, paragraph 11]

19

Furthermore, IAS 32 defines a financial asset as:

'any asset that is:

(a)   cash;
(b)   an equity instrument of another entity;
(c)   a contractual right:

   (i)    to receive cash or another financial asset from another entity; or
   (ii)   to exchange financial assets or financial liabilities with another entity under conditions that are potentially favourable to the entity; or

(d)   a contract that will or may be settled in the entity's own equity instruments and is:

   (i)    a non-derivative for which the entity is or may be obliged to receive a variable number of the entity's own equity instruments; or
   (ii)   a derivative that will or may be settled other than by the exchange of a fixed amount of cash or another financial asset for a fixed number of the entity's own equity instruments. For this purpose the entity's own equity instruments do not include instruments that are themselves contracts for the future receipt or delivery of the entity's own equity instruments.'

[IAS 32, paragraph 11]

and a financial liability as:

'any liability that is:

(a)   a contractual obligation:

   (i)    to deliver cash or another financial asset to another entity; or
   (ii)   to exchange financial assets or financial liabilities with another entity under conditions that are potentially unfavourable to the entity; or

(b)   a contract that will or may be settled in the entity's own equity instruments and is:

   (i)    a non-derivative for which the entity is or may be obliged to deliver a variable number of the entity's own equity instruments; or
   (ii)   a derivative that will or may be settled other than by the exchange of a fixed amount of cash or another financial asset for a fixed number of the entity's own equity instruments. For this purpose the entity's own equity instruments do not include instruments that are themselves contracts for the future receipt or delivery of the entity's own equity instruments.'

[IAS 32, paragraph 11]

**3.5**   While these definitions capture what the IASB requires, they are not easy to intuitively apply. The following paragraphs discuss the application of these definitions in more detail.

## APPLICATION OF THE DEFINITIONS

### Cash

**3.6** The most basic financial instrument is cash. An English bank note evidences this in the form of the statement from the Bank of England, 'I promise to pay the bearer on demand the sum of [five, ten, twenty pounds, etc]', engraved directly on the note. It is a promise from the Bank of England to deliver, in return for presentation of the note.

**3.7** A deposit of cash with a bank or other deposit-taking institution is a financial asset of the depositor because it represents the contractual right of the depositor to receive cash from the institution or to draw a cheque or similar instrument against the balance in favour of a creditor in payment of a financial liability. Similarly, the deposit is a financial liability of the bank, being a contractual obligation to deliver cash when demanded by the depositor.

### Receivables and payables

**3.8** A number of common financial instruments involve one party having a contractual right to receive (or obligation to deliver) cash in the future which is matched by the other party's corresponding obligation to deliver (or right to receive) cash in the future. These include:

(a)   trade accounts receivable and payable;
(b)   notes receivable and payable;
(c)   loans receivable and payable; and
(d)   bonds receivable and payable.

These are commonly collectively referred to as debt instruments.

**3.9** The economic benefit to be received or given up does not have to be cash; it can be another financial asset.

### EXAMPLE 3.1

Company A has invested in a note receivable which requires another party to make payments to it in treasury bills. The note gives Company A the contractual right to receive, and the other party (the issuer) the contractual obligation to deliver, treasury bills, not cash. The treasury bills are financial assets because they represent obligations of the issuing government to pay cash. The note receivable is, therefore, a financial asset of Company A and a financial liability of the note issuer.

21

**EXAMPLE 3.2**

Company B borrows money from a bank at a fixed interest rate of 8 per cent per annum. The loan represents a contractual obligation for Company B to deliver cash (interest payments of 8 per cent per annum plus the repayment of the principal amount) to the bank. Therefore, it is a financial liability of Company B. It also provides a contractual right for the bank to receive principal and interest payments in the form of cash from Company B. Therefore, it is a financial asset of the bank.

## Equity instruments

**3.10**   An equity instrument is defined in IAS 32 as:

'any contract that evidences a residual interest in the assets of an entity after deducting all of its liabilities.'

[IAS 32, paragraph 11]

The most obvious example is common shares, but the definition also encompasses certain types of preferred shares and warrants or options to subscribe for or purchase common shares in the issuing company.

**3.11**   The definitions of a financial asset and a financial liability have been modified in the improved version of IAS 39 to specifically address contracts that will or may be settled in the company's own equity instruments. A company's obligation to deliver or receive a variable number of its own equity instruments is a financial asset or financial liability, rather than an equity instrument. However, if the obligation is for a fixed number of the company's own equity instruments, it is an equity instrument.

**EXAMPLE 3.3**

Company C enters into a contract to deliver 300 of its own common shares to another party in settlement of an obligation. The contract results in a distribution from the residual assets of Company C. It is an equity instrument.

**3.12**   An option or other similar instrument acquired by a company that gives it the right to reacquire a variable number of its own equity instruments is also a financial asset or financial liability of the company, rather than an equity instrument. However, if it is for a fixed number of the company's own equity instruments or for a fixed amount of cash or another financial asset, it is an equity instrument. In the latter circumstance, exercise of the option is not potentially favourable or unfavourable to the company since it results in a reduction in equity and an inflow or outflow of assets.

**EXAMPLE 3.4**

Company D enters into a contract giving it the right to repurchase up to 100,000 of its own shares at the then market price on a future date. The amount of cash that Company D will deliver to repurchase those shares at that date will vary depending on the market price of the shares. The contract is potentially favourable or unfavourable to Company D. It is a financial asset or financial liability.

**3.13** **Chapter 15** provides additional explanation of the distinction between financial liabilities and equity instruments from the perspective of the issuer.

## Derivative financial instruments

*Definition of a derivative*

**3.14** A derivative is defined in IAS 39 as:

'a financial instrument or other contract within the scope of this Standard ... with all three of the following characteristics:

(a)  its value changes in response to the change in a specified interest rate, financial instrument price, commodity price, foreign exchange rate, index of prices or rates, credit rating or credit index, or other variable, provided in the case of a non-financial variable that the variable is not specific to a party to the contract (sometimes called the "underlying");

(b)  it requires no initial net investment or an initial net investment that is smaller than would be required for other types of contracts that would be expected to have a similar response to changes in market factors; and

(c)  it is settled at a future date.'

[IAS 39, paragraph 9]

**3.15** Once again the definition is not altogether clear on its own, but a number of examples illustrate its applicability.

**3.16** Worth noting first is the fact that a derivative financial instrument meets the definition of a financial asset or financial liability. This is important, since all derivative financial instruments, therefore, qualify as items to be recognised on the balance sheet. On inception, derivative financial instruments give a company a contractual right to exchange financial assets or financial liabilities with another party under conditions that are potentially favourable or unfavourable to the company. Some instruments include both a right and an obligation to make an exchange. Since the terms of the exchange are determined on inception of the derivative instrument, as prices in financial markets change, those terms may become either favourable or unfavourable.

**3.17** The underlying on which changes in a derivative's value are based can be any variable whose changes are observable or can otherwise be objectively verified. Examples include:

(a)   an interest rate or interest rate index;
(b)   the price of a common share or stock exchange price index;
(c)   the price of a commodity or commodity price index;
(d)   a foreign exchange rate or exchange rate index;
(e)   a measure of creditworthiness;
(f)   an insurance risk index or catastrophe loss index; and
(g)   a climatic or geological condition (although excluded from the scope of IAS 39).

The underlying is often not delivered at settlement; it is merely the 'reference' by which value changes are calculated.

**EXAMPLE 3.5**

Company E enters into a foreign currency forward contract. The value of the contract varies based on changes in the relative exchange rate between two currencies. The underlying is the foreign exchange rate.

A non-financial variable may not be specific to a party to the contract. If it is, then the contract is an insurance contract, rather than a derivative. Such a non-financial variable may include the occurrence or non-occurrence of a hurricane that destroys an asset of a party to the contract. However, an index of hurricane losses in a particular region would not be specific to a party to the contract and thus, an instrument based on such a variable would be a derivative.

**3.18**   A derivative does not usually require an initial net investment of the notional amount. If that is the case, then the instrument does not meet the definition of a derivative. IAS 39, paragraph AG11 clarifies that whether a net investment is smaller than would be required for other similar contracts is to be evaluated on a relative rather than an absolute basis. Thus, the consideration is whether the value of the instrument in question varies in relation to the amount invested in a manner greater than a contract in the underlying.

**EXAMPLE 3.6**

Company F enters into a contract that gives it the option to acquire 1,000 shares in ABC Company at 35p per share, when the current price is 38p per share. It pays a fee of £50 to acquire the contractual right. The fee of £50 is less than the investment that would be required to obtain the shares themselves (£38,000).

**3.19**   The third criterion in the definition of a derivative is that the contract is settled at a future date. Of significance here is the fact that, unlike in US GAAP, settlement being net or gross does not affect determination of whether a contract is a derivative.

*Common types of derivatives – option contracts*

**3.20**  An option contract gives the option-holder the right, but not the obligation, to buy or sell an underlying instrument or commodity at a predetermined price, called the 'strike' or 'exercise' price. Options normally are in the form of a 'call' or a 'put'. Calls enable the holder to acquire the underlying instrument or commodity at the strike price. If the strike price is unfavourable to the option-holder, then they will not exercise the option and all that the contract will have cost will have been the, usually relatively small, upfront premium or fee. If the strike price is favourable, the option-holder will be able to benefit. Puts enable the option-holder to deliver the underlying instrument or commodity at the strike price. Again, the option-holder will be able to exercise the option if favourable, but would not generally do so if it is unfavourable.

**EXAMPLE 3.7**

Company G enters into a contract that enables it to buy a certain financial instrument for £10 per unit during a specified future period. If the market price per unit of that instrument falls below £10 per unit, it would not be beneficial to exercise the option. The company can buy the unit in the market for a lesser amount. Therefore, Company G would let the option expire and purchase the instrument in the market. However, if the market price per unit rises above £10 per unit, then the company can exercise the option to purchase the instrument for £10 – an amount less than the market price.

**3.21**  A company may either 'write' or 'purchase' an option. A written put option obligates the option-writer to buy an instrument or commodity for a fixed price in the future if the option-holder exercises the put. The other party to this contract – the option-holder – has a purchased put option – the right to deliver an instrument or commodity for a fixed price in the future. Similarly, a written call option obligates the writer of the option to deliver an instrument or commodity for a fixed price in the future if the option-holder exercises the call. The other party to this contract – the option-holder – has a purchased call option – the right to buy an instrument or commodity for a fixed price in the future.

**3.22**  An option meets the definition of a financial instrument because the option-holder has the right to obtain potential future economic benefits associated with changes in the fair value of the financial instrument underlying the contract. Conversely, the writer of an option assumes an obligation to forego potential future economic benefits or bear potential losses of economic benefits associated with changes in the fair value of the underlying financial instrument. The contractual right of the option-holder and obligation of the option-writer meet the definition of a financial asset and a financial liability, respectively.

**3.23**  An option contract may require the option-writer to issue another financial instrument rather than transfer a financial asset. However, the instrument underlying the option still constitutes a financial asset of the option-holder if the option were exercised. The option-holder's right to exchange the assets under potentially favourable conditions and the option-writer's obligation to exchange the assets under potentially unfavourable conditions are distinct from the underlying assets to be exchanged upon exercise of the option.

**3.24**   The nature of the option-holder's rights and the option-writer's obligations are not affected by the likelihood that the option will be exercised. If the contract is 'out of the money', ie it is currently more beneficial to undertake a transaction at the current market price than at the strike price specified in the option contract, it may have little value. However, this does not change the nature of the rights or obligations.

**3.25**   An option to buy or sell an asset other than a financial asset (such as a commodity) does not give rise to a financial asset or financial liability because it does not require the receipt or delivery of financial assets or exchange of financial instruments. However, as discussed in paragraphs **3.34–3.38** and in **Chapter 4**, many such contracts are included in the scope of IAS 32 and IAS 39, in addition to financial instruments.

*Common types of derivatives – forward contracts*

**3.26**   A forward contract differs from an option contract in that it obligates both parties to buy and sell instruments or commodities at a future date – whether or not the exercise is favourable to one or other party – whereas performance under an option contract occurs only if and when the holder of the option chooses to exercise it.

**EXAMPLE 3.8**

Company H enters into a contract whereby it promises to deliver, in three months' time, £500,000 in exchange for US$750,000, and the other party (the seller) promises to deliver US$750,000 in exchange for £500,000. During the three-month period, both parties have a contractual right and a contractual obligation to exchange financial instruments. If the £/US$ exchange rate moves to, say, 1:1.4 the conditions will be favourable to Company H and unfavourable to the seller (Company H will receive US$750,000 when the market price would result in delivery of only US$700,000). Correspondingly, if the £/US$ exchange rate moves to, say, 1:1.6 the effect will be the opposite (Company H will receive US$750,000 but the market price would result in delivery of US$800,000).

**3.27**   In this case, the purchaser (Company H in Example 3.8) has both a contractual right (a financial asset) similar to the right under a purchased call option and a contractual obligation (a financial liability) similar to the obligation under a written put option; the seller has a contractual right (a financial asset) similar to the right under a purchased put option and a contractual obligation (a financial liability) similar to the obligation under a written call option. As with options, these contractual rights and obligations constitute financial assets and financial liabilities separate and distinct from the underlying financial instruments (the currency amounts to be exchanged).

*Other types of derivatives*

**3.28** Most other types of derivatives are variations, or combinations, of options, forward contracts or non-derivative instruments. For example, a swap contract may be viewed as a variation of a forward contract in which the parties agree to make a series of future exchanges of cash amounts rather than a single exchange in the future. Futures contracts are another variation of forward contracts, differing primarily in that the contracts are standardised and traded on an exchange.

### EXAMPLE 3.9

Company I enters into a contract whereby it agrees to pay to another party a fixed rate of interest of 5.75 per cent based on a notional principal of £1,000,000 in exchange for receiving interest at a floating rate based on the London Inter-Bank Offered Rate (LIBOR) and a notional principal of £1,000,000. The parties to the contract do not exchange principal amounts. However, if LIBOR is above 5.75 per cent, Company I receives a payment based on the difference between LIBOR and 5.75 per cent. If LIBOR is below 5.75 per cent, Company I makes a payment based on the difference between LIBOR and 5.75 per cent. Payments may be exchanged on each payment date or the overall difference in payments may be accumulated for settlement at the end of the contract.

**3.29** Various risks may underlie derivative contracts. Common risks are foreign currency, interest rate and commodity price risks, but other risks may also be involved, such as prepayment risk, liquidity risk, etc. Risks may also be combined.

### EXAMPLE 3.10

Company J enters into a contract to exchange fixed rate interest, domestic currency flows for floating rate interest, foreign currency cash flows (a cross-currency interest rate swap). This contract involves both interest rate risk and foreign currency risk.

**3.30** Interest rate caps, collars and floors are contracts that place a floor or a ceiling on interest rate payments. A cap and a floor are essentially option contracts which provide the holder with the right not to pay interest at a rate above a specified rate, or to receive interest at no lower than a specified rate. A combination of a cap and a floor creates a collar, whereby interest payments remain within a specified range, by the use of two option contracts. Such contracts may also be based on underlying risks other than interest rates.

**3.31**   Loan commitments are also option contracts. Often a financial institution will give a borrower the right to enter into a mortgage contract at a specified interest rate if the borrower purchases a house within, say, 90 days. The borrower has entered into an option contract which may be valuable to it if interest rates rise but which it would not exercise if interest rates fall. Conversely, the financial institution has a risk that the borrower will exercise the option and it will be obligated to lend at a below-market interest rate.

**3.32**   Other examples of more complex financial instruments include:

(a)   a structured note (a debt instrument with an embedded option or swap contract);

(b)   a variation on the 'plain vanilla' swap (illustrated in Example 3.9), which may include embedded options or leverage features; or

(c)   a 'swaption', which is the option to enter into a swap.

**3.33**   There are an infinite variety of manners in which primary financial instruments (non-derivatives) and derivatives can be combined. This provides great flexibility to companies in managing risk positions, but can also result in accounting complexity. It is important that a company fully understands the risk that it is exposed to as a result of entering into financial instruments, as well as the accounting consequences.

## Commodity contracts

**3.34**   Contracts that provide for settlement by receipt or delivery of a physical asset only (for example, an option, futures or forward contract to acquire or sell silver) are not financial instruments. Such contracts do not give rise to a financial asset of one party and a financial liability of the other party, unless any corresponding payment is deferred past the date on which the physical assets are transferred. Such is the case with the purchase or sale of goods on trade credit.

**3.35**   Many commodity contracts are of this type. Some are standardised in form and traded on organised markets in much the same manner as some derivative financial instruments. For example, a commodity futures contract may be readily bought and sold for cash because it is listed for trading on an exchange and may change hands many times. However, the parties buying and selling the contract are, in effect, trading the underlying commodity. The ability to buy or sell a commodity contract for cash, the ease with which it may be bought or sold and the possibility of negotiating a cash settlement of the obligation to receive or deliver the commodity do not alter the fundamental character of the contract in a way that creates a financial instrument.

**3.36**   Some contracts are commodity-linked but do not involve settlement through physical receipt or delivery of a commodity. They specify settlement through cash payments that are determined according to a formula in the contract rather than through payment of fixed amounts.

**EXAMPLE 3.11**

Company K issues a bond whereby the principal amount of the bond is calculated by applying the market price of natural gas prevailing at the maturity of the bond to a fixed quantity of natural gas. The principal is indexed by reference to a commodity price but is settled only in cash. Such a contract constitutes a financial instrument.

**3.37**   The definition of a financial instrument also encompasses a contract that gives rise to a non-financial asset or liability in addition to a financial asset or liability. Such financial instruments often give one party an option to exchange a financial asset for a non-financial asset.

**EXAMPLE 3.12**

Company L acquires an oil-linked bond that gives it the right to receive a stream of fixed periodic interest payments and a fixed amount of cash on maturity, with the option to exchange the principal amount for a fixed quantity of oil. The desirability of exercising this option will vary from time to time based on the fair value of oil relative to the exchange ratio of cash for oil (the exchange price) inherent in the bond. The intentions of the bond-holder concerning the exercise of the option do not affect the substance of the component assets. The financial asset of the bond-holder and the financial liability of the bond-issuer make the bond a financial instrument regardless of the other types of assets and liabilities also created.

**3.38**   Although many commodity-based contracts are not financial instruments, IAS 32 and IAS 39 include within their scope those contracts that operate in the same manner as financial instruments (essentially those that are other than for physical delivery of the underlying commodity). This aspect is discussed in more detail in **Chapter 4**.

GAAP COMPARISON

**Financial assets, financial liabilities and equity instruments**

**3.39**   While the definitions of a financial instrument, financial asset and financial liability differ slightly from the manner in which those terms are used in US and UK GAAP, it is unlikely that any significant difference in application would arise.

**Derivatives**

**3.40**   The first two parts of the definition of a derivative in IAS 39 are essentially the same as the definition in FASB Statement 133. However, the third part differs.

**3.41**   Initially, it appears that the IASB definition would result in more items meeting the definition of a derivative than under the US definition, since it merely requires 'future settlement' rather than 'net settlement'[1].

---

[1]   FASB Statement 133 and 14 DIG issues provide extensive guidance as to what constitutes 'net settlement'.

**3.42**   The basis for conclusions to the exposure draft preceding FASB Statement 133 explains that the FASB included the net settlement provision:

> 'to exclude from the scope contracts that require ownership of the underlying or settlement by delivery of the underlying because (a) those contracts are difficult to distinguish from ordinary purchase and sale contracts and some insurance contracts and (b) the accounting for those contracts is not currently the subject of wide concern.'

> [FASB, 'Exposure Draft of Proposed Statement of Financial Accounting Standards, Accounting for Derivative and Similar Financial Instruments and for Hedging Activities' No 162-B, 20 June 1996, paragraph 66]

It subsequently turned out that many of the ordinary purchase and sale contracts that the FASB did not intend to include in FASB Statement 133 contained net settlement clauses, or there were other market mechanisms allowing net settlement. Accordingly, FASB Statement 138 was issued to modify FASB Statement 133 by explaining that 'normal purchases and sales' are not derivatives, so long as it is probable at inception and throughout the term of the contract that there will be no net settlement and the contract will result in physical delivery.

**3.43**   IAS 39 seeks to achieve the same objective in a different manner. Rather than incorporating the net settlement provision in the definition of a derivative, it excludes:

> 'contracts that were entered into and continue to be held for the purpose of the receipt or delivery of a non-financial item in accordance with the entity's expected purchase, sale, or usage requirements.'

> [IAS 39, paragraph 5]

**3.44**   In the vast majority of circumstances there will be no difference between the items accounted for as a derivative in accordance with FASB Statement 133 and those accounted for as such in accordance with IAS 39. However, the following paragraphs identify a few items where differences may arise.

**3.45**   An area where there might remain some difference between IAS 39 and US GAAP is with regard to certain financial instruments that require gross settlement. The Guidance on Implementing IAS 39, Section B.3, makes it clear that whether there is gross or net settlement is irrelevant to the definition of a derivative under IAS 39. It concludes that it makes no difference whether parties to an interest rate swap pay the interest payments to each other (gross settlement) or settle on a net basis. In many cases, the same result would be achieved under

FASB Statement 133. For example, one of the FASB's criteria for net settlement is, 'one of the parties [to a contract] is required to deliver an asset [that is associated with the underlying] … but that asset either is readily convertible to cash or is itself a derivative instrument' (FASB Statement 133, paragraph 9(c)). The interest payments of the swap are cash and hence the contract meets the FASB definition of a derivative. This seems a longer way to get to essentially the same answer. However, it also seems possible that, at least in theory, some contracts might be included in the IAS 39 scope but excluded from FASB Statement 133. This could lead to an instrument qualifying as a derivative in accordance with IAS 39 but not in accordance with US GAAP. However, it is worth noting that this situation is not one that has been identified as giving rise to issues in practice.

**3.46** Some have suggested that the IAS 39 requirement for settlement at a future date appears to exclude contracts for goods and services where the settlement amount is prepaid. This could lead to an instrument qualifying as a derivative in accordance with US GAAP but not in accordance with IAS 39. However, this has also not been identified as an issue in practice.

**3.47** It is also possible that a loan commitment that can only be settled by issuing a mortgage that will remain on the reporting company's balance sheet would be treated differently, since in accordance with US GAAP it would not meet the definition of a derivative as a result of the lack of the ability for net settlement whereas IAS 39 would treat such an instrument as a derivative.

Chapter 4

# Scope – inclusions and exclusions

Principal IFRS references:

- IAS 32, paragraphs 4–10, 14.
- IAS 39, paragraphs 2–7, AG1–AG4.

## INTRODUCTION

**4.1**  Before considering the rest of the requirements of IAS 32 and IAS 39 it is important to understand what is included in the scope of the two standards and what is not included.

**4.2**  The starting point is that IAS 32 and IAS 39 apply to all financial instruments (see the explanation of the definition of a financial instrument in **Chapter 3**) of all entities. Thus, IAS 32 and IAS 39 are likely to need to be considered to some degree by almost any company. There are no exclusions for any type of entity. The standards would apply to not-for-profit organisations and smaller entities[1], just as they would to any other entities. The standards also apply to partnerships, trusts, co-operatives, etc, just as they apply to incorporated entities. When this book refers to 'company' or 'companies' the analysis applies equally to these unincorporated entities.

---

[1]  The IASB has commenced a project considering the needs of smaller and medium-sized entities. The outcome of that project is not yet clear, but may result in some different requirements for such entities, although these are unlikely to be scope exclusions.

**4.3**  Some financial instruments are excluded from the scope of the standards. These are mainly items that meet the definition of a financial instrument, but are appropriately addressed by other IFRS, such as subsidiaries, associates and joint ventures, leases, and an issuer's own equity. In some cases items are excluded because they are the subject of another active IASB project, such as insurance contracts. Some circumstances are excluded from IAS 39 that are not excluded from IAS 32 because they relate to recognition and measurement only. Other circumstances are excluded because it is considered necessary for presentation and disclosure to be provided in the same manner as required by IAS 32 even though recognition and measurement is addressed in another IFRS, or is not yet dealt with in an IFRS.

**4.4**   In addition to financial instruments, IAS 32 and IAS 39 include in their scope certain contracts to buy or sell non-financial items, when those contracts can be settled in the same way as a financial instrument. This does not include, however, a contract for physical receipt or delivery of a non-financial item within a company's expected purchase, sale or usage requirements. Therefore, the standards do not affect inventory accounting, but they do apply to those companies that purchase or sell commodities in active markets.

**4.5**   It is important for companies to understand the financial instruments that they hold or have issued, in order to determine whether they fall within the scope of the standards. Most straightforward financial instruments, such as debt and equity investments, accounts receivable and payable, long-term debt, and most derivatives, etc will clearly fall within the scope. For other instruments, a company may have to carefully consider the scope inclusions and scope exclusions to determine whether IAS 32 and IAS 39 relate to them.

**4.6**   A company should also institute procedures to identify contractual relationships entered into by the company that may constitute or include financial instruments but which may not regularly come to the attention of those responsible for financial reporting. Certain commodity contracts (see paragraphs **4.39–4.45**) and embedded derivatives (see **Chapter 6**) are examples of instruments that may not ordinarily be identified as falling within the scope of the accounting requirements.

**4.7**   This chapter considers companies included in the scope, reviews the financial instruments excluded from IAS 32 or IAS 39 and discusses the extent to which contracts to buy or sell non-financial items are included in the scope.

## COMPANIES INCLUDED IN THE SCOPE

**4.8**   Both IAS 32 and IAS 39 apply to all companies. A financial instrument has the same economic benefits and risks, and is affected by financial market forces in the same manner, irrespective of the type of company that holds or issues it. Accordingly, the accounting is consistent with the attributes of the financial instrument rather than being based on the industry or type of company in which certain instruments may be prevalent. To the extent that a company enters into sophisticated financial instrument contracts, or elects to adopt hedge accounting, it will be affected by the more complex aspects of the standards. However, a company that enters into straightforward contracts only should not be affected by many of the more complex aspects of the standards. To some extent, complex financial instruments give rise to complex accounting.

**4.9**   No exemption from IAS 32 or IAS 39 is provided for any company on the grounds that it has specialised accounting practices. FASB Statement 115 excludes from its scope companies with specialised accounting practices that require substantially all investments in debt and equity securities to be measured at fair value or market value, such as brokers/dealers, defined benefit pension plans and investment companies. However, an exemption from IAS 32 or IAS 39 for such companies is unnecessary since an option to measure almost all financial instruments that such companies may hold at fair value with gains and losses recognised in profit or loss is available, thus enabling, but not requiring, such companies to measure all financial instruments at fair value if they so desire.

## SCOPE EXCLUSIONS

### Subsidiaries, associates and joint ventures

**4.10**   Interests in subsidiaries, associates and joint ventures are financial instruments. However, most such interests are accounted for in accordance with existing requirements in IAS 27, 'Consolidated and Separate Financial Statements', IAS 28, 'Investments in Associates' or IAS 31, 'Interests in Joint Ventures', for consolidation, proportionate consolidation or equity accounting and, hence, they are excluded from the scope of IAS 32 and IAS 39. The exception to this is for certain interests in subsidiaries, associates and joint ventures that IAS 27, IAS 28 or IAS 31 permit or require to be accounted for in accordance with IAS 39. These include the following:

(a)   an investment in a subsidiary in a parent company's separate financial statements. The parent company may choose to account for that subsidiary in accordance with IAS 39[1] (see IAS 27, paragraph 37);

(b)   an investment in an associate in an investor's separate financial statements. The investor may choose to account for that investment in accordance with IAS 39[2] (see IAS 28, paragraph 35 and IAS 31, paragraph 46); and

(c)   an investment in a subsidiary, associate or a jointly-controlled entity that is acquired and held exclusively with a view to its disposal within twelve months from acquisition and for which management is actively seeking a buyer. The investment should be accounted for as a financial asset held for trading in accordance with IAS 39 (see IAS 27, paragraph 16, IAS 28, paragraph 13 and IAS 31, paragraph 42).

In these cases the disclosure requirements of IAS 32, as well as those of IAS 27, IAS 28 or IAS 31, apply.

[1]   Alternatively, the parent company may choose to account for a subsidiary at cost.
[2]   Alternatively, the investor may account for an investment in an associate at cost.

**4.11**   In common with the basic principle that IAS 32 and IAS 39 apply to all derivatives, they also apply to a derivative with an underlying that is an interest in a subsidiary, associate or joint venture. However, when such a derivative is classified as an equity instrument of the company, the presentation and disclosure requirements of IAS 32 apply, but it is excluded from the scope of IAS 39.

### Leases

**4.12**   A company needs to take care with the scope of IAS 32 and IAS 39 for leases since, as will be explained in paragraphs **4.13–4.15** below, while most accounting for leases is specified in IAS 17, 'Leases', certain aspects of IAS 32 and IAS 39 do apply.

**4.13**   In accordance with IAS 17, a finance lease is accounted for as a sale with delayed payment terms. The lease contract is considered to be primarily an entitlement of the lessor to receive, and an obligation of the lessee to pay, a stream of payments that are substantially the same as blended payments of principal and interest under a loan agreement. The lessor accounts for its investment in the amount receivable under the lease contract rather than the leased asset itself. An operating lease, on the other hand, is considered to be primarily an uncompleted contract committing the lessor to provide the use of an asset (not a financial instrument) in future periods in exchange for consideration similar to a fee for a service. The lessor continues to account for the leased asset itself rather than any amount receivable in the future in accordance with the contract. Accordingly, a finance lease is considered to be a financial instrument and an operating lease is considered not to be a financial instrument (except as regards individual payments currently due and payable).

**4.14**   Since IAS 17 addresses accounting for leases, IAS 39 excludes from most of its scope any transaction accounted for in accordance with IAS 17. However, a lease contract might contain sets of rights and obligations that, if separated from the contract, would be a derivative. The embedded derivatives requirements of IAS 39 (see **Chapter 6**) apply to derivatives that are embedded in leases. In addition, there is no exclusion from the scope of IAS 32 for leases. Therefore, a company is required to consider the presentation requirements (probably limited to presenting a lease payable as debt rather than equity) and the disclosure requirements as they apply to leases.

**4.15**   The derecognition requirements of IAS 39 (see **Chapter 13**) also apply to lease receivables recognised by a lessor and finance lease payables recognised by a lessee. Furthermore, the impairment requirements (see **Chapter 8**) apply to lease receivables recognised by a lessor.

### Employee benefit plan rights and obligations

**4.16**   Most employers' assets and liabilities under employee benefit plans are financial instruments. However, these items present unique estimation and other issues that are addressed in IAS 19, 'Employee Benefits'. Thus, these items are excluded from the scope of both IAS 32 and IAS 39.

### Insurance contracts

**4.17**   Rights and obligations with insurance risk arising from insurance contracts are financial instruments. However, the IASB has a separate project that is considering the unique aspects of accounting for insurance contracts. Some aspects of that project have been addressed in IFRS 4, 'Insurance Contracts' issued in March 2004. However, the majority of the issues are being addressed in a second phase of the project to be exposed for comment sometime in 2005. Accordingly, contracts that are dealt with by IFRS 4 or are being dealt with by that project are excluded from the scope of the financial instruments project.

**4.18**    For purposes of this scope exclusion, the IASB has retained the definition of an insurance contract presently in IAS 32. However, it plans to replace this with a new definition once the second phase of its current project on insurance contracts is complete. Companies may wish to refer to the new definition and additional background about the definition being developed in that project to clarify marginal circumstances.

**4.19**    To ensure that a policy-holder cannot avoid accounting for a derivative embedded in an insurance contract in accordance with IAS 39, any derivative embedded in an insurance contract would be subject to IAS 32 and IAS 39, as would any contract that takes the form of an insurance (or reinsurance) contract but which principally involves the transfer of financial risks.

**4.20**    It should be made absolutely clear here that this scope exclusion applies to insurance *contracts* only. Any other financial instruments held or issued by an insurance *company*, including most of its assets, are subject to the requirements of IAS 39. The IASB is proposing, in the first phase of its insurance contracts project, to put in place certain requirements that will deal with the interaction between IAS 39 and other accounting practices for insurance companies, in time for application by those companies adopting IFRS in 2005. Standards more comprehensively addressing accounting for insurance contracts will then follow.

### Equity instruments issued by the reporting company

**4.21**    Equity instruments of the reporting company are subject to different measurement considerations than those relevant for financial assets and financial liabilities as a result of their nature as residual interests in the assets and liabilities of the company. Accordingly, such instruments are excluded from the scope of IAS 39 for reporting by the issuing company. IAS 32 addresses what qualifies to be presented as an equity instrument. Any instrument classified as an equity instrument in accordance with IAS 32, including certain options, warrants and other financial instruments based on a company's own equity, is excluded from the scope of IAS 39. A company considering this scope exception, therefore, needs to consider whether a financial instrument is presented as equity in accordance with IAS 32 (see **Chapter 15**) before determining whether it qualifies for exclusion from the scope of IAS 39.

### Financial guarantee contracts

**4.22**    Certain financial guarantee contracts are excluded from the scope of IAS 39 but not from IAS 32[1]. A financial guarantee contract is described as one that provides for specified payments to be made to reimburse the holder for a loss it incurs because a specified debtor fails to make payment when due under the original or modified terms of a debt instrument.

---

[1]    Note that on the issue of IFRS 4, 'Insurance Contracts', IAS 39 was amended to delete the scope exception for financial guarantee contracts, requiring that those

transferring significant risk to the issuer be accounted for in IFRS 4 and the remainder be accounted for in accordance with IAS 39. The IASB is expected to issue an exposure draft in April 2004 proposing to revert to the original text of IAS 39 and exclude such contracts from IFRS 4. Accordingly, this book discusses the original text.

### EXAMPLE 4.1

A common example of a financial guarantee is a contract whereby Company A guarantees repayment by one of its subsidiaries of loans made to that subsidiary by a financial institution.

**4.23**  The holder of such a guarantee (the financial institution in Example 4.1) does not account for the guarantee in accordance with IAS 39 – it accounts for the financial asset in accordance with the loan agreement instead. However, it may take the guarantee into account when determining whether its financial asset is impaired.

**4.24**  IAS 39 does address the accounting by the issuer of such a guarantee (Company A in the previous example). These requirements are contained directly in the scope section of the standard, but are discussed in **Chapter 8** of this book (see paragraphs **8.19–8.22**).

**4.25**  Note that a derivative with payments based on a change in credit rating, rather than a failure by another party to pay, is not subject to this scope exclusion and falls within IAS 39. Similarly, financial guarantee contracts that provide for payments to be made in response to changes in a specified interest rate, financial instrument price, commodity price, foreign exchange rate, index of prices or rates, or other variables, also fall within the scope of IAS 39.

### EXAMPLE 4.2

Company B enters into a contract that will result in a payment to another party in the event of a reduction in the credit rating of a third company's debt instruments. In this example, the triggering event is not the failure of the third party to pay the debt issuer, but the credit downgrade. This is not excluded from the scope of IAS 39.

### Contingent consideration in a business combination

**4.26**  A company that accounts for a business combination by the purchase method might issue financial instruments as contingent consideration for the purchase. The accounting for such contracts by the acquiring company is addressed in IAS 22, 'Business Combinations'. Accordingly, such contracts are excluded from the scope of IAS 32 and IAS 39. However, the acquired company applies IAS 32 and IAS 39 to such contracts.

**Contracts based on climatic, geological or other physical variables**

**4.27**    Contracts that require a payment based on climatic, geological or other physical variables are commonly considered to be insurance contracts. These may include contracts where the underlying is an amount of rain or snow in a particular location, the temperature in a particular location for a specified period of time, or the severity of earthquakes, hurricanes or other natural phenomenon. In many cases, the payment made is based on an amount of loss suffered by an insured party as a result of an underlying event. Such contracts are insurance contracts and they are excluded from the scope of IAS 32 and IAS 39, by the scope exclusion for insurance contracts, being accounted for in accordance with IFRS 4, 'Insurance Contracts'.

**4.28**    However, in accordance with some contracts, payments arise that are not based on a loss suffered by a party to the contract as a result of an event. For example, a contract might require a payment based on whether more than a specified amount of rain falls in a certain location during a certain time period, regardless of whether this causes a loss to the contract-holder due to flooding. Such contracts are economically no different from financial instruments such as conditional receivables. Accordingly, contracts based on such variables are included in the scope of IAS 32 and IAS 39, both from the issuer's and the holder's perspective.

**EXAMPLE 4.3**

Company C expects that if the maximum daily temperature in June is less than 20°C for more than 15 days it will suffer £100,000 in lost ice cream sales. Company C could enter into a contract that specifies that it would receive £100,000 if the maximum daily temperature in June is less than 20°C for more than 15 days. Alternatively, Company C could enter into an insurance contract that will reimburse it for lost sales. In the first case, the contract is included in the scope of IAS 32 and IAS 39 as the £100,000 does not have to correlate with lost sales, but in the latter case the contract is excluded from the scope of IAS 32 and IAS 39.

**4.29**    Other types of derivatives that are embedded in contracts excluded from the scope because they are insurance contracts are within the scope of IAS 32 and IAS 39 (see **Chapter 6**).

**4.30**    US GAAP results in similar treatment, since EITF 99–2, 'Accounting for Weather Derivatives' requires companies that enter into such contracts for trading purposes, or for the purposes of speculation, to account for such contracts at fair value.

**Loan commitments**

**4.31**    Excluding certain loan commitments from the scope of IAS 39 simplifies the accounting for both holders and issuers of commitments to issue loans. The effect is that a company does not have to recognise and measure the change in fair value of the loan commitment that results from changes in market interest rates or credit spreads prior to recognising the loan. This is consistent with the measurement of the loan that is originated when the holder of the loan commitment exercises its right to obtain financing, since changes in market interest rates do not affect the measurement of an asset measured at amortised cost (assuming it is not designated in a category other than loans and receivables).

**4.32** IAS 39 permits a company to measure a loan commitment at fair value through profit or loss, in which case it is subject to the standard. This may be appropriate, for instance, if the company manages risk exposures related to loan commitments on a fair value basis – perhaps using credit derivatives. In addition, if the company has a past practice of selling the assets resulting from its loan commitments shortly after origination, it is required to apply IAS 39 to all its loan commitments in the same class. Thus, the company may, for example, apply IAS 39 to commitments for mortgage loans that are regularly securitised, but not to other loan commitments.

**4.33** Further, a loan commitment is included in the scope of IAS 39 if it can be settled net in cash or another financial instrument. If the value of the loan commitment can be settled net in cash or by some other financial instrument, including by selling the resulting loan assets shortly after origination, it is difficult to justify its exclusion from the requirement to measure similar instruments that meet the definition of a derivative at fair value. IAS 39 explains that a loan commitment is not regarded as settled net merely because the loan is paid out in instalments (for example, a mortgage construction loan that is paid out in instalments in line with the progress of construction).

**4.34** Accounting requirements for a commitment to extend a loan at a below-market interest rate are contained directly in the scope section of the standard, but are discussed in **Chapter 8** of this book (see paragraphs **8.23–8.25**).

**4.35** Loan commitments are included in the scope of IAS 32. Hence, the presentation and disclosure requirements apply.

## Contracts with settlements based on the volume of items sold or services rendered

**4.36** Differences of opinion exist about whether contractual rights and contractual obligations that are contingent on the future use of, or right to use, a non-financial item are financial instruments. US GAAP excludes from the scope of FASB Statement 133 contracts that require a payment based on specified volumes of sales or service revenues of one of the parties to a contract and that are not traded on an exchange. This results in royalty agreements not being treated as derivatives under US GAAP. IAS 39 achieves a similar effect by noting, in paragraph AG2, that the standard does not change the accounting for royalty agreements based on the volume of sales or service revenues that are accounted for under IAS 18, 'Revenue'. US GAAP appears to exclude more contracts than IAS 39 since, for example, IAS 39 would include a foreign currency contract based on sales volume.

## Derivatives that serve as impediments to recognition of a sale

**4.37**   The existence of certain derivatives affects the accounting for the transfer of an asset or a pool of assets. For example, a call option retained by the transferor may prevent a transfer of financial assets from being accounted for as a sale (see **Chapter 13**). The consequence is that to recognise the call option would be to count the same thing twice. The holder of the option already recognises in its financial statements the assets that it has the option to purchase. Thus, those types of derivatives are effectively excluded from the scope of IAS 39, since they are not recognised as a derivative asset. Nonetheless, they would be subject to disclosure in accordance with IAS 32.

## Share-based payments

**4.38**   Generally, contracts for share-based payments are equity instruments of the issuer and are outside the scope of IAS 39. However, to the extent that they are required to be settled in cash or can be settled in cash at the option of the holder, they do not meet the definition of equity and, thus, would fall within the scope. The IASB issued IFRS 2, 'Share-based Payment' in February 2004. At that time, a consequential amendment was made to IAS 39 to explain that a contract falling within the scope of the new IFRS on share-based payment would be excluded from the scope of IAS 32 and IAS 39, unless the contract falls within the scope of IAS 32 or IAS 39 as a result of the inclusion of certain contracts to buy or sell non-financial items discussed in paragraphs **4.39–4.45**.

## CERTAIN CONTRACTS TO BUY OR SELL NON-FINANCIAL ITEMS

**4.39**   IAS 32 and IAS 39 apply not only to financial instruments. Some contracts to buy or sell a non-financial item (such as a commodity) may be settled net by a financial instrument. That could be because the terms of the contract explicitly permit, or implicitly allow, settlement in that way, or because there is an established market mechanism, or side agreement, outside the contract that facilitates settlement net by a financial instrument, or because the non-financial item that is the subject of the contract has interchangeable (fungible) units that are exactly the same as those for which an active market exists, in which offsetting contracts might be obtained. Although such contracts are not financial instruments, the distinction between such contracts and financial instruments for which the net settlement amount is indexed to an underlying price has little economic significance. In addition, if such contracts were not accounted for in the same manner as financial instruments, it would be possible to circumvent the requirements of IAS 32 and IAS 39 by including a non-substantive delivery provision in a contract that otherwise would be considered a financial instrument. Therefore, the scope of the standards includes such contracts.

**4.40**  Not all contracts to buy or sell a non-financial item are settled net by a financial instrument. Many are entered into for delivery of the non-financial item. It is not the IASB's objective to prescribe accounting principles for inventory or capital expenditures, for example, both of which are outside the scope of the project. Accordingly, contracts entered into and continuing to be held for the purpose of receipt or delivery of a non-financial item in accordance with the company's expected purchase, sale or usage requirements are excluded from the scope of IAS 32 and IAS 39.

**4.41**  IAS 32 and IAS 39 explain circumstances in which a contract to buy or sell non-financial items can be settled net in cash or another financial instrument or by exchanging financial instruments. These include:

(a)  when the terms of the contract explicitly specify that either party may settle net in cash or another financial instrument or by exchanging financial instruments;
(b)  when the company has a practice of settling similar contracts net in cash or another financial instrument or by exchanging financial instruments;
(c)  when the company has a practice of taking delivery, selling it within a short period for the purpose of generating a profit from short-term fluctuations in price or dealer's margin; or
(d)  when the non-financial item that is the subject of the contract is readily convertible to cash (for example it is gold).

**EXAMPLE 4.4**

Company D purchases coffee beans as an ingredient in manufacturing chocolate. To manage the price at which it purchases coffee beans, Company D frequently enters into forward contracts for delivery of coffee beans on the open market. Only when Company D requires the coffee beans for its manufacturing process does it take delivery. Otherwise it 'settles' the contracts by entering into offsetting contracts (exchanging financial instruments). Because the company has a practice of settling similar contracts by exchanging financial instruments, none of the contracts qualify for the 'normal purchases and sales' exemption. Hence they are within the scope of IAS 32 and IAS 39.

**EXAMPLE 4.5**

Company E, a brewer, has historically used approximately 500,000 kg of hops annually in brewing beer. Company E enters into a forward contract to purchase 400,000 kg of hops each year for the next three years. The price is fixed per kilogram, with delivery of the hops to Company E's brewery.

Unless there is a history of net settling contracts with similar terms and conditions, the contract is likely to qualify as a normal purchase, sale or usage contract and, thus, fall outside the scope of IAS 32 and IAS 39.

**4.42**   The dividing line between a contract falling within the scope of IAS 32 and IAS 39 and one that does not is fine. A company that trades commodities as well as using them in production processes will need to establish and document very clear policies on the purposes of its commodity contracts to ensure that it is clear which fall within the scope of the standards and which do not.

**4.43**   The terminology in IAS 32 and IAS 39 differs from US GAAP. In particular, US GAAP focuses on an asset to be delivered that is readily convertible into cash, rather than focusing on the company's past practice of taking delivery of the underlying and selling it within a short period after delivery for the purpose of generating a profit from short-term fluctuations in price or dealer's margin. US GAAP also requires that the basis for concluding that a contract is for the receipt or delivery of a non-financial item in accordance with its expected purchase, sale or usage requirements be documented. This provides a discipline to the assessment that contracts are for this purpose, as well as a verifiable source of evidence.

**4.44**   FASB Statement 133 specifies additional criteria that must be met in order to be excluded from the scope of that Statement. Accordingly, it is possible that a contract might fall outside the scope of IAS 39 but fall within the scope of FASB Statement 133. A company wishing to comply with US GAAP and IASB GAAP at the same time could identify the additional contracts included within the scope of FASB Statement 133 and account for them in accordance with that Statement without being in conflict with IASB GAAP.

**4.45**   Companies previously applying IAS 32 should note that the applicability of IAS 32 to such contracts is new: they were not previously included in the scope of IAS 32.

GAAP COMPARISON

**4.46**   A number of differences between the scope of FASB Statement 133 and IAS 32 and IAS 39, as they apply to derivatives, are noted in the text above. However, the biggest difference is the greater scope of IAS 39 to specify recognition and measurement requirements for all financial instruments, when compared to FASB Statement 115 (which deals only with certain debt and equity securities). Thus, a company applying IAS 32 and IAS 39 may have to apply those standards to more financial instruments than are addressed by US GAAP.

**4.47**   Furthermore, US GAAP does not have a standard comprehensively addressing presentation of financial instruments. Therefore, instruments falling within the scope of IAS 32 may be presented differently in accordance with IAS 32 compared to US GAAP.

**4.48**  *Scope – inclusions and exclusions*

**4.48**    Since UK GAAP does not have a comprehensive standard dealing with recognition and measurement of financial instruments, there is no comparable standard with which to compare the scope.

Chapter 5

# Classification of financial instruments

---

Principal IFRS references:

●   IAS 39, paragraphs 9, AG14–AG26.

---

## INTRODUCTION

**5.1**   The starting point for determining the accounting that will be followed for a particular financial asset or financial liability is to decide how that financial instrument will be classified. The choice as to which category to place a financial instrument in can significantly affect the resultant accounting for that instrument – whether it will be measured at fair value or amortised cost, and, if measured at fair value, whether gains and losses arising from changes in fair value will be recognised directly in profit or loss, or temporarily in the statement of changes in equity.

**5.2**   The decision as to how to classify the instrument generally has to be made before the instrument is acquired, originated or issued. Accordingly, careful advance planning is necessary to achieve the appropriate accounting.

**5.3**   This chapter describes and explains each of the four primary categories of financial assets and two categories of financial liabilities that will determine the accounting required by IAS 39. The classifications are derived from US GAAP (principally FASB Statement 115). There is no corresponding UK GAAP. Therefore GAAP comparisons are contained in each section of the chapter.

## CLASSIFICATION OF FINANCIAL ASSETS

### Four primary categories of financial asset

**5.4**   IAS 39 defines four primary categories of financial assets. These are:

(a)   financial assets at fair value through profit or loss;
(b)   held-to-maturity investments;
(c)   loans and receivables; and
(d)   available-for-sale financial assets.

Each of these categories is discussed in the next few sections.

**Financial assets at fair value through profit or loss**

*Overview*

**5.5** Financial assets classified as at fair value through profit or loss are required to be measured at fair value with all gains and losses arising from changes in fair value recognised in profit or loss in the period in which they arise. Certain financial assets must be included in this category, but others may be included by designation.

*Financial assets required to be classified as at fair value through profit or loss*

**5.6** Certain financial assets are required to be classified as at fair value through profit or loss. These are financial assets 'held for trading', defined as any financial asset that is:

'(i) acquired or incurred principally for the purpose of selling or repurchasing it in the near term;
(ii) part of a portfolio of identified financial instruments that are managed together and for which there is evidence of a recent actual pattern of short-term profit-taking; or
(iii) a derivative (except for a derivative that is a designated and effective hedging instrument).'

[IAS 39, paragraph 9]

**5.7** The measurement of all derivatives at fair value is consistent with the basic principle (see **Chapter 1**) that fair value is the only relevant measure for derivatives – it is the only measure that makes the exposures as assets or liabilities to which the company is subject at the balance sheet date visible on the balance sheet. Furthermore, unless the derivative is a designated and effective hedging instrument, in which case special accounting applies (see **Chapter 12**), gains and losses arising as a result of changes in fair value of a derivative represent economic events of the period in which they arise, and are recorded in profit or loss in that period. Thus, all free-standing derivatives and embedded derivatives that are required to be separated from their host contracts (see **Chapter 6**) are classified as held for trading.

**5.8** Companies may also manage financial instruments for trading purposes. For example, a bank or other financial institution will typically have a 'trading book' within which it actively buys and sells financial instruments with a view to making profits from those trading transactions. In such circumstances, the most relevant financial statement presentation for such items is at fair value through profit or loss. Indeed, that is the manner in which most such instruments are accounted for today by banks and similar financial institutions.

46

**5.9** The requirement to include financial assets in this category because they are acquired or incurred principally for the purposes of selling or repurchasing in the near term, or because they are part of a portfolio of identified financial instruments that are managed together and for which there is evidence of a recent pattern of short-term profit-taking, is a question of fact rather than intent – although professional judgment would need to be applied to determine whether an instrument meets the requirements. Past practices would be considered in determining whether a financial asset should be classified as held for trading in accordance with these requirements.

**5.10** An evaluation of those practices would consider the company's policies and procedures for using financial instruments in general, rather than the specific practice related to an individual instrument. Thus, if a company frequently trades financial instruments for short-term profit, it is more likely that additional financial instruments acquired for that purpose would be used for similar purposes than for a company that never undertakes such trading. Similarly, if a company enters into large numbers of financial instruments in excess of the normal volume that it has used in the past to manage its operational and financial exposures, this may be an indication that it has entered into financial instruments for trading purposes. Other indicators of trading may include the nature of the counter-parties to the instruments (for example, active dealers with high volumes of transactions), the management and organisational policies associated with such instruments (for example, management is remunerated based on profits arising from trading such instruments) or the nature of the contracts themselves (for example, commodity contracts that are not capable of physical delivery).

**5.11** The Implementation Guidance to IAS 39 explains that a financial instrument placed in a portfolio held for trading would itself be held for trading, even if it were held for a longer period of time (see 'Guidance on Implementing IAS 39', Section B.11). Section B.12 of the Guidance on Implementing IAS 39 also clarifies that buying and selling instruments to balance risks in a portfolio that is not otherwise held for trading does not necessarily result in the instruments bought and sold being classified as held for trading. The company would look to the overall purpose of the transactions, rather than merely the fact that buying and selling occurred. An investment in an investment fund or mutual fund is also not held for trading, merely because the assets in the fund are actively traded. The company holding the fund investment considers its practice regarding the investment in the fund – it does not look through the fund to the activities relating to the underlying assets.

*Financial assets designated as at fair value through profit or loss*

**5.12** In addition to those financial instruments required to be included in the category at fair value through profit or loss, a company may choose, on initial recognition of a financial asset falling within the scope of IAS 39[1], to designate it as one to be measured at fair value through profit or loss. This choice is available for any financial asset except for investments that do not have a quoted market price in an active market and whose fair value cannot be reliably measured (see **Chapter 8** for information about the circumstances in which fair value cannot be reliably measured)². However, once this category has been chosen for a particular financial asset, it must remain in this category until subsequent disposition or other derecognition. Thus, a company should take care in deciding whether to designate a financial asset to be classified as at fair value through profit or loss.

¹    See **Chapter 4** for an explanation of which financial assets fall within the scope of IAS 39.

²    At the time of writing, the IASB is considering placing some restrictions on the circumstances in which the option may be used. These may restrict the use of the option to circumstances in which the financial instrument contains one or more embedded derivatives, is a financial liability linked to the performance of assets that are measured at fair value, or the exposure to changes in fair value of the financial instrument is substantially offset by the exposure to changes in fair value of another financial instrument. This would not greatly restrict the legitimate use of the option to reflect risk management policies, but would preclude application of the option to only one part of a position, thus introducing volatility to profit or loss. In order to accommodate investment companies, and the like, the IASB is considering allowing an option for gains and losses on a financial asset classified as available for sale, other than a loan or receivable, to be recognised in profit or loss. The IASB is also considering restricting the use of the option to those circumstances when the fair value of the financial instrument is verifiable. An exposure draft is expected in April 2004.

**5.13** This represents one of the more significant changes to present practice. Among the benefits are the following:

(a) It mitigates problems arising from a mixed-measurement model where assets are measured at fair value and related liabilities are measured at amortised cost. In particular, it allows a company to eliminate the artificial volatility in net profit or loss and equity that results when matched positions of assets and liabilities are not measured consistently.

(b) It makes interpretive issues of what constitutes trading less significant.

(c) It reduces the burden of separating embedded derivatives, since they need only be separated when the contract as a whole is not measured at fair value.

(d) Permitting companies to designate at inception financial instruments as held for trading reduces the need for hedge accounting for hedges of fair value exposures and the resulting complexity in accounting for such hedges. The hedged item could, instead of being designated as a hedged item, be designated as held for trading to achieve symmetrical recognition of offsetting fair value gains and losses in the same periods, thereby eliminating the related burden of designating, documenting, tracking and analysing hedge effectiveness (see **Chapter 12**).

**EXAMPLE 5.1**

Company A has made several loans for which it is concerned about the ability of the borrower to repay. To protect itself against that risk, at the same time as entering into the loans, it enters into credit derivative contracts with a third party that will pay Company A if there is a decline in creditworthiness of the specified borrowers. In accordance with IAS 39, all derivatives are measured at fair value. Therefore, the credit derivatives are measured at fair value. However, loans and receivables are measured at amortised cost. Fluctuations in fair value of the credit derivatives will affect profit or loss immediately. However, similar fluctuations in the loans will not affect profit or loss in the same period.

Company A may elect to designate the credit derivatives as a hedge of the loans and apply hedge accounting as specified in **Chapter 12**. Alternatively, Company A may choose to measure the loans at fair value through profit or loss on initial recognition so that gains and losses on the loans are recognised in profit or loss in the same period as those on the related credit derivatives. This avoids the need for designation and documentation of a hedging relationship. However, it should be noted that the loans would be measured at fair value not only for changes in creditworthiness but also for other changes, such as interest rate changes. Therefore, a company needs to carefully determine the optimal strategy in such circumstances.

*US GAAP comparison*

**5.14** The ability to irrevocably elect, on initial recognition, that financial instruments be accounted for at fair value through profit or loss is not available in accordance with US GAAP. Accordingly, a company also desiring to apply US GAAP would probably not choose to use this option.

**5.15** Furthermore, even though the four categories into which financial instruments are to be classified in IAS 39 are derived from FASB Statement 115, they are of greater applicability, since IAS 39 applies these categories to all financial assets whereas FASB Statement 115 applies only to debt securities and equity securities with a readily determinable fair value. Thus, certain financial assets may be required to be accounted for at fair value through profit or loss in accordance with IAS 39, but not in accordance with US GAAP.

**Held-to-maturity investments**

*Overview*

**5.16** A financial asset classified as held to maturity is measured at amortised cost. Generally, this will be little different from the way in which such a financial asset is measured today. However, the strict 'tainting' provisions applying to this category (see paragraphs **5.23–5.29**) mean that a company must take care in deciding whether to include a financial asset in this category.

**5.17** IAS 39 defines held-to-maturity investments as:

'non-derivative financial assets with fixed or determinable payments and fixed maturity that an entity has the positive intention and ability to hold to maturity ... other than:

(a)   those that the entity upon initial recognition designates as at fair value through profit or loss;
(b)   those that the entity designates as available for sale; and
(c)   those that meet the definition of loans and receivables.'

[IAS 39, paragraph 9]

**5.18**   This definition reflects the view that when a financial asset is intended to be held to maturity, changes in the value of that asset while it is held are of limited relevance. However, in order for that view to hold, and for a company to classify a financial asset in this category, it must meet certain criteria:

(a)   it must have a fixed maturity with fixed or determinable payments; and
(b)   the entity must have both a positive intention and the ability to hold the asset to maturity.

The company is required to assess whether these criteria are met on initial recognition of held-to-maturity investments, as well as at each balance sheet date.

*Fixed maturity and fixed or determinable payments*

**5.19**   Without a fixed maturity and fixed or determinable payments, a financial asset cannot qualify to fall within this category. Equity instruments do not have a fixed maturity, or if they do – such as in the case of options, warrants and similar rights – they do not have predetermined payments. Therefore, they would not be classified as held-to-maturity investments. Many debt instruments may be candidates for inclusion in this category. However, a perpetual debt instrument would not qualify, since it has no maturity date. A significant risk of non-payment does not preclude classification as held to maturity, as long as the company intends to hold the instrument until maturity or non-payment arises.

*Positive intention to hold to maturity*

**5.20**   Rather than explain what constitutes a positive intention to hold a financial asset to maturity, IAS 39 focuses on those factors that do not constitute a positive intention to hold to maturity. If any of these factors are present, the asset cannot be classified as a held-to-maturity investment in the first place or, perhaps more seriously, can no longer be classified as a held-to-maturity investment if previously classified as such; at which time the tainting rules (see paragraphs **5.23–5.29**) take effect.

**5.21**   IAS 39 specifies that a company does not have a positive intention to hold a financial asset to maturity in the following circumstances:

(a)   The company intends to hold the financial asset for an undefined period.

Thus, it is insufficient for a company to be uncertain whether it will hold the asset for the entire period to maturity.

(b)  The company stands ready to sell the financial asset in response to changes in circumstances. Thus, it is insufficient for a company to state that it intends to hold the financial asset until maturity unless market conditions change (other than certain situations that are non-recurring and could not have been reasonably anticipated by the entity – see paragraphs **5.27– 5.28**).

(c)  The issuer has a right to settle the financial asset at an amount significantly below its amortised cost. The assumption here is that if this is the case then the issuer would rationally make such a settlement and, therefore, the company holding the instrument would be unable to hold the instrument to maturity. However, if the settlement would not be significantly below its carrying amount (after taking into account any premium paid and capitalised transaction costs), the held-to-maturity classification may still be appropriate.

(d)  The financial asset is puttable. In this case it is assumed that when a company pays for a put feature in an instrument it is an indication that it does not intend to hold the investment to maturity regardless of the circumstances. Note that this differs from US GAAP: FASB Statement 115 allows a financial asset that is puttable to be classified as held to maturity when the holder has the positive intent and ability to hold it until maturity.

*Ability to hold to maturity*

**5.22**  Not only must a company have a positive intention to hold a held-to-maturity investment to maturity, it must also have the ability to do so. A lack of ability to hold an investment to maturity may result from a lack of financial resources. For example, when it is evident that the instrument will need to be sold before its maturity for liquidity purposes, it would not be classified as held to maturity. An existing legal or other constraint, such as a requirement to dispose of an investment before maturity for legislative reasons that were known of at the time the instrument was acquired, may also demonstrate a lack of ability to hold the instrument to maturity. However, a disaster scenario that may be only remotely possible would not affect the classification. For practical purposes, if there is any known, more than remote, possibility that an entity would not have the ability to hold an investment to maturity, then this category would not be used, because of the effects of the 'tainting' provisions if that ability is no longer available.

*Tainting*

**5.23**  The so-called 'tainting' provisions in IAS 39 are intended to ensure that an entity cannot change its mind about whether an instrument is held-to-maturity at will. Although these rules are slightly more lenient than those in FASB Statement 115 (see paragraphs **5.24–5.25**), they are intended to be strict. Generally, any sales or reclassifications of more than an insignificant amount of financial assets out of the held-to-maturity category will result in an inability to use the held-to-maturity category for any financial assets for a period of two years. Thus, any other assets in the category would have to be reclassified as 'held for trading' or 'available for sale' and measured at fair value. There are some exceptions to the rule for circumstances outside the entity's control.

**5.24** The IAS 39 reference to 'more than an insignificant amount' of financial assets is to be assessed in relation to the total amount of held-to-maturity investments. Thus, this is likely to be an amount less than 'materiality' as it is commonly used for the financial statements as a whole. However, no guidance is provided as to what constitutes more than an insignificant amount. This also differs from US GAAP, since FASB Statement 115 does not contain any provision for a sale of an insignificant amount of held-to-maturity investments. A company also wishing to be in compliance with US GAAP would, therefore, apply the tainting rule more strictly.

**5.25** The two-year time frame after which 'tainting' is cured applies to the current financial year and the two preceding years.

**EXAMPLE 5.2**

Company B has sold more than an insignificant amount of held-to-maturity investments in its financial year ending 31 December 2005. Accordingly, it is not permitted to use the held-to-maturity category again until its financial year ending December 31, 2008.

The two-year time frame is a difference from US GAAP: FASB Statement 115 does not contain the ability for tainting to be cured after two years. A company also wishing to be in compliance with US GAAP would, therefore, be subject to a stricter requirement.

**5.26** The tainting provisions apply to the reporting entity as a whole. Thus, when tainting of the held-to-maturity category has occurred in a subsidiary company, the parent company is precluded from using that category for its consolidated financial statements (but not in its separate financial statements). It is, therefore, important that the circumstances in which the held-to-maturity category is to be used, and the consequences of breaching the requirements, are clearly understood throughout a group of companies.

*Exceptions to tainting*

**5.27** There are some exceptions to when the tainting provisions apply, mainly related to circumstances in which a held-to-maturity investment is sold for reasons outside the company's control, or when the effect would be immaterial.

**5.28** IAS 39 provides an exclusion for:

'sales or reclassifications that ... are attributable to an isolated event that is beyond the entity's control, is non-recurring and could not have been reasonably anticipated by the entity.'

[IAS 39, paragraph 9]

The standard continues to provide examples of sales or reclassifications as a result of:

(a)   a significant deterioration in the issuer's creditworthiness, such as a downgrade in rating by an external credit rating agency;
(b)   a change in tax law that eliminates or significantly eliminates the tax-exempt status of interest on a held-to-maturity investment;
(c)   a major business combination or major disposition necessitating a need to sell held-to-maturity investments to maintain the company's interest rate risk position or credit risk policy;
(d)   a change in statutory or regulatory requirements causing a disposition;
(e)   a significant increase in industry regulatory capital requirements causing sales; or
(f)   a significant increase in risk-weights of held-to-maturity investments used for regulatory risk-based capital purposes.

**5.29**   Sales or reclassifications that would not have a material effect on the financial asset are:

(a)   sales or reclassifications so close to maturity or the financial asset's call date that changes in the market rate of interest would not have a significant effect on the financial instrument's fair value (an example is provided in IAS 39 of 'so close to maturity' being less than three months, but whether three months is an appropriate period would depend on the magnitude of the premium or discount on the instrument and its overall terms, as well as other factors); or
(b)   sales or reclassifications occurring after the company has collected substantially all of the financial asset's original principal through scheduled payments or prepayments (FASB Statement 115 provides guidance that 'substantially all' constitutes at least 85 per cent. This guidance is not included in IAS 39).

*US GAAP comparison*

**5.30**   Even though the definition of a held-to-maturity investment is essentially the same as that in FASB Statement 115, FASB Statement 115 applies only to securities whereas IAS 39 applies to all financial instruments. Accordingly, more instruments may qualify for classification as held-to-maturity investments in accordance with IAS 39 than in accordance with US GAAP. However, there is no obligation to classify any financial asset as held to maturity. Therefore, possible GAAP differences should be capable of being avoided.

**5.31** Other differences between IAS 39 and US GAAP in this respect are mentioned in the text above. In summary, they are:

(a)  FASB Statement 115 allows a financial asset that is puttable to be classified as held to maturity when the holder has the positive intent and ability to hold it until maturity (see (d) in paragraph **5.21**), whereas IAS 39 precludes any puttable instrument from being classified as held to maturity.

(b)  FASB Statement 115 does not contain an ability to sell or reclassify an 'insignificant amount' of held-to-maturity investments before the tainting provisions apply (see paragraph **5.24**).

(c)  FASB Statement 115 does not contain an ability to reinstate the held-to-maturity category two years after a tainting (see paragraph **5.25**).

(d)  FASB Statement 115 provides guidance that collection of 'substantially all' of a financial asset's principal for an exception to the tainting provisions to apply means at least 85 per cent (see (b) in paragraph **5.29**).

**Loans and receivables**

*Overview*

**5.32**  Like the held-to-maturity classification, loans and receivables are measured at amortised cost – little different from the way in which such assets are measured today.

**5.33**  IAS 39 defines loans and receivables as:

'non-derivative financial assets with fixed or determinable payments that are not quoted in an active market, other than:

(a)  those that the entity intends to sell immediately or in the near term, which shall be classified as held for trading, and those that the entity upon initial recognition designates as at fair value through profit or loss;

(b)  those that the entity upon initial recognition designates as available for sale; or

(c)  those for which the holder may not recover substantially all of its initial investment, other than because of credit deterioration, which shall be classified as available for sale.'

[IAS 39, paragraph 9]

*No need for a fixed maturity*

**5.34**  The significant difference between this category and the held-to-maturity category is that loans and receivables do not need to have a fixed maturity. The accounting is the same as for a held-to-maturity investment, with the significant exception that 'tainting' provisions do not apply. Such provisions would not be possible when there is no fixed maturity and are not practical for many loans and receivables, which may be frequently settled before maturity (for example because a homeowner moves house and decides to repay a mortgage loan early or a debtor settles an account receivable before the due date). Furthermore, such assets generally form part of a customer relationship and there is no active market for the asset. Therefore, there is no need to consider the company's intent and ability to hold such assets until maturity. This category may include investments in debt instruments (other than those quoted in an active market) and bank deposits, as well as more traditional loans and receivables.

*Instruments not classified as loans and receivables*

**5.35**   Certain financial assets that meet the definition of loans and receivables must be classified otherwise:

(a)   those quoted in an active market, which may be classified as held-to-maturity investments, at fair value through profit or loss, or available for sale;

(b)   those that the entity intends to sell immediately or in the near term, which are classified as held for trading; and

(c)   those for which the holder may not recover substantially all of its initial net investment, other than because of credit deterioration, which are classified as available for sale.

Also, a company may choose to classify any financial instrument that meets the definition of a loan or receivable as at fair value through profit or loss[1], or as available for sale, by designation on initial recognition.

[1]   The IASB considerations of restricting the ability to classify any financial instrument as at fair value through profit or loss, discussed in footnote 2 to paragraph **5.12**, may limit the ability to classify a loan or receivable as at fair value through profit or loss.

**5.36**   Like the held-to-maturity category, amortised cost accounting is considered the less desirable choice and, hence, every opportunity is provided to elect to measure loans and receivables at fair value. That said, it is likely that many companies will not avail themselves of this option unless it is, say, convenient to avoid the need for hedge accounting because a corresponding risk management position is also measured at fair value.

**5.37**   IAS 39 also specifies that an interest acquired in a pool of assets that are not loans or receivables, such as an investment or mutual fund, is not a loan or receivable. This seems to imply that one must look through the fund to its contents in this circumstance to determine whether the investment is one in loans and receivables.

*US GAAP comparison*

**5.38**   In accordance with US GAAP, loans that are securities would be generally accounted for in the same manner as under IAS 39. Such loans would not generally qualify for the category of loans and receivables in IAS 39 since they would be quoted in an active market. They would also be accounted for in accordance with FASB Statement 115, rather than FASB Statement of Financial Accounting Standards No 114, 'Accounting by Creditors for Impairment of a Loan', in accordance with US GAAP.

**5.39**   Loans that are not securities are excluded from the scope of FASB Statement 115 and would generally be carried at amortised cost less any impairment provision. Accordingly, most loans would be accounted for in the same manner. It may be questionable whether loans measured at fair value in accordance with IAS 39, for example because they are classified as at fair value through profit or loss, would be capable of being so measured in accordance with US GAAP. Therefore, such elections would not be made by a company seeking to comply with US GAAP as well as IFRS. A US GAAP difference may be impossible to avoid for those loans required to be classified as held for trading in accordance with IAS 39, for example because they are actively managed together with evidence of a recent pattern of short-term profit-taking.

**5.40**   In addition, US GAAP requires certain mortgage loans held for sale by a mortgage banking enterprise to be accounted for at the lower of cost or market value. This valuation may differ from both amortised cost and fair value.

**Available-for-sale financial assets**

*Overview*

**5.41**   A financial asset classified as 'available for sale' is, generally, measured at fair value but gains and losses resulting from changes in fair value, rather than being included directly in profit or loss, are temporarily recognised in equity through the statement of changes in equity[1]. There is an exception for investments in equity instruments that do not have a quoted market price in an active market, which would be measured at cost (see **Chapter 8** for further details).

[1]   As discussed in paragraph **5.12**, footnote 2, the IASB is considering introducing an option for gains and losses on available for sale financial assets, other than loans and receivables designated as such, to be recognised in profit or loss.

**5.42**   IAS 39 defines available-for-sale financial assets as:

'those non-derivative financial assets that are designated as available for sale or are not classified as:

(a)   loans and receivables;
(b)   held-to-maturity investments; or
(c)   financial assets at fair value through profit or loss.'

[IAS 39, paragraph 9]

*Examples*

**5.43** The most common instrument required to be classified as available for sale would probably be an equity instrument held as a portfolio investment, although other non-derivative financial instruments may be classified as available for sale by election.

*US GAAP comparison*

**5.44** This category is essentially the same as that in FASB Statement 115, although, as noted previously, FASB Statement 115 applies only to debt and equity securities, so additional financial instruments might be accounted for in this manner in accordance with IAS 39 rather than in accordance with US GAAP. There are also differences in the exceptions for measurement at cost. These are discussed in **Chapter 8**.

## CLASSIFICATION OF FINANCIAL LIABILITIES

**5.45** Most financial liabilities, including trade payables and long-term debt, would be measured at amortised cost representing little, if any, change from current practice. However, those financial liabilities that meet the definition of held for trading (see paragraph **5.6**) would be measured at fair value with gains and losses resulting from changes in fair value recognised in profit or loss in the period in which they arise.

**5.46** Like financial assets, a company may elect to designate a financial liability on initial recognition as one to be measured at fair value through profit or loss.[1]

---
[1] See paragraph **5.12**, footnote 2.

**5.47** Financial liabilities held for trading include:

(a) derivative liabilities that are not hedging instruments, such as a forward contract or swap contract whose value is unfavourable to the company at the balance sheet date;

(b) the obligation to deliver financial assets borrowed by a short seller (ie the obligation to deliver financial assets that the company does not yet own); and

(c) financial liabilities incurred with the intent to buy them back in the near term for purposes of short-term profit-taking (perhaps, trading in the issuer's own quoted debt instruments).

**5.48** It is the nature, or use, of the financial liability that determines whether it must be classified as held for trading, rather than the company's intent. IAS 39 notes that the fact that a financial liability is used to fund trading activities does not make that financial liability one held for trading.

## US GAAP comparison

**5.49** US GAAP does not address the measurement of non-derivative liabilities. Accordingly, a company may be required to classify a financial liability as held for trading in accordance with IAS 39, but not in accordance with US requirements. It is questionable whether it would be permissible to measure such a financial liability at fair value in accordance with US GAAP. Therefore, a company would probably not avail itself of the option to classify a financial liability as at fair value through profit or loss. A difference may arise for those financial liabilities required to be classified as held for trading in accordance with IAS 39.

## SUMMARY

**5.50** The following table summarises the potential classifications for various types of financial asset.

| Category/type of instrument | Held for trading[1] | Designated on initial recognition as at fair value through profit or loss[2] | Held to maturity (if have fixed maturity and positive intent and ability to hold to maturity) | Loans and receivables | Available for sale |
|---|---|---|---|---|---|
| **Derivatives** | ✓ | N/A | x | x | x |
| **Non-derivative debt instruments** | | | | | |
| ● With fixed or determinable payments quoted in an active market | ✓ | ✓ | ✓ | x | ✓ |
| ● With fixed or determinable payments not quoted in an active market[3] | ✓ | ✓ | ✓ | ✓ | ✓ (by designation) |
| ● Without fixed or determinable payments | ✓ | ✓ | x | x | ✓ |

| Category/type of instrument | Held for trading[1] | Designated on initial recognition as at fair value through profit or loss[2] | Held to maturity (if have fixed maturity and positive intent and ability to hold to maturity) | Loans and receivables | Available for sale |
|---|---|---|---|---|---|
| **Non-derivative equity instruments** | | | | | |
| • With a quoted market price or whose fair value is reliably determinable | ✓ | ✓ | x | x | ✓ |
| • With no quoted market price and whose fair value is not reliably determinable | ✓ | x | x | x | ✓ |

[1]     Any instrument acquired or incurred principally for the purpose of selling or repurchasing in the near term, or which is part of a portfolio of identified financial instruments that are managed together and for which there is evidence of a recent actual pattern of short-term profit-taking, must be classified as held for trading.

[2]     See paragraph **5.12**, footnote 2.

[3]     Except those for which the holder may not recover substantially all of its initial investment, other than because of credit deterioration, which are classified as available for sale.

**5.51**    Financial liabilities are classified in one of two categories:

(a)    derivatives, which must be held for trading (unless they are designated and effective hedging instruments); or

(b)    debt instruments, which may be designated as at fair value through profit or loss, or which may meet the definition of held for trading. Otherwise, they are accounted for at amortised cost.

Chapter 6

# Embedded derivatives

---

Principal IFRS references:

- IAS 39, paragraphs 10–13, AG27–AG33.

---

## INTRODUCTION

**6.1** The need to search for and identify embedded derivatives requires a company to institute procedures to ensure that all contracts that might contain embedded derivatives come to the attention of those who have the knowledge to determine the accounting consequences. This may require education of those outside the accounting department to identify embedded derivatives in contracts on an ongoing basis, as well as a search for such contracts on initially adopting IAS 39.

**6.2** IAS 39 requires that all derivatives within its scope are recognised and measured in accordance with the requirements of the standard. However, sometimes a derivative is not a separate contract, but is contained within a contract that also provides other rights and obligations – this is an 'embedded derivative'.

### EXAMPLE 6.1

Company A enters into a mortgage contract to finance the purchase of a building. The contract permits Company A to settle the contract before its maturity on payment of a specified amount that varies to compensate the issuer for the difference between the contractual interest rate on the mortgage and the current market interest rate. These rights constitute a prepayment option – a derivative contained within the contract that otherwise specifies the principal and interest amounts required to pay off the mortgage.

Many other contracts such as leases, insurance contracts or contracts for the purchase or sale of goods may include terms and conditions that are the same as a derivative, which vary based on variables such as interest rates, foreign currency rates or commodity prices.

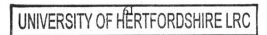

**6.3**   The basic principle that all derivatives are measured at fair value (see **Chapter 1**) could be circumvented if derivatives that are embedded in other contracts were to be excluded from the scope of IAS 39. Indeed, in the extreme, it would be possible to create a contract that operates in all principal terms as if it were a derivative, but by including some non-derivative terms (such as a small component of insurance risk) avoid the application of IAS 39 to that contract.

**6.4**   To avoid a situation whereby a company would be able to circumvent the recognition and measurement requirements for derivatives merely by embedding a derivative in a non-derivative financial instrument or other contract, and to achieve consistency in the accounting for such embedded derivatives, IAS 39 requires that embedded derivatives that would otherwise fall within the scope of IAS 39 be accounted for separately from the rest of the contract in which they are contained – unless the entire contract is measured at fair value with gains and losses reported in profit or loss. As a practical expedient, however, the proposals provide that an embedded derivative need not be separated when it is closely related[1] to the rest of the contract in which it is contained.

[1]   US GAAP refers to 'clearly and closely related'. On developing IAS 39, the IASC concluded that the words 'clearly and' were redundant, although the intent of the phrase is identical.

**6.5**   This chapter reviews common types of embedded derivative, the circumstances in which an embedded derivative is required to be separately accounted for and the accounting that is required in such circumstances.

## TERMINOLOGY

**6.6**   The following terms are used in explaining the accounting for embedded derivatives:

(a)   A 'hybrid contract' is the entire combined contract, containing the embedded derivative and other terms and conditions.

(b)   A 'host contract' is the part of the combined contract other than the embedded derivative (the contract in which the derivative is embedded).

(c)   An 'embedded derivative' is the derivative that is contained in the combined contract.

Host contract + embedded derivative = hybrid contract

**EXAMPLE 6.2**

In Example 6.1, the 'hybrid contract' is the mortgage contract as a whole. The 'host contract' is the part of the contract that specifies the principal and interest amounts required to pay off the mortgage. The 'embedded derivative' is the prepayment option.

## NEED TO SEPARATE AN EMBEDDED DERIVATIVE

**6.7**   There are three criteria that need to be evaluated in determining whether an embedded derivative should be accounted for separately.

**6.8**   The first step is to consider whether the entire hybrid contract is measured at fair value with gains and losses arising from changes in fair value recognised in profit or loss. When this is the case, then there is no need to account for the embedded derivative separately, since it will be measured at fair value with gains and losses in profit or loss as part of the measurement of the hybrid contract.

### EXAMPLE 6.3

Company B actively buys and sells mortgage contracts with a view to generating profits from short-term profit-taking. The mortgage contracts contain options to prepay at specified dates. Because the mortgage contracts are actively traded they are required to be classified as financial instruments held for trading, accounted for by measuring them at fair value with gains and losses from changes in fair value recognised in profit or loss (see **Chapters 5** and **8**). Accordingly, there is no need to separate the embedded prepayment option and account for it at fair value with gains and losses in profit or loss, since it will be accounted for in that manner as part of the hybrid contract.

**6.9**   The second criterion is whether the embedded derivative would meet the definition of a derivative on its own. In other words, does the embedded derivative change in value in response to changes in an underlying variable, does it not require an initial net investment (or one that is smaller than would be required for similar contracts) and will it be settled in the future? When these criteria are present, the embedded derivative would meet the definition of a derivative on a stand-alone basis.

**6.10**   The third criterion is to consider whether the economic characteristics and risks of the embedded derivative are closely related to those of the host contract. This is probably the most difficult of the three criteria to apply. The basic idea is that when the value changes of the derivative depend on the same factors as value changes in the host contract, they are considered to be closely related. However, when the value changes of the embedded derivative depend on different factors and, thus, have the potential to significantly modify the cash flows arising from the host contract, they are not closely related.

### EXAMPLE 6.4

Company C has issued a debt instrument containing an embedded derivative. If the embedded derivative varies based on changes in interest rates, inflation or creditworthiness, generally the embedded derivative would be considered to be closely related to the host contract, because these variables also affect the fair value of the host debt instrument. However, if the embedded derivative varies based on changes in value of an equity underlying, such as common stock, the equity underlying does not change in value in the same manner as the host debt instrument. Therefore, it is not closely related to the debt host.

**6.11** If all three of the above criteria are met, then the company is required to separate the embedded derivative from the host contract and account for it in accordance with IAS 39.

**Figure 6.1: Need to separate an embedded derivative?**

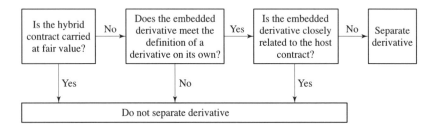

**6.12** The Application Guidance to IAS 39 provides an extensive list of examples of contracts in which the embedded derivative is, or is not, closely related to the host contract.

**EXAMPLE 6.5**

Examples of contracts in which the embedded derivative is not closely related to the host contract include:

(a)  An equity-indexed, or commodity-indexed, note for which principal or interest payments are based on changes in value of an equity security other than that of the issuer, such as the FTSE 100 index or the price of a commodity such as gold.

(b)  Debt with an option for repayment in a fixed amount of foreign currency.

(c)  A contract entered into by a UK company to purchase oil from another UK company, where the price will be denominated in South African Rand. The Rand is neither the functional currency of either party to the contract, the currency in which oil is normally traded in international markets nor the currency used in the company's local environment (ie the UK) for purchasing or selling oil. If the purchase were in US dollars, the contract would be considered closely related and the embedded derivative would not require separation because the US dollar is the currency in which oil is normally traded in international markets.

(d)  An investment in convertible debt which provides the investor with the option to convert its debt instrument into common shares of the issuer at an established conversion rate. Note that the investor would separately account for the derivative whereas the issuer would not, since the embedded option would be an equity instrument of the issuer, which falls outside the scope of IAS 39. (The issuer would present the separate components of the instrument as liabilities or equity in accordance with IAS 32 – see **Chapter 15**.)

(e) A prepayable debt instrument, unless the option's exercise price is approximately equal to the debt instrument's amortised cost on each exercise date. Thus, in a prepayable mortgage for which the penalty for prepayment is approximately equal to the loss that the issuer would incur as a result of the prepayment, there would be no need to separate the prepayment option. However, if the penalty is disproportionate to that loss, it may be required to be separated.

## EXAMPLE 6.6

Examples of contracts in which the embedded derivative is closely related to the host contract include:

(a) A debt instrument containing a derivative whose value varies based on changes in interest rates or an interest rate index, unless:
  (i) the contract can be settled in such a way that the holder will not recover substantially all (greater than or equal to 90 per cent) of its investment; or
  (ii) the embedded derivative could at least double the holder's initial rate of return on the host contract and could result in a rate of return that is at least twice what the market return would be for a contract with similar terms as the host contract.
(b) A contract to purchase a commodity, which contains a cap or floor on the price to be paid – provided the cap or floor is not leveraged and is out of the money at inception.
(c) A debt instrument for which principal or interest is payable in a foreign currency. There is no need to separate the embedded derivative because foreign currency gains and losses on the contract would be recognised in profit or loss, in accordance with IAS 21.
(d) A lease contract containing an inflation-price index, contingent rentals based on related sales or contingent rentals based on variable interest rates.
(e) An option to extend the term of a debt instrument, as long as the interest rate resets to a current market rate at the date the option is exercised.

**6.13** In practice, it may be difficult to identify embedded derivatives – particularly when first applying IAS 39. Derivatives may be embedded in contracts that have been entered into many years ago or in contracts that do not usually come to the attention of the accounting department, such as sale and purchase orders. Therefore, a company needs to put in place procedures to identify such contracts and bring them to the attention of those who can determine whether an embedded derivative exists. This may require educating other members of the company as to what to look for to identify a contract that may contain an embedded derivative.

**EXAMPLE 6.7**

The purchasing department of Company D enters into a contract with a supplier to purchase 100,000 units of product for £250,000 for delivery in 30 days. However, because the supplier has to acquire the raw materials to make the product from a foreign country, Company D also agrees that if the sterling/foreign currency exchange rate moves beyond a certain paramotor, Company D will make an additional payment to the supplier. This contract contains an embedded foreign currency derivative that would need to be accounted for from the date of entering into the contract. However, in normal circumstances the contract might not come to the attention of the accounting department until the purchase has been made in 30 days.

**6.14** A contract may contain more than one embedded derivative. When those embedded derivatives relate to different risk exposures and are readily separable and independent from one another they are separated. Embedded derivatives that are classified as equity, in accordance with IAS 32, are also separated from those that are classified as financial assets or financial liabilities.

**6.15** If a contract contains two or more embedded derivatives but one of them is excluded from the scope of IAS 39 (for example, it is an insurance contract), then only the embedded derivative that does not qualify for the exemption is required to be separated. This differs from US GAAP, which would require the predominant characteristics of the combined variables to be considered in determining whether the combined variable is an embedded derivative.

**6.16** There may be different ways in which a contract may be divided to separate a derivative. However, it must be divided in a manner such that an embedded forward or swap has a fair value of zero at inception. This prevents the creation of combinations of host contracts and embedded derivatives that create leverage or some other risk exposure not present in the hybrid instrument. It is also inappropriate to identify a cash flow that does not exist.

**EXAMPLE 6.8**

Company E has an equity-linked debt instrument whereby the principal to be paid at maturity is determined based on the change in an equity price index and interest payments are at fixed amounts. Company E might identify this as a fixed rate host contract with an embedded equity-based derivative. However, it would be inappropriate for the company to identify this as a variable rate host contract with an embedded equity swap because there are no floating rate cash flows in the hybrid contract.

## ACCOUNTING FOR A SEPARATED DERIVATIVE

**6.17** As noted in paragraph **6.11**, when the criteria discussed in paragraphs **6.8–6.10** are met, the company is required to separate the embedded derivative from the host contract and account for the embedded derivative in accordance with IAS 39. The host contract continues to be accounted for in accordance with whatever accounting standards apply to that instrument. Thus, when the host contract is a lease, it is accounted for in accordance with IAS 17, 'Leases'; when it is a financial instrument other than one measured at fair value with gains and losses in profit or loss when they arise, it is accounted for in accordance with the appropriate provisions of IAS 39.

**6.18** IAS 39 assumes that fair value can be reliably measured for all derivative instruments, except for certain derivatives whose values are based on changes in value of underlying, non-quoted equity instruments. Therefore, in the vast majority of cases it will be possible to determine the fair value of the embedded derivative. However, if it is not possible to determine the fair value of the embedded derivative, it may be possible to determine the fair value of the hybrid contract and that of the host contract – in which case the fair value of the embedded derivative is the difference between that of the hybrid contract and the host contract.

**6.19** If the company is unable to determine the fair value of either the host contract or the embedded derivative as a separate item, it is required to treat the entire hybrid contract (including both the host and the derivative) as a financial asset or financial liability that is held for trading. Thus, the entire hybrid contract is measured at fair value, with gains and losses arising from changes in fair value recognised in profit or loss.

## TRANSITION

**6.20** Derivatives may be embedded in many different types of contracts. A company should institute procedures to identify embedded derivatives. This may include considering any of the following types of contracts:

(a)   debt and equity instruments;
(b)   leases;
(c)   insurance contracts;
(d)   purchase and sale contracts;
(e)   service agreements (royalty, franchise, advertising, etc); and
(f)   financing arrangements.

**6.21** In some instances, it may not be practical to identify all embedded derivatives in existing contracts, some of which may have been entered into many years ago. US GAAP provides an option for a company not to account separately for some pre-existing embedded derivatives. However, no such option is provided in accordance with IAS 39, even for first-time adoption of IFRS. The IASB notes that if it is not practical to measure the embedded derivative, then the entire contract should be measured at fair value. However, it does not address circumstances when it is difficult to identify an embedded derivative. Presumably, if a company fails to identify an embedded derivative, and subsequently identifies that fact, it must treat the subsequent identification of the embedded derivative as a correction of an error in accordance with IAS 8, 'Accounting Policies, Changes in Accounting Estimates and Errors' with retrospective application unless impractical.

## GAAP COMPARISON

**6.22**   The requirements for embedded derivatives in IAS 39 are essentially the same as those in US GAAP. However, one important difference is the treatment of a sale or purchase contract that is not in the reporting currency of either party to the currency and is not routinely priced in this currency in international commerce. In addition to circumstances that are the same as US GAAP, IAS 39 states that an embedded foreign currency derivative in a host contract that is not a financial instrument is closely related to the host contract – provided it is not leveraged, does not contain an option feature and requires payments denominated in a currency that is commonly used in contracts to purchase or sell non-financial items in the economic environment in which the transaction takes place (for example, a relatively stable and liquid currency that is commonly used in local business transactions or external trade). US GAAP is more restrictive in that it allows only the use of the currency in which any substantial party to that contract measures the items in its financial statements (or the currency in which the price of the related good or service that is acquired or delivered is routinely denominated in commercial transactions around the world – such as the US dollar for crude oil transactions).

**EXAMPLE 6.9**

Company F, with a reporting currency in sterling, enters into a contract with Company G, whose reporting currency is the US dollar, to purchase product denominated in yen. Provided that yen is a commonly used currency for purchasing or selling that type of product in the economic environment in which the transaction takes place, an embedded derivative need not be separated. However, in accordance with US GAAP, it is likely that an embedded derivative would require separation, unless yen is the currency for routine, worldwide transactions in that product – an interpretation that has been strictly applied in accordance with US GAAP.

**6.23**   Accounting for embedded derivatives will be new to most UK companies. It is not a requirement that presently exists in UK GAAP.

Chapter 7

# Recognition

---

Principal IFRS references:

- IAS 39, paragraphs 9, 14, 38, AG34–AG35, AG53–AG56.

---

## INTRODUCTION

**7.1** The basic recognition requirement in IAS 39 is quite straightforward. A company is required to:

> 'recognise a financial asset or a financial liability on its balance sheet when, and only when, the company becomes a party to the contractual provisions of the instrument.'

[IAS 39, paragraph 14]

**7.2** This chapter discusses the implications of this requirement, as well as considering the exception for regular-way purchases and sales.

## BASIC RECOGNITION REQUIREMENTS

**7.3** The decision to recognise a financial asset or financial liability does not depend on whether a reliable measurement is possible. The IASB takes the view that it is possible to measure all financial instruments with sufficient reliability for them to be recognised. Sometimes subsequent measurement will be fair value. In other cases it will be another measurement basis, such as amortised cost or cost. However, in all cases a reliable measurement will be available.

**7.4** This means that all financial instruments are included on the balance sheet – a change for many UK companies that presently keep derivatives 'off-balance-sheet'. The contract establishing a financial instrument creates, at inception, rights and obligations to obtain or receive economic benefits resulting from the instrument. These rights and obligations are assets or liabilities of the company and, thus, qualify for balance sheet recognition. The act of becoming a party to a financial instrument contract (either initially on issue of the contract, or subsequently as a result of taking over rights or obligations arising from the contract) determines the time at which a company should recognise the financial asset or financial liability on its balance sheet.

### EXAMPLE 7.1

Company A purchases goods on credit. At the point in time when delivery of the goods reaches a stage where Company A has a legal obligation to pay for the goods, albeit at a future date, a financial liability is established.

### EXAMPLE 7.2

Company B enters into an agreement with a car dealer to purchase a particular car for an agreed price, for delivery in six weeks' time. At the time of entering into the agreement there is no obligation to be recognised as a liability by Company B or right to be recognised by the car dealer as an asset. However, once the car has been delivered (or is available for pick up), Company B has an obligation to pay for the car (and a financial liability is recognised) and the car dealer has a right to payment (and a financial asset is recognised).

**7.5**   Directly entering into a financial instrument contract, or other contract within the scope of IAS 39, establishes rights and obligations at the time of entering into the contract. Thus, on entering into a derivative contract, or a commitment to acquire or deliver non-financial items that can be settled net, a financial asset or financial liability is established immediately.

### EXAMPLE 7.3

Company C enters into a forward contract on 1 November 2004 to purchase US$60,000 on 31 March 2005 for £40,000. At the date of entering into this contract, Company C has an obligation to deliver £40,000 on 31 March 2005 and to receive US$60,000 on that same date – a right and an obligation. That right and obligation cannot be settled independently of one another. Therefore, only the net position is recognised as an asset or liability. At inception the value will often be zero. Nonetheless there is an asset or liability recognised.

### EXAMPLE 7.4

Company D enters into an agreement to purchase 300 tonnes of aluminium for a fixed price per tonne, for delivery in three months' time, by entering into a contract on the London Metals Exchange. Unlike the situation in Example 7.2, the contract is exchange traded and capable of being settled net before the three-month period expires. In this case, Company D has a contractual obligation to deliver payment for the aluminium and to take delivery of the aluminium, in accordance with the contract. Any gain or loss on the contract as a result of changes in price of aluminium is readily available to the company through the Exchange. Therefore, Company D has a financial asset or financial liability to be recognised as soon as it enters into the contract.

**EXAMPLE 7.5**

Company E enters into a contract that gives it the option to acquire 145,000 euros for £100,000 at any time from the inception of the contract until 31 March 2005. Company E has the ability to benefit from the contract as soon as it is entered into. Therefore, it recognises a financial asset from that time.

**7.6**   Future transactions for which there is no firm commitment, no matter how likely, are not recognised as financial assets or financial liabilities. There is no benefit or obligation to the company until it has entered into, or become a party to, a contract.

**7.7**   At the inception of a financial guarantee contract a guarantor recognises a liability for that guarantee, even though it is not probable that payments will be required under that guarantee. The asset recognised represents the guarantor's standby commitment to deliver if it is required to do so in accordance with the terms of the financial guarantee contract.

## REGULAR-WAY PURCHASE OR SALE OF A FINANCIAL ASSET

**7.8**   In accordance with the basic recognition requirement in paragraph **7.1**, a company would be required to recognise a forward contract whenever it enters into a transaction to buy or sell a financial asset in the future (the trade date). In regulated securities markets and the like, the time period during which a forward contract exists and the actual delivery of the financial asset (the settlement date) is often very short. Strict application of the principle would require a company to record a forward contract for a short period of time only. Therefore, IAS 39 provides an exception to the recognition principle, to permit a company to adopt settlement-date accounting rather than trade-date accounting for such regular-way transactions. In such circumstances, both sale and purchase contracts are accounted for in accordance with the chosen accounting policy. This exception does not apply to a contract that requires or permits net settlement of the change in the value of the contract. Thus, it applies primarily to purchases and sales of debt and equity instruments on organised exchanges. Furthermore, it does not apply to a contract entered into on an exchange for settlement other than in accordance with the regulations or conventions governing that exchange, or to a non-exchange contract that settles in a time longer than reasonably required for normal preparation and execution of documents to finalise the transaction.

**EXAMPLE 7.6**

Company F enters into a contract to purchase investments on an exchange where settlement is usually required three days following the trade date. However, Company F enters into an agreement that its contract should settle ten days following the trade date. The contract does not qualify as a regular-way purchase. Accordingly, it is accounted for as a forward contract prior to the settlement date, and as an investment at the settlement date.

**7.9**   Trade-date accounting results in a financial asset being recognised at the trade date, together with a liability to pay for it, or a financial asset being derecognised at the trade date, together with a receivable from the buyer and any gain or loss on derecognition. Settlement-date accounting results in a financial asset not being recognised until it is received by the company, and a financial asset being derecognised, together with recognition of any corresponding gain or loss, only when it is delivered. Sections D.2.1 and D.2.2 of the Guidance on Implementing IAS 39 contain detailed examples of trade-date and settlement-date accounting.

**7.10**   If a company makes an election settlement-date accounting, it is required to apply that accounting policy consistently to all purchases and sales of financial assets within a particular category of financial assets and to disclose its accounting policy for such transactions.

A NOTE ON HEDGES

**7.11**   Other amounts may be recognised on the balance sheet as a result of hedge accounting. For example, when a previously unrecognised firm commitment is designated as a hedged item in a fair value hedge, any change in the net fair value attributable to the hedged risk is recognised as an asset or liability subsequent to the inception of the hedge. Hedge accounting is discussed in more detail in **Chapter 12**.

GAAP COMPARISON

**7.12**   While US GAAP does not explicitly address recognition of a financial instrument, it is not expected that significant differences would arise between US practice and IAS 39.

**7.13**   US GAAP regarding trade-date and settlement-date accounting is very similar to that permitted by IAS 39.

Chapter 8

# Measurement

Principal IFRS references:

● IAS 39, paragraphs 2, 9, 43–47, 58–70, AG5–AG8, AG13, AG64–AG68, AG80–AG81, AG84–AG93.

## INTRODUCTION

**8.1**  The basic measurement principle underlying IAS 39 is that fair value is the most relevant measure for financial instruments. On initial recognition financial instruments are measured at fair value. However, for subsequent measurements there are significant exceptions, when an alternative measure is considered appropriate. Some financial instruments are required to be measured at fair value, some at amortised cost, and a few at cost. The manner in which a financial instrument is measured depends on its classification (see **Chapter 5**). Therefore, a company's decisions about how to classify a financial instrument will have a significant effect on the subsequent accounting measurement that is required – and, as a result, on the period in which gains and losses are recognised in profit or loss.

**8.2**  This chapter considers not only the basic measurement requirements on initial recognition and subsequently, but also provides guidance on when and how to undertake impairment testing. **Chapter 9** provides guidance on how to determine fair values.

## MEASUREMENT ON INITIAL RECOGNITION

**8.3**  On initial recognition, fair value of the consideration given or received should be readily determinable in all cases and is, therefore, the basis for measurement.

**8.4**  Fair value on initial recognition does not necessarily equal the face amount of a financial instrument. In some cases, a financial asset or financial liability may be acquired at what appears to be an amount that differs from fair value. In such cases, there is an additional factor to be considered and accounted for separately.

**EXAMPLE 8.1**

Company A receives an interest-free loan from a government agency. In the absence of evidence to the contrary, the difference between the fair value of the loan and the cash received is accounted for as a government grant.

**EXAMPLE 8.2**

Company B extends an interest-free loan to an employee. In the absence of evidence to the contrary, the difference between the fair value of the loan and the cash paid to the employee is accounted for as employee compensation.

**8.5**   Usually, the fair value of the financial instrument is that on the date it is initially recognised. However, when a company elects to use settlement-date accounting as its accounting policy for regular-way transactions (see **Chapter 7**) that are subsequently measured at amortised cost or cost (see paragraphs **8.11** and **8.13–8.15** for circumstances in which a financial asset may be subsequently measured at amortised cost or cost), the fair value on the trade date is the measurement amount on initial recognition.

**EXAMPLE 8.3**

Company C acquires a financial asset on 15 April 2004, for settlement on 17 April 2004. The financial asset is to be subsequently measured at amortised cost. Its fair value on 15 April 2004 is £1.20. Its fair value on 17 April 2004 is £1.22. Company C elects settlement-date accounting as its accounting policy.

Company C recognises the financial asset on 17 April 2004, but initially measures it at the fair value on 15 April 2004 (£1.20), which is the amount that it has paid for the asset.

**Transaction costs**

**8.6**   The fair value of a financial instrument does not include transaction costs. However, IAS 39 requires transaction costs that are directly attributable to the acquisition of a financial asset or issue of a financial liability to be included in the initial measurement amount, except for a financial asset or financial liability at fair value through profit or loss. This is consistent with the normal historical cost basis of accounting for held-to-maturity investments, loans and receivables and financial liabilities other than those held for trading.

**EXAMPLE 8.4**

Company D acquires a held-to-maturity investment for £100, with transaction costs of £2. The initial measurement amount is the fair value of £100, plus the transaction costs of £2.

**8.7**   For financial assets classified as available for sale, since such assets would initially be measured at their fair value plus transaction costs, but immediately thereafter would be subsequently measured at fair value, the initial transaction costs would immediately be adjusted to equity, resulting in an expense in the statement of profit or loss only if it was considered that impairment had arisen or the asset were subsequently derecognised. (In the previous example, if the instrument were classified as available for sale, the £2 would be included in the initial measurement of the asset, but the asset would be immediately written down to its fair value of £100 in the next period, assuming no other change in fair value, with the £2 charged to equity.)

**8.8**   It is possible that the treatment of transaction costs in some instances will differ from US GAAP, which is largely based on practice. In some instances that practice does not include transaction costs in the measurement amount on initial recognition.

## SUBSEQUENT MEASUREMENT

**8.9**   Subsequent measurement depends, primarily, on the manner in which a financial asset or financial liability has been classified (see **Chapter 5**).

### Financial assets and financial liabilities classified as at fair value through profit or loss

**8.10**   There are no exceptions to fair value measurement for financial instruments held for trading or designated as at fair value through profit or loss. For such instruments, fair value reflects the purpose for which they are held. In particular, there are no exceptions for derivative financial instruments (except those with an underlying that is an unquoted equity instrument – see paragraph **8.12**) because fair value is the only method that provides sufficient transparency of derivatives in financial statements. In many cases the 'cost' of a derivative is a very small amount relative to the potential exposure that may arise. It is only by measuring these instruments at fair value that the exposure can be reflected in the financial statements.

### Held-to-maturity investments and loans and receivables

**8.11**   For held-to-maturity investments and loans and receivables, many expect that, absent default, the initial measurement amount will be realised and any interim unrealised gains and losses will reverse. Accordingly, amortised cost, using the effective interest method (see paragraph **8.18**), is the subsequent measurement basis, subject to appropriate testing for impairment, for these categories.

**Available-for-sale financial assets**

**8.12** Other than for held-to-maturity investments and loans and receivables, there is no basis for measuring other financial assets at other than fair value. Therefore, available-for-sale financial assets are measured at fair value.

**8.13** It may not be possible to estimate fair values for some investments in equity instruments that do not have a quoted market price in an active market or for derivatives that are linked to, and must be settled by, such unquoted equity instruments. Accordingly, when such instruments are not reliably measurable, they are measured at cost.

**8.14** IAS 39 considers that the circumstances in which such instruments would not be reliably measurable would be rare. It specifies that, so long as the variability in the range of reasonable fair value estimates for that instrument is not significant, or the probabilities of various estimates within the range can be reasonably assessed, a fair value is reliably determinable.

**8.15** This requirement differs from US GAAP (FASB Statement 115), in that US GAAP requires cost measurement whenever securities do not have a quoted market price in an active market. This would include an equity security traded only in a non-US market unless the breadth and scope of that foreign market is comparable to a US market. There is no further consideration as to whether other reliable measures of fair value can be obtained. Therefore, more financial instruments are likely to qualify for cost measurement in accordance with US GAAP than with IAS 39. The exemption for derivatives in accordance with US GAAP also differs slightly in that it provides an exemption only for forwards and options on unquoted equity instruments that must be settled by delivery.

**Financial liabilities**

**8.16** The subsequent measurement of financial liabilities depends only on whether the instrument is held for trading or designated as at fair value through profit or loss. Those held for trading or designated as at fair value through profit or loss are measured at fair value. All others are measured at amortised cost using the effective interest method.

**8.17** This too goes beyond US GAAP, in that US GAAP does not require financial liabilities other than derivatives to be measured at fair value.

**Figure 8.1: Summary of subsequent measurement requirements**

| | |
|---|---|
| Financial assets at fair value through profit or loss (including those held for trading) | Fair value |
| Held-to-maturity investments | Amortised cost |
| Loans and receivables | Amortised cost |

76

| | |
|---|---|
| Available-for-sale financial assets for which fair value is reliably determinable | Fair value |
| Available-for-sale financial assets for which fair value is not reliably determinable | Cost |
| Financial liabilities at fair value through profit or loss (including those held for trading) | Fair value |
| Other financial liabilities | Amortised cost |

### Determining amortised cost using the effective interest method

**8.18**   Amortised cost is determined using the effective interest method. That method determines the effective interest rate inherent in the financial instrument as the rate that exactly discounts the estimated cash flows associated with the instrument through its expected life or, when appropriate, a shorter period, to the net carrying amount at initial recognition.

### EXAMPLE 8.5

On 1 January 2004, Company E acquires a debt instrument which matures on 30 June 2006. The debt instrument has a principal amount of £1,000 and pays fixed interest of 5 per cent annually. Company E acquires the debt instrument for its fair value of £934.14, representing an annual yield of 8 per cent.

| Year | Opening amortised cost | Interest income | Cash | Closing amortised cost |
|---|---|---|---|---|
| 2004 | £934.14 | £74.73 | £50 | £958.87 |
| 2005 | £958.87 | £76.71 | £50 | £985.58 |
| 2006 | £985.58 | £39.42 | £1,000 + £25 | £0 |

The total gains and losses recognised in profit or loss in each of the three years are £124.73 in 2004, £126.71 in 2005 and £64.42 in 2006.

It is possible that application of the effective yield method in IAS 39 may, in some circumstances, differ from that specified in US GAAP. In particular, a revision of the estimate of cash flows is accounted for by adjusting the opening balance of the instrument in IAS 39, whereas it may be accounted for prospectively in accordance with US GAAP.

### Special situations – financial guarantees

**8.19**   As discussed in **Chapter 4**, a financial guarantee contract that provides for specified payments to be made to reimburse the holder for a loss it incurs because a specified debtor fails to make payment when due in accordance with the original or modified terms of a debt instrument is excluded from the scope of IAS 39. However, in the paragraph excluding this type of financial instrument from the scope, measurement requirements are specified.

**8.20** On initial recognition of such a financial guarantee contract, the issuer treats it no differently than any other financial instrument – it is measured at fair value, which would usually be the amount of the premium received for issuing the contract.

**8.21** However, subsequent to initial recognition, the measurement differs from other financial instruments. The premium received would be amortised to profit or loss in accordance with IAS 18, 'Revenue'. However, if there becomes a possibility that the issuer will have to make a payment in accordance with the guarantee contract, a provision is measured in accordance with IAS 37, 'Provisions, Contingent Liabilities and Contingent Assets'. The financial guarantee is then measured at the higher of the amount determined in accordance with IAS 37 and the amount initially recognised, less any amortisation.

**EXAMPLE 8.6**

Company F issues a guarantee to Financial Institution G, guaranteeing to reimburse Financial Institution G if Subsidiary Company H fails to make payment on a £50,000 debt to Financial Institution G. In return for the guarantee, Company F receives a fee of £100. Company F initially measures the guarantee as a financial liability of £100. This is amortised to revenue over the life of the guarantee. If it becomes, say, 10 per cent probable that Subsidiary Company H will not be able to repay the debt to Financial Institution G, Company F would measure the financial liability at 10 per cent times the outstanding amount remaining payable to Financial Institution G (this is greater than £100).

**8.22** It should be noted that the financial guarantee contract is separate from the guaranteed liability. The financial guarantee is a contract between the guarantor and the creditor and is reported as a liability by the guarantor and as an asset by the creditor (usually included as part of the loan asset). The debtor's obligation is not affected by the guarantee. Consequently, a financial guarantee does not affect the measurement of the guaranteed liability by the debtor.

**Special situations – loan commitment at below-market interest rate**

**8.23** Loan commitments that cannot be settled net in cash or another financial instrument are excluded from the scope of IAS 39, unless they are designated as, or meet the requirements for, measurement at fair value through profit or loss (see **Chapter 4**). However, in the paragraph excluding this type of financial instrument from the scope of IAS 39, measurement requirements are specified.

**8.24**   Like a financial guarantee, the issuer of a loan commitment measures it initially at fair value and subsequently at the higher of the amount recognised in accordance with IAS 37 and the amount initially recognised less, where appropriate, cumulative amortisation recognised in accordance with IAS 18.

---

### EXAMPLE 8.7

Financial Institution I enters into a contractual commitment to make a five-year, £100,000 loan to Borrower J at an interest rate of 5 per cent per annum, at a time when market interest rates for similar five-year loans are 6 per cent per annum, should Borrower J choose to draw down that loan in the next 30 days. In return for the commitment, Financial Institution I receives a fee of £100. Financial Institution I initially measures a financial liability reflecting the fair value of the loan commitment (which may be equal to the fee received). If it becomes possible that Borrower J will draw the loan down, Financial Institution I measures the liability using the difference between the committed interest rate (5 per cent) and the then market rate of interest multiplied by the probability of the loan being drawn down. (Note: It is more usual for there to be a number of loan commitments on similar terms, so that the probability of some being drawn down is determinable based on economic circumstances, past history, etc.)

---

**8.25**   IAS 39 also specifies that an issuer of loan commitments should apply IAS 37 to loan commitments that do not fall within the scope of IAS 39.

## IMPAIRMENT AND UNCOLLECTABILITY OF FINANCIAL ASSETS

### Introduction

**8.26**   Whenever a financial instrument is measured other than at fair value with gains and losses recognised in profit or loss, it is required to be tested for impairment. This includes available-for-sale financial assets, even though they are measured at fair value. This is necessary because gains and losses on such instruments would be recognised in equity, rather than profit or loss. In order to be consistent with the treatment of impairment losses on all other financial assets, when the loss included in equity includes an impairment loss, that amount is required to be transferred to profit or loss.

### Objective evidence of impairment

**8.27**   The starting point is to consider whether there is any objective evidence that a financial asset or a group of financial assets is impaired. Only if such evidence exists is it necessary to determine whether there is a need to recognise an impairment loss. A company is required to make the assessment as to whether there is objective evidence of impairment at each balance sheet date.

**8.28** IAS 39 makes it clear that the objective assessment of impairment is based on there having been a 'loss event' between the time that the financial asset was originally recognised and the balance sheet date. Impairment testing of a financial asset considers the asset's condition at the balance sheet date and does not take into account future events. Thus, for example, impairment of a portfolio of accounts receivable would take into account the bankruptcy of customers before the balance sheet date, but would not take into account the probability that other customers that were not bankrupt at the balance sheet date might become bankrupt at some date in the future and thus be unable to pay their debts. Those customers are assessed based on their condition at the balance sheet date.

**8.29** IAS 39 provides examples of several events that provide objective evidence that a financial asset or group of financial assets is impaired, as well as examples of events that are not, on their own, evidence of impairment.

**8.30** Once a company determines that there is objective evidence of impairment for a financial asset or group of financial assets, it then needs to consider whether there is an impairment loss and, if so, how it should be accounted for. This will differ depending upon the financial asset being considered.

**Financial assets measured at amortised cost**

**8.31** For financial assets measured at amortised cost, the amount of any impairment loss is determined as the difference between the asset's carrying amount and the present value of estimated future cash flows, excluding credit losses that have not been incurred, discounted at the financial asset's original effective interest rate.

**EXAMPLE 8.8**

Company K holds a debt instrument with five years remaining to maturity that it has classified as held to maturity and measured at amortised cost. Company K purchased the debt instrument for its fair value of £100,000 (including transaction costs). The instrument has a principal amount of £125,000 and carries an interest rate of 4.7 per cent paid annually. It has an effective interest rate of 10 per cent.

At the end of the first year the amortised cost of the debt instrument is £104,100 (£100,000 + (£100,000 × 10 per cent) − (£100,000 × 4.7 per cent)). At this time Company K determines that there is objective evidence of impairment and that it expects that no further interest payments will be paid on the debt. Company K recalculates the present value of the principal repayment in four years' time as £85,377 ($£125,000/(1.10)^4$) and recognises an impairment loss of £104,100 − £85,377 = £18,723.

**8.32** The carrying amount of the asset may be reduced either directly or through the use of an allowance account. Either way, the impairment loss is recognised in profit or loss in the period in which the impairment is identified.

**8.33**   If in a subsequent period the amount of the impairment loss decreases, it can be reversed as long as the decrease can be related objectively to an event occurring after the impairment loss was recognised (for example, the debt issuer announces that it will be making interest payments once again). Any reversal affects either the carrying amount of the asset or the allowance account, depending on the manner in which the impairment was originally recognised, and is recognised in profit or loss. The amount of the reversal must not result in a carrying amount exceeding what the amortised cost would have been had no impairment been recognised. Therefore, a company needs to track the original amortised cost, as well as the impaired amount, if it might reverse an impairment loss.

**8.34**   Frequently, an impairment loss is not only determined for an individual financial asset, but also for a portfolio of financial assets such as loans or receivables. In such cases, a company first determines whether objective evidence of impairment exists for individually significant financial assets. A company may then assess impairment collectively for the financial assets as a group. The company excludes from the collective assessment any financial assets for which an impairment loss is or continues to be recognised. However, it includes in the collective assessment any financial assets that were previously assessed, but for which no objective evidence of impairment was identified.

**8.35**   When estimating the future cash flows of an impaired loan asset, a company would consider the effects of collateral or other factors that affect the probability of collection.

**8.36**   Cash flows expected on short-term accounts receivable are generally not discounted, unless the effect is likely to be material.

#### Financial assets measured at cost

**8.37**   For financial assets carried at cost, the amount of any impairment loss is determined as the difference between the asset's carrying amount and the present value of estimated future cash flows, discounted at the current market rate of return for a similar financial asset. Since these financial assets are ones for which fair value cannot be reliably measured, the amount may be difficult to determine. If it is possible to determine a range of values, then the asset is written down to the best estimate within the range. Any impairment loss is recognised in profit or loss and, because of the uncertainty in measuring the amount of such a loss, is not reversed if future circumstances change.

#### Available-for-sale financial assets

**8.38**   Available-for-sale financial assets are measured at fair value. However, gains and losses are recognised in equity, rather than profit or loss. Since all impairment losses are recognised in profit or loss, it is necessary to determine whether a decline in fair value on an available-for-sale financial asset is an impairment loss. Accordingly, such financial assets are assessed to see if there is objective evidence that the asset is impaired.

**8.39** If it is concluded that there is objective evidence that an available-for-sale financial asset is impaired, any remaining debit in equity relating to that financial asset is removed and recognised in profit or loss.

### EXAMPLE 8.9

Company L acquires a financial asset for £500 and classifies it as available for sale. In the first year that Company L holds the financial asset its fair value declines to £475. Accordingly, Company L has recognised £25 as a debit to equity. Early in the second year the fair value declines rapidly to £400. Company L determines that there is objective evidence that the asset is impaired. Therefore, Company L transfers £100 from equity to profit or loss, reflecting the impairment loss on the asset. If, at the end of the second year, the fair value has continued to decline to, say, £360, and there remains objective evidence of impairment, the further loss of £40 is also recognised in profit or loss, rather than equity.

**8.40** Impairment losses on available-for-sale equity instruments are not reversed if future circumstances change. However, if in a subsequent period the amount of an impairment loss on an available-for-sale debt instrument decreases it can be reversed as long as the decrease can be related objectively to an event occurring after the impairment loss was recognised.

**Summary**

**8.41** The following table summarises impairment testing for financial assets.

**Figure 8.2: Summary of impairment testing**

| Asset classification | Impairment adjustment | Reversals |
|---|---|---|
| Financial assets at amortised cost | Difference between carrying amount and present value of estimated future cash flows discounted at original effective interest rate recognised in profit or loss | Reversal permitted |

| Asset classification | Impairment adjustment | Reversals |
|---|---|---|
| Financial assets at cost | Difference between carrying amount and present value of estimated future cash flows discounted at current market rate of return for similar financial asset recognised in profit or loss | Reversal not permitted |
| Available-for-sale financial assets | Difference between acquisition cost and current fair value recognised in profit or loss (rather than equity) | Reversal permitted for debt instruments. Not permitted for equity instruments |

**GAAP comparison**

**8.42**   Impairment testing of loans and receivables is consistent with that in US GAAP. However, impairment testing of held-to-maturity investments, financial assets carried at cost and available-for-sale financial assets might result in earlier recognition of impairment in accordance with IAS 39 than in accordance with US GAAP, because US GAAP requires an impairment loss to be recognised for such financial assets only when the loss is other than temporary. This is, in part, because US GAAP does not permit reversal of impairment losses for such financial assets.

**8.43**   UK GAAP does not presently contain comprehensive guidance on impairment testing of loans and receivables.

Chapter 9

# Determining fair value

---

Principal IFRS references:

- IAS 39, paragraphs 9, 48–49, AG69–AG82.

---

## INTRODUCTION

**9.1**   Measuring financial instruments is by no means the only place in IFRS that fair value is required. Indeed, requirements to use fair values can be found in a long list of IFRS, including IAS 16, 'Property, Plant and Equipment', IAS 17, 'Leases', IAS 18, 'Revenue', IAS 19, 'Employee Benefits', IAS 20, 'Government Grants', IAS 21, 'The Effects of Changes in Foreign Exchange Rates', IAS 22, 'Business Combinations', IAS 33, 'Earnings per Share', IAS 38, 'Intangible Assets', IAS 40, 'Investment Property,' IAS 41, 'Agriculture' and IFRS 2, 'Share-based Payment'. Furthermore, fair value is likely to be used in other current IASB projects, including business combinations and insurance contracts. Fair value is, therefore, by no means a new concept, or unique to accounting for financial instruments. In some cases, guidance on determining fair values can be found in these other standards or is being developed in conjunction with current projects.

**9.2**   Fair values determined for financial instruments need to be no more precise than for other financial statement estimates. Estimation is an inherent part of measuring many financial instruments – the objective being to determine a fair value that is sufficiently precise for financial reporting purposes. In some cases, it may not be necessary to incur the full cost of developing a precise fair value measure if simplified assumptions can determine a fair value that can be demonstrated (for example, by use of sensitivity analysis) to be within tolerable limits.

**9.3**   The definition of fair value is consistent in all IFRS:

> 'the amount for which an asset could be exchanged or a liability settled, between knowledgeable, willing parties in an arm's length transaction.'

[IAS 39, paragraph 9]

This definition is also consistent with those used in most other jurisdictions.

**9.4** The objective of fair value is to determine the price at which the instrument being measured would trade in an active market at the valuation date. Thus, the value is not for the instrument in some repackaged form or a projection of what the value might be at some future date.

**9.5** This chapter considers sources of fair value, as well as the determination of fair value in some specific situations. It also comments on policies and procedures that a company should have in place to support reliable and consistent determination of fair values. For more detailed guidance on determining fair values a company might need to refer to valuation text books or involve outside expertise.

## SOURCES OF FAIR VALUE

**Quoted market prices**

**9.6** The best evidence of fair value comes from published price quotations in an active market. IAS 39 states:

> 'A financial instrument is regarded as quoted in an active market if quoted prices are readily and regularly available from an exchange, dealer, broker, industry group, pricing service or regulatory agency and those prices represent actual and regularly occurring market transactions on an arm's length basis.'

[IAS 39, paragraph AG71]

Thus, the fair value of shares regularly traded on the London Stock Exchange would be the number of shares multiplied by the price in the Stock Exchange Daily Official List. Quoted prices for a range of traded financial instruments are regularly available from such sources as the financial pages of national newspapers and Internet sites linked to official price quotes. These are generally available, not only for exchange markets such as the London Stock Exchange, New York Stock Exchange, London International Financial Futures Exchange, etc, but also bid and ask quotations are generally available for securities, corporate bonds, commercial and industrial loans, and asset-backed and mortgage-backed securities traded on dealer markets such as NASDAQ. Other potential sources of market quotations include quoted valuations from appraisers or specialist firms that offer pricing services, or from database services.

**9.7** Quoted prices from exchange markets are generally more reliable than from other sources. If prices are available from non-exchange markets, they might vary widely according to the source. In such cases, a company might consider obtaining quotations from more than one source to ensure that the fair value estimate is appropriate.

**9.8** Often quotations include a bid and an asking price. For example, shares may be quoted as bid £1.54, offer £1.56. Generally, the difference between these two quotes represents transaction costs. The 2p difference in quote reflects that fact that the market-maker would bid £1.54 to purchase shares but would require £1.56 to offer to sell those same shares – thus earning a 2p transaction fee. IAS 39 explains that the appropriate quoted market price for an asset held or a liability issued would usually be the current bid price – £1.54 in the above example – since that is what the company could sell the asset or settle the liability for. The appropriate quoted market price for an asset to be acquired or liability held would be the asking price – £1.56 in the above example – since that is what the company would be required to pay to acquire the asset or issue the liability.

**9.9**  Mid-market prices (the average of the bid and asking prices) are not generally appropriate to be used, unless the effect is immaterial. This may represent a departure from current practice for some – particularly for investment funds. It may, however, be useful to use mid-market prices to establish fair values for offsetting positions, so long as appropriate bid or asking prices are used for the net open positions.

**9.10**  When published price quotations in an active market representing transactions at the valuation date are not available, the most recent transaction may, nonetheless, provide evidence of fair value, so long as there has not been a significant change in economic circumstances since the most recent transaction. This is likely to be the case if the quoted price was on the same day as the valuation date and no price changing event occurred later in the day, or even if the transaction was in the few days prior to the valuation date. If there has been a change in conditions since the recent transaction it may be possible to adjust the price of the recent transaction to reflect the effects of that change in conditions.

**9.11**  Principal-to-principal or brokered trades, significant announcements or other events may have occurred after the close of the market in which a financial instrument is traded. A company would not be expected to seek out information about after-hours trading, but it would take into account information that is available. Awareness of changes is particularly important for instruments traded in foreign markets that close before the end of the business day in the reporting jurisdiction.

**EXAMPLE 9.1**

Company A has an investment in shares of ABC Company quoted on the London and New York Stock Exchanges. At its year-end, the closing price on the London Stock Exchange is £1.50 per share. However, after the close of the London Stock Exchange ABC Company announces the loss of major contracts, with the result that by the time trading on the New York Stock Exchange closes its share price is quoted at an equivalent of £1.34 per share. The fair value of the shares for purposes of Company A's financial reporting is £1.34 per share.

**9.12**  Fair value is the price that would be obtained between a willing buyer and a willing seller. Thus, it is not an amount that would arise on a forced transaction, such as an involuntary liquidation or distress sale. It is possible that the last transaction price may not be at fair value – for example, if it were the result of a sale to meet a court order in a bankruptcy situation. If the company can demonstrate this, it would adjust the quoted price to reflect this. In contrast, if the entire market for a particular financial instrument is affected by a lack of liquidity or financial difficulties of many participants, the observed prices are evidence of fair value.

**9.13**  Adjustments to reflect the perceived effects of holding a greater or lesser number of units of a financial instrument than is reflected in the market quote (blockage or control premiums or discounts) is precluded. IAS 39 specifies that the fair value of a portfolio of financial instruments is the product of the number of units of the instrument and its unit price.

**EXAMPLE 9.2**

Company B has an investment representing 15 per cent of the voting shares of Company C. The market price of the shares of Company C on Company B's balance sheet date is 120p, quoted in a market which trades 2 per cent of the issued share capital of Company C on average per day. Company B believes that if it were to dispose of its investment, it would need to accept a discount, since an orderly disposition of this number of shares would depress the market price. In spite of Company B's belief that it would need to accept a discount, Company B is required to value its stake at 120p per share.

Just as Company B is closing its balance sheet for the year, it becomes aware that Company D, who already holds 40 per cent of the voting shares of Company C, is interested in acquiring Company B's stake in Company C. Company B now believes that it will be able to sell its stake for a premium, since it would give Company D control of Company C. In spite of Company B's belief that it would be able to dispose of its stake at a premium, Company B is required to value its stake at 120p per share.

**9.14**  If a company has access to more than one active market for a financial instrument and prices in those markets are different, the instrument's fair value would be based on the price in the most advantageous active market to which the company has immediate access. This reflects the fact that it is the market that the company would most rationally access. IAS 39 is silent on the extent to which a company would have to search for such markets. However, it seems reasonable to assume that while a company need not conduct an exhaustive search for markets to which it could have access, it would be expected to make reasonable efforts to become aware of significant differences in prices in known markets to which it had access.

**9.15**  In determining which is the most advantageous market a company would take into account any significant difference in costs that would have to be incurred to sell a financial asset or obtain relief from a financial liability. These costs would include any incremental costs that would have to be incurred to access a market for a financial instrument.

### EXAMPLE 9.3

Company E can observe that the quoted market price of a financial asset on its balance sheet date is £100 in Market A and £110 in Market B. Costs to sell the asset in Market A are £2 and in Market B are £15. The most advantageous price is that of Market A. Thus, the fair value of the financial asset is £100.

**Valuation techniques**

**9.16**   When quoted market prices are not available, a company uses valuation techniques to establish a fair value for a financial instrument. There are many techniques that could be used – far too many to deal with in detail in this book. Valuation techniques range from adjusting prices for similar items to reflect the different attributes of the item the company is trying to value, through discounted cash flow analysis, option pricing models and more complex valuation models for complex financial instruments with multiple variables. However, there are some important principles that must be applied in determining a fair value by way of a valuation technique. Appendix A to IAS 39 identifies many of the inputs to valuation techniques that would be taken into account, including interest at the basic, or risk-free rate, credit risk, foreign currency exchange prices, commodity prices, equity prices, volatility, prepayment risk and surrender risk, and servicing costs.

**9.17**   Since the objective of a valuation technique is to establish what the transaction price would have been on the measurement date in an arm's length transaction motivated by normal business considerations, any valuation technique maximises the use of market inputs and relies as little as possible on entity-specific inputs. Therefore, it is required to incorporate all factors that market participants would consider in setting a price, and to be consistent with accepted economic methodologies for pricing financial instruments. It is not acceptable to ignore a market-driven factor in preference to an entity-specific factor, unless there are clearly different attributes attributable to the instrument that the company is valuing compared to the one observable in the market. In particular, it should be noted that it is the attributes of the instrument that are important – not the manner in which the company is using the instrument.

**9.18**   Any factor included in a valuation technique should be supportable and verifiable. It is not appropriate to include a non-verifiable adjustment for 'model risk'. The valuation model itself should be sufficiently robust that it produces a fair value within a reasonable range of variability.

**9.19**   If a quoted market price becomes available for a financial instrument that a company is valuing using a valuation technique, then the company calibrates its valuation technique by reference to that quoted market price. If the quoted market price differs from that determined using the valuation technique, it is possible that there is a factor missing from the valuation technique and that technique may require modification.

## FAIR VALUE – SPECIFIC SITUATIONS

### Fair value on initial recognition

**9.20**   The best evidence of fair value on initial recognition is usually the transaction price, ie the fair value of the consideration given or received – unless there is objective evidence that the transaction has been undertaken at an off-market price, such as in the case of an interest-free loan.

**9.21**   When fair value is available on initial recognition, but not subsequently, so that a valuation technique must be used to determine subsequent measurement amounts, that valuation technique would be calibrated against the fair value on initial recognition and, hence, a company would not use a technique that results in a gain or loss on initial recognition.

### Fair value based on recent market transactions

**9.22**   Even though there may not be an observable market price for a particular financial instrument at the balance sheet date, there may be a price for a market transaction close to the balance sheet date. If such a price is available, a company may use that price as the base for a valuation technique, adjusting it for changes in circumstances between the date of the recent transaction and the balance sheet date.

### EXAMPLE 9.4

Company F has an investment in an interest-sensitive financial instrument that it has classified as available for sale. It therefore needs to determine the fair value of that instrument at the balance sheet date. The instrument held by the company is not regularly traded. However, a market transaction in such an instrument is observable two days previously. Since that date a change in market interest rates has occurred. The company can measure the fair value of its financial instrument by reference to the market price of the previous transaction by adjusting the price at which that transaction occurred to reflect the new interest rate for the period between the transaction and the measurement date, the effect on fair value of the change in rates and any cash distribution in that period.

### Fair value based on similar financial instruments

**9.23**   A fair value may not be available for the financial instrument that the company has, but is available for a similar financial instrument. In this case, estimating the fair value of the company's financial instrument involves the following process:

(a)     Identify the significant risk attributes and projected cash flows of the company's financial instrument.

(b)     Identify another financial instrument for which a market price is available that has risk attributes and projected cash flows that are similar to the financial instrument the company is trying to measure.

(c)     Quantify the effects on fair value of differences in cash flows and risks between the two financial instruments (including differences in marketability) and adjust the market price of the similar instrument for those effects to estimate the fair value of the company's financial instrument.

**EXAMPLE 9.5**

Company G holds a private placement corporate bond for which there is no observable market price. Company G identifies an actively traded corporate bond that appears to be similar to its bond. The major elements on which the two bonds would be compared are:

(a)     The pattern of contracted cash flows, including prepayment expectations.

(b)     The currency in which the bonds are payable.

(c)     The credit risk rating and the factors on which changes in the credit risk rating are dependent. For example, the fair values of bonds issued by companies with different industry and geographical bases would be expected to respond differently to changes in market factors. However, the two issuers need not necessarily be in the same industry or geographic region if the difference would not be expected to affect fair value.

(d)     Any other terms or conditions that could affect the fair value of the bonds.

Company G determines the price of its bond by adjusting the market price of the similar bond for the differences in factors identified.

**9.24**   By definition, similar financial instruments are not identical, and some of the differences will cause the fair values of the instruments to be different. For similar financial instruments to be used in estimating fair value, measurement of the effect of the differences must be practicable. If not practicable, then a different valuation technique may be necessary.

**9.25**   It may be clear that some factors have not changed since initial recognition of the company's financial instrument. For example, a company may observe that the price at which it acquired its financial instrument differs from the price of the similar financial instrument as a result of a lack of marketability of the company's instrument. It may be reasonable to assume that any premium for marketability differences between the two financial instruments remains unchanged from period to period, except if an observable event that could be expected to significantly affect marketability takes place.

**9.26**   A valuation technique based on similar financial instruments is unlikely to be effective for equity instruments, since each equity investment is unique in significant respects. For example, even if two companies are similar with respect to size, products and clientele, there will be differences in their management, employee personnel and other intangible factors that could lead to very different future cash flow patterns and potential variability. Thus, with the exception of equity instruments that are contractually structured to replicate other equity instruments, it would not be appropriate to estimate fair values of equity investments directly by comparison to the market prices of other traded equity instruments. However, observable prices of traded equity instruments may be helpful as an input or check on estimations developed using internal valuation techniques such as multiples of earnings or discounted cash flow analysis.

## Fair value based on observable changes in market conditions

**9.27** Even though a particular financial instrument is not quoted in an active market, it may be possible to determine fair value by observing changes in market conditions that affect that financial instrument and adjusting the initial recognition amount to reflect those changes in conditions.

### EXAMPLE 9.6

Company H holds a non-traded debt instrument acquired two years ago, when market interest rates were 4 per cent per annum. Company H classified the debt instrument as available for sale. Company H can observe that market interest rates have now risen to 6 per cent per annum, based on rates currently charged for similar instruments, and has no reason to believe that there have been any other changes in its instrument relative to the market. Company H can estimate the fair value of its debt instrument by recalculating the discounted cash flows from the instrument using an interest rate based on the market rate of 6 per cent per annum rather than the original rate of 4 per cent per annum.

## Fair value using discounted cash flows

**9.28** A common valuation technique is to use a discounted cash flow analysis. Such an analysis uses a set of projected cash flows from the contractual rights or obligations constituting the financial instrument and an appropriate discount rate to determine the present value of the future cash flow stream flowing from an asset or liability. The discount rate would be that which is applicable to the prevailing rate of return on financial instruments having substantially the same terms and characteristics. The cash flows are only those contractually expected to arise from the financial instrument. Thus, they do not include additional expected cash flows that a company might expect as a by-product of the financial instrument (such as those that might arise from other contractual relationships with the same customer) or those from renewals or extensions of the contract.

**9.29** Either the discount rate may be adjusted to reflect expectations about the future or the cash flows may be adjusted. These are referred to as a discount rate adjustment approach and a cash flow adjustment approach, respectively. It is important to ensure that all variables are included once, and only once, in the estimate so that there is no double-counting by adjusting the discount rate and the estimated cash flows for the same factor, or omission of information.

**9.30**   The discount rate adjustment approach uses the stream of contracted cash flows as the basis for the present value computation. The rate used to discount those cash flows reflects the uncertainties of the cash flows. This approach is most readily applied to financial instrument contracts to receive or pay fixed cash flows at fixed future dates (ie instruments for which the only significant uncertainties in amount and timing of cash flows are caused by credit risk).

**9.31**   The discount rate adjustment approach is consistent with the manner in which assets and liabilities with contractually specified cash flows are commonly described (as in 'a 9 per cent bond') and it is useful and well accepted for those instruments. However, because the discount rate adjustment approach places the emphasis on determining the interest rate, it is more difficult to apply to complex financial instruments where cash flows are conditional or optional, and where there are uncertainties in addition to credit risk that affect the amount and timing of future cash flows.

**9.32**   The cash flow adjustment approach uses the projected cash flows for a financial instrument, reflecting the uncertainties in timing and amount (ie they are weighted according to the probability of their occurrence). These cash flows are then discounted using the appropriate market interest rate. The cash flow adjustment approach has advantages over the discount rate adjustment approach when an instrument's cash flows are conditional, optional or otherwise particularly uncertain for reasons other than credit risk.

**EXAMPLE 9.7**

Company I holds a derivative financial asset that has no specified cash flows. Company I estimates that there is a 10 per cent probability that it will receive £100, a 60 per cent probability that it will receive £200 and a 30 per cent probability that it will receive £300. The cash flows are expected to occur one year from the measurement date regardless of the amount. The expected cash flow is then 10 per cent of £100 plus 60 per cent of £200 plus 30 per cent of £300, which gives a total of £220. The discount rate used to estimate the instrument's fair value based on that expected cash flow would then be the basic (risk-free) rate adjusted for the premium that market participants would be expected to receive for bearing the uncertainty of expected cash flows with the same level of risk.

**9.33**   The cash flow adjustment approach also can incorporate uncertainties with respect to the timing of projected cash flows. The discount rate adjustment approach is difficult to apply when timing uncertainties are involved because it is difficult to incorporate those uncertainties in determining the appropriate discount rate.

**EXAMPLE 9.8**

Company J holds a derivative financial asset that has no specified cash flows. Company J estimates that the cash flow is certain to be £200. There is a 60 per cent chance it will be received in one year and a 40 per cent chance it will be received in three years. The present value computation weights those possibilities accordingly. Because the interest rate for a two-year instrument is not likely to be the weighted average of the rates for one-year and three-year instruments, two separate present value computations are required. One computation discounts £200 for one year at the basic interest rate for a one-year instrument (say 4 per cent) and the other discounts £200 for three years at the basic interest rate for a three-year instrument (say 4.5 per cent). The ultimate result is determined by probability-weighting the results of the two computations as follows:

Fair value = 0.60 × (200/1.04) + 0.40 × (200/(1.045)$^3$) = £186.63

**9.34**  Typically, financial instruments are priced along a yield curve. The interest rate for a one-year instrument differs from that for a two-year instrument, and so on. Accordingly, the rate used to discount particular cash flows will vary depending on how far out they are into the future. In simple situations, the yield curve may be obtained by referring to quotes for one-year, two-year, three-year, etc, government bonds in published sources. However, the curve may differ for particular types of instruments depending on other characteristics – including credit risk – that cause them to differ from government bonds.

**Fair value of non-traded equity instruments**

**9.35**  Techniques for measuring the fair value of equity instruments are commonly based on discounting expected cash flows, which may be estimates of future dividend payments or of net cash flows to be generated by the issuing company. Estimates are also made on the basis of multiples of earnings or the present value of expected future earnings, both of which are surrogates for expected future cash flows.

**9.36**  It is normally possible to estimate the fair value of an equity instrument acquired from a third party on initial recognition. However, it may be difficult to estimate the fair value of certain non-traded equity instruments subsequently (for example, investments in private companies that have little history or track record). In many cases, the difficulties can be overcome, but on rare occasions making a reasonable estimate of fair value will not be practicable. IAS 39 explains that cost is used to measure such instruments if they are classified as available-for-sale financial assets and the range of fair value estimates for the instrument is significant and the probabilities of various estimates cannot be reasonably assessed.

**Fair value of non-traded options and other derivatives**

**9.37**  Option pricing models (such as the Black-Scholes Option Valuation Model or the Binomial Option Pricing Model and models derived therefrom) are available in standard computer packages that enable computations of stock and equivalent options at a reasonable cost. Valuations using such models with appropriate market-based data inputs are likely to be sufficiently reliable for financial reporting purposes in many circumstances. However, standard option pricing models require adaptations or modifications to fit custom-tailored instruments with unusual or unique characteristics and to reflect the appropriate counter-party credit risk.

**9.38**   Volatility of the variable on which an option is based is an important factor in determining the option's fair value. Estimating expected future volatility generally begins with calculating historical volatility and then considering the effects of ways in which the future is expected to differ from the past. Guidance on determining the fair value of share-based payments may be useful in determining fair values for other option-based contracts.

**9.39**   For more complex derivatives it is likely that a company will either need to enlist the assistance of a valuation service or, for more sophisticated companies such as financial institutions, develop its own internal valuation model. As noted previously, if an internal valuation model is developed it should maximise the use of market inputs and be calibrated against external sources whenever possible.

**Fair values obtained from pricing services**

**9.40**   It is not generally appropriate to obtain a fair value from the counter-party to a financial instrument – particularly one that has been custom-designed for the company. However, it may be reasonable to obtain a valuation from the counter-party for generic instruments for which one could expect that the valuation from one party would be no different from that from any other party – such as for straightforward option and forward contracts. Otherwise, fair values may be obtained from independent sources such as bond dealers, brokers or other pricing services. A company may periodically check pricing service quotations with estimates made by other qualified third parties on a test basis.

**Fair value of financial liabilities**

**9.41**   Fair value will require determination for far fewer financial liabilities than for financial assets since, other than those measured at fair value through profit or loss, financial liabilities are measured at amortised cost. The fair value of financial liabilities that are derivatives is determined in the same manner as for any other derivatives. For other financial liabilities some additional considerations need to be taken into account.

**9.42**   Perhaps the most difficult aspect of fair valuing a financial liability is to take account of the effects of changes in the issuing company's own credit risk. IAS 39 specifies that this must be taken into account in determining the fair value of a financial liability. This is because it is the financial instrument as a stand-alone contract that is being valued, not the value of the instrument to the company.

**9.43** If a company's credit rating declines, then, all other things being equal, the fair value of its financial liabilities will also decline – perhaps below the amount that would contractually be payable. This appears counter-intuitive to many – particularly since the corresponding entry may be recognition of a gain in income. However, many overlook the fact that if a company's credit rating has declined there may well be expenses recognised in income as a result of declines in asset values, as well as the fact that debt- and equity-holders do not bear the effects of general declines in creditworthiness equally. However, because of the apparently counter-intuitive effects, additional disclosures are required of any difference between the fair value of a financial liability and the amount contractually required to be paid on settlement.

**9.44** In addition, IAS 39 specifies that the fair value of a financial liability with a demand feature is not less than the amount payable on demand, discounted from the first date that the amount could be required to be paid. Thus, when determining the fair value of a financial liability, it is not acceptable for a company to assume that not all liabilities that are due on demand will actually be demanded immediately. For example, a financial institution is precluded from including in the fair value of a financial liability its assessment that depositors do not, on average, withdraw their deposits immediately, even though they might have that right.

**9.45** When there are no observable market prices for a company's own financial liabilities, determining the appropriate interest rate to reflect the company's credit standing may require internal estimates and assumptions. At the date a financial liability is incurred, the company has a transaction price that usually represents the market price at that date. That price will be useful in determining such factors as the interest spread over the basic interest rate. At subsequent measurement dates, the company probably will not have a transaction price to observe (unless it has recently incurred a similar liability), and it may be difficult to determine the spread over the basic interest rate that market participants would demand on that measurement date. However, a company may assume that the net interest rate spread over the basic interest rate has not changed unless available information indicates otherwise. The company need not conduct an exhaustive search of possible changes in the net rate spreads of its financial liabilities since the last reporting date. However, it would be expected to make reasonable efforts to identify and consider available information as to whether one or more of the following events have occurred since the end of the last reporting period:

(a)    A significant change in the market credit risk spread for liabilities of similar credit risk. If overall interest rates have changed significantly, a company would consider whether the credit spread as a proportion of the basic interest rate has changed.

(b)   The company has issued or settled similar liabilities at a significantly different net rate spread.

(c)   The fair value of collateral, or the extent of coverage, has changed to such an extent that it could change the credit risk quality of the liability.

(d)   An external rating of the credit quality of the liability or of the company has changed.

(e)   A major change in the company's operating activities (for example, a large business combination or major decline in revenues or operating income), in the market value of the company, or in the technological, economic or legal environment in which it operates, which could be expected to affect the credit quality of the liability.

(f)   The expected variability of the projected cash outflows of a liability that are dependent on the resolution of uncertainties other than credit risk has changed to such an extent that it could have affected the net rate spread of the liability.

If one or more of the above events has occurred, the company would evaluate whether the spread over the basic interest rate has changed. If it has, the fair value of the liability would be estimated taking into account best estimates of the effects of this change.


## FAIR VALUE ESTIMATION POLICIES AND PROCEDURES

**9.46**   Consistent approaches to determining fair value measurements are impor-
tant to avoid the effects of volatility from the use of different valuation sources or techniques. A company should establish policies and procedures specifying how fair values are to be determined for its financial instruments. These would include identification of the methods to be used to determine the fair value of particular instruments, as well as identification and senior management review of especially difficult measurements (such as those affected by events after the close of trading in an instrument) and other unusual measurement issues. Senior management also would be responsible for effective monitoring to ensure appropriate application and continued validity of its policies to the company's financial activities, instruments held and issued, and market developments.

**9.47**   The nature and extent of policies and procedures will vary considerably between companies depending on the nature and extent of financial instruments held and issued. A company with only short-term trade receivables and payables, and perhaps a short-term bank loan, will not need an extensive fair value estimation system. However, many companies will need more extensive and rigorous processes to estimate fair values of such financial instruments as non-traded loan assets, long-term debt and derivatives.

**9.48**   Policies and procedures for estimating the fair value of financial instru-
ments should be consistent from period to period – except when a change will result in more accurate estimates. The validity and accuracy of fair value estimates would be assessed by comparing the results of valuation techniques to observable market prices (including back testing of previous estimations and

comparing to actual outcomes). If a company makes a change in its valuation techniques, the resulting effects on fair value estimates would be treated as a change in estimate as of the first measurement date when the new technique is used.

## GAAP COMPARISON

**9.49**    Some guidance is available in US and UK GAAP to assist with determining fair values. Generally, this is consistent with that in IAS 39. The FASB is presently undertaking a project to consolidate its fair value measurement guidance in one place. An exposure draft is expected in mid-2004.

Chapter 10

# Gains and losses

Principal IFRS references:

• IAS 1, paragraphs 96–101.
• IAS 39, paragraphs 55–57, AG83.

## INTRODUCTION

**10.1**  Whether financial instruments are measured at fair value, amortised cost or cost, it is necessary to specify how gains and losses arising over the life of those financial instruments are to be recognised.

**10.2**  This chapter considers gains and losses on financial instruments arising from changes in fair value, as well as gains and losses on financial instruments measured at amortised cost. **Chapter 12** discusses gains and losses on financial instruments that are part of designated hedging relationships. **Chapter 13** discusses gains and losses on derecognition of a financial instrument. **Chapter 15** discusses presentation of gains and losses on an issuer's own equity instruments.

## FINANCIAL INSTRUMENTS MEASURED AT FAIR VALUE

### Nature of the gains and losses

**10.3**  As discussed in **Chapter 6**, a financial asset that is not part of a hedging relationship is measured at fair value when it is held for trading, designated as at fair value through profit or loss or is available for sale. A financial liability that is not part of a hedging relationship is measured at fair value when it is held for trading or designated as at fair value through profit or loss.

**10.4**  When a financial instrument is measured at fair value it is necessary to consider how to account for the changes in fair value. As the asset or liability carrying amount is adjusted to reflect the change in value, the other side of the entry must be recognised somewhere.

**10.5** Such losses and gains do not meet the definition of assets or liabilities in the IASB Framework (or any other conceptual framework). Neither do they meet the definition of equity. Accordingly, conceptually, they should be recognised in profit or loss.

## Financial instruments measured at fair value through profit or loss

**10.6** For financial instruments that are actively managed (held for trading), as well as those designated as at fair value through profit or loss, this is the accounting that is required by IAS 39. Recognition of gains and losses in profit or loss in the period in which they arise reflects the economic consequences of the events of the reporting entity (such as changes in fair value).

## Available-for-sale financial assets

**10.7** Many companies are concerned about the potential non-representative volatility that would be recorded in profit or loss from measuring financial instruments that are not actively traded at fair value and recognising the resultant gains and losses in profit or loss. Accordingly, IAS 39 requires that unrealised gains and losses on changes in fair value of financial assets that are classified as available for sale be reported outside profit or loss[1] – directly in equity, through the statement of changes in equity – until the financial asset is derecognised, at which time the cumulative gain or loss previously recognised in equity is recognised in profit or loss.

### EXAMPLE 10.1

On 1 July 2004, Company A acquires a financial asset for £100 and classifies it as an available-for-sale investment. By 31 December 2004 the fair value of the financial asset has increased to £113. On 15 April 2005 the company sells the financial asset for its then fair value of £108. The following are the journal entries to account for the asset (transaction costs are ignored):

| | | |
|---|---|---|
| Debit: | Financial asset | £100 |
| Credit: | Cash | £100 |

(1 July 2004. To record acquisition of financial asset.)

| | | |
|---|---|---|
| Debit: | Financial asset | £13 |
| Credit: | Equity | £13 |

(31 December 2004. To record increase in value of financial asset.)

| | | |
|---|---|---|
| Debit: | Cash | £108 |
| Credit: | Financial asset | £113 |

| Debit: | Equity | £13 |
|---|---|---|
| Credit: | Profit on sale | £8 |

(15 April 2005. To record sale of financial asset.)

1  At the time of writing, the IASB was considering the possibility of introducing an option for gains and losses on available for sale financial assets, except for loans and receivables that are in this category by election, to be recognised in profit or loss in the period in which they arise, to allow those companies, such as investment funds, that wish to account for financial instruments in this manner to do so even though they might be unable to classify the financial asset as at fair value through profit or loss in accordance with proposed requirements discussed in **Chapter 5**. An exposure draft is expected to be issued in the second quarter of 2004.

**10.8**  The gain or loss on change in fair value of financial assets classified as available for sale is recognised directly in equity, through the statement of changes in equity. This statement is established in accordance with IAS 1, which requires an entity to present a statement of changes in equity showing on the face of the statement:

'(a)  profit or loss for the period;
(b)  *each item of income and expense that, as required by other Standards or by Interpretations, is recognised directly in equity, and the total of these items;*
(c)  total income and expense for the period (calculated as the sum of (a) and (b)), showing separately the total amounts attributable to equity holders of the parent and to minority interest; and
(d)  for each component of equity, the effects of changes in accounting policies and corrections of errors recognised in accordance with IAS 8.'

[IAS 1, paragraph 96. *Emphasis added.*]

**10.9**  The statement may be presented in a manner that presents all changes in equity, or only those that arise from transactions with equity-holders acting in their capacity as equity-holders, such as distributions and capital contributions. The following provides an example of a statement of changes in equity assuming there are no other transactions with equity-holders.

**EXAMPLE 10.2**

| Statement of changes in equity (£000) | | | |
|---|---|---|---|
| | | 2005 | 2004 |
| Profit for the period | | £651 | £22 |
| Items recognised directly in equity: | | | |
| Exchange differences on translation of foreign operations[1] | | £2 | £9 |
| Unrealised gains and losses on available-for-sale financial assets arising during the period | £1,689 | £277 | |

| Statement of changes in equity (£000) | | |
|---|---|---|
| | **2005** | **2004** |
| Reclassification adjustment for gains and losses included in net income | (£317) | £62 |
| Change in unrealised gains and losses on available-for-sale financial assets | £1,372 | £339 |
| Gains and losses on derivatives designated as cash flow hedges | £1,723 | £687 |
| Gains and losses on derivatives designated as cash flow hedges in prior periods transferred to net income in the current period | (£995) | (£333) |
| Change in gains and losses on derivatives designated as cash flow hedges | £728 | £354 |
| Tax on items charged or credited directly to equity | (£500) | (£300) |
| Total items recognised directly in equity | £1,602 | £402 |
| Total recognised gains and losses for the period | £2,253 | £424 |

¹  It is assumed that there was no reduction in the net investment in a foreign operation. Therefore, there is no reclassification adjustment.

**10.10**   IAS 12, 'Income Taxes' specifies that the aggregate current and deferred tax relating to items that are charged or credited to equity be separately disclosed.

**10.11**   The joint IASB/UK Accounting Standards Board (UK ASB) project on reporting comprehensive income, which the FASB is also actively considering, proposes that gains and losses on available-for-sale investments ultimately be presented in a single statement to report all components of financial performance. However, the future conclusions of that project are by no means certain and international consensus on implementing a standard is probably at least two years away. A discussion paper, or perhaps an exposure draft on certain aspects of the project, is expected in the second half of 2004.

**10.12**   In accordance with regular accounting for any asset, impairment losses and foreign exchange gains and losses are recognised directly in profit or loss. This is no different for an available-for-sale investment. Thus, if the investment becomes impaired, a transfer is made from equity to profit or loss to reflect the impairment loss. If the investment is denominated in a foreign currency, foreign exchange gains and losses are recognised directly in profit or loss, but other gains and losses are recognised in equity.

**EXAMPLE 10.3**

On 1 July 2004, Company B acquires a financial asset for £100 and classifies it as an available-for-sale investment. By 31 December 2004 the fair value of the financial asset has declined to £94. On 31 March 2005 the issuer of the financial asset announces that it is entering bankruptcy proceedings. Company B determines that the financial asset is impaired and that its fair value is £50. The following are the journal entries to account for the asset (transaction costs are ignored):

| | | |
|---|---|---|
| Debit: | Financial asset | £100 |
| Credit: | Cash | £100 |

(1 July 2004. To record acquisition of financial asset.)

| | | |
|---|---|---|
| Debit: | Equity | £6 |
| Credit: | Financial asset | £6 |

(31 December 2004. To record decrease in value of financial asset.)

| | | |
|---|---|---|
| Debit: | Impairment (profit or loss) | £50 |
| Credit: | Financial asset | £44 |
| Credit: | Equity | £6 |

(31 March 2005. To record impairment of financial asset.)

**10.13**   If the available-for-sale investment is a debt instrument, interest calculated using the effective interest method (see **Chapter 8**) is recognised in profit or loss. Dividends on available-for-sale equity investments are also recognised in profit or loss.

## FINANCIAL INSTRUMENTS MEASURED AT AMORTISED COST

**10.14**   A financial asset designated as held to maturity, a loan or receivable, or a financial liability other than one classified as held for trading or designated as at fair value through profit or loss is measured at amortised cost using the effective interest method. Gains and losses on these instruments are not recognised in profit or loss while they are held other than when they relate to impairment losses, foreign exchange gains and losses, or the amortisation process.

**10.15**   Amortised cost is calculated using the effective interest method. That method determines the effective interest rate inherent in the financial instrument as the rate that exactly discounts the estimated cash flows associated with the instrument through its expected life, or where appropriate a shorter period, to the net carrying amount at initial recognition. An example is provided in paragraph **8.18**.

**10.16**   Foreign exchange gains and losses are recognised in profit or loss in accordance with IAS 21.

## SUMMARY

**10.17** The following table summarises the treatment of gains and losses in each measurement situation.

**Figure 10.1: Summary of recognition of gains and losses**

| Measurement requirement | Recognition of gains and losses |
|---|---|
| Financial assets or financial liabilities held for trading or at fair value through profit or loss | Change in fair value to profit or loss |
| Held-to-maturity investments | Gain or loss on amortisation or impairment to profit or loss. Foreign exchange gains and losses to profit or loss in accordance with IAS 21. |
| Loans and receivables | Gain or loss on amortisation or impairment to profit or loss. Foreign exchange gains and losses to profit or loss in accordance with IAS 21. |
| Available-for-sale financial assets at fair value | Change in fair value to equity[1] (except impairment losses and foreign exchange gains and losses, which go to profit or loss. Dividends and interest also go to profit or loss). Transfer to profit or loss when derecognised. |
| Available-for-sale financial assets at cost | Gain or loss on impairment to profit or loss. Foreign exchange gains and losses to profit or loss in accordance with IAS 21. |
| Financial liabilities other than held for trading or at fair value through profit or loss | Gain or loss on amortisation to profit or loss. Foreign exchange gains and losses to profit or loss in accordance with IAS 21. |
| Financial asset that is part of a hedging relationship | See **Chapter 12** |

[1] With possible option for gains and losses in profit or loss. See paragraph **10.7**, footnote 1.

## GAAP COMPARISON

**10.18** The treatment for financial assets and financial liabilities measured at amortised cost, and for those held for trading, is consistent with US GAAP.

**10.19**    The treatment for available-for-sale financial assets is consistent with US GAAP, except that, in accordance with US GAAP, the entire change in fair value of a monetary available-for-sale financial asset, including foreign exchange gains or losses, is recognised directly in other comprehensive income rather than in net income. The recognition of foreign exchange gains and losses on an available-for-sale financial asset in other comprehensive income, in accordance with US GAAP, as opposed to profit or loss in accordance with IAS 39, is an unavoidable reconciling item.

**10.20**    The statement of changes in net assets, required by IAS 1, is similar to the statement of other comprehensive income in US GAAP. In some respects US GAAP is less restrictive:

(a)    IAS 1 requires presentation of the components of changes in net assets in the statement of changes in net assets, whereas US GAAP permits this display in the notes to the financial statements.
(b)    IAS 34, 'Interim Financial Reporting' requires more detail in interim financial statements, whereas US GAAP requires only that total comprehensive income be presented in interim financial statements prepared by public companies. However, the FASB noted that a company with a large difference between net income and comprehensive income would be inclined to explain that difference by disclosing the components.

**10.21**    In other respects US GAAP is more restrictive:

(a)    US GAAP specifies more detail about the presentation of accumulated balances of comprehensive income by component in equity.
(b)    US GAAP requires separate display of reclassification adjustments between other comprehensive income and the income statement. IAS 1 does not have such an explicit requirement, although many companies may provide such disclosure in reconciling the components of the statement of changes in equity.

**10.22**    Some of the presentation options for the statement of changes in equity differ from the statement of total recognised gains and losses in existing UK GAAP. However, it is possible to present the statement in a very similar manner to existing UK GAAP. The transfer of gains and losses on available-for-sale investments from equity to profit or loss when certain circumstances occur differs from the existing UK GAAP requirements which do not incorporate 'recycling'. However, the requirement for classification of financial assets as available for sale is, itself, new to UK GAAP.

Chapter 11

# Reclassification

Principal IFRS references:

● IAS 39, paragraphs 50–54.

## INTRODUCTION

**11.1** Under certain circumstances it may be appropriate to reclassify a financial instrument from one category to another. Generally, such reclassifications should be supported by changes in circumstances, such as the availability of quoted market prices, or changes in intent or ability associated with held-to-maturity investments. Reclassifications are generally not permitted on a discretionary basis.

**11.2** Furthermore, when a reclassification is permitted, the effects of the original classification on profit or loss generally continue, so that any change in accounting affects periods subsequent to the reclassification only.

**11.3** Companies should take great care in planning how they intend to classify financial instruments, since this can have a significant effect on accounting in the future. In many instances, initial classification will determine the accounting for an instrument throughout the time that it is held or issued. However, companies should be aware of the limited circumstances in which reclassifications are possible and their accounting consequences.

**11.4** This chapter considers each of the categories of financial assets and financial liabilities, the possibilities for reclassification and, when reclassification is permitted, the accounting consequences of reclassification.

## FINANCIAL ASSETS AND FINANCIAL LIABILITIES AT FAIR VALUE THROUGH PROFIT OR LOSS

**11.5** For a financial instrument to be classified as measured at fair value through profit or loss, it must be designated as such on initial recognition – either because it meets the requirements to be classified as held for trading or because the company chooses to classify it in this category. Once a company has made such a classification it would be inappropriate for it to have the ability to change its mind, since this would open up a very easy opportunity for profit manipulation – for example, an unscrupulous company could elect to have an instrument classified as at fair value through profit or loss while it is making profits and classified otherwise when it is making losses so as to maximise profit for a particular period. Accordingly, reclassification in or out of the fair value through profit or loss category is precluded while an instrument is held or issued. If a company wishes to transfer a financial instrument in or out of this category it must do so by entering into a transaction to derecognise the instrument and a new transaction to recognise a new instrument.

**11.6** Because voluntary reclassification in or out of this category is not permitted, the only time that reclassification is a consideration is in those rare circumstances when a company has a derivative financial instrument that is linked to and must be settled by delivery of equity instruments that do not have a quoted market price in an active market and whose fair value cannot be reliably measured. An instrument may be classified in the fair value through profit or loss category, but during the time that it is held the holder becomes unable to reliably measure the fair value. On the other hand, a company may hold an instrument for which it is not able to reliably determine the fair value, but circumstances change such that a fair value becomes reliably determinable. The accounting when a reliable fair value measure becomes available or unavailable is considered in paragraph **11.19**.

**11.7** It should be noted that, in accordance with US GAAP, FASB Statement 115 appears to allow some limited reclassification into or out of this category, since it states that reclassification in or out of the held-for-trading category should be 'rare'. However, in practice such reclassifications are not made.

## HELD-TO-MATURITY INVESTMENTS

**11.8** For a financial asset to be classified as a held-to-maturity investment a company must have the positive intention and ability to hold that instrument to maturity. If that intention or ability changes, then the held-to-maturity assumption is no longer valid and that instrument is required to be reclassified as available for sale. (Note that the fair value through profit or loss category is not available as a result of the preclusion on reclassification in or out of that category, except on initial recognition.)

**11.9** Once the held-to-maturity assumption no longer applies the instrument is required to be immediately re-measured at fair value. Any gain or loss arising as a result of a difference between carrying amount and fair value at that date is recognised in equity, through the statement of changes in equity (except to the extent that it is a foreign exchange gain or loss on a monetary financial asset or it is a loss that represents an impairment loss – in which case it is recognised in profit or loss).

**EXAMPLE 11.1**

Company A has an investment in a debt instrument that it originally acquired for £9,500 and has been accounting for at amortised cost, such that its carrying amount is now £9,700. Company A no longer has an intention to hold the debt instrument to maturity, but it does not comprise a significant amount of its held-to-maturity category (therefore, the entire category is not 'tainted'). The fair value of the debt instrument at that date is £9,780. The following journal entries are made by Company A to reclassify the investment:

| Debit: | Available-for-sale investments | £9,780 |
| Credit: | Held-to-maturity investments | £9,700 |
| Credit: | Equity (through the statement of changes in equity) | £80 |

**11.10**   If the instrument in the previous example was denominated in a foreign currency the situation might be as follows.

**EXAMPLE 11.2**

Company B has an investment in a debt instrument that it originally acquired for FCU9,400 when the exchange rate was £1 = FCU2. The original carrying amount was, therefore, £4,700. When the instrument is no longer to be classified as a held-to-maturity investment its carrying amount is FCU9,600, its fair value is FCU9,900 and the exchange rate is £1 = FCU1.8. At that time the investment is carried at £5,333 (FCU9,600/1.8) and its fair value is £5,500 (FCU9,900/1.8). The average exchange rate between the date of investing in the instrument and the date of change in classification is £1 = FCU1.9. The company makes the following entries:

| Debit: | Held-to-maturity investment | £4,700 |
| Credit: | Cash | £4,700 |

(To reflect acquisition of the investment.)

| Debit: | Held-to-maturity investment | £633 |
| Credit: | Amortisation of held-to-maturity investment (FCU200/1.9) | £105 |
| Credit: | Profit and loss – foreign exchange gain | £528 |

(To reflect amortisation and foreign exchange gain on investment to date of reclassification.)

| Debit: | Available-for-sale asset | £5,500 |
| Credit: | Equity | £167 |
| Credit: | Held-to-maturity investment | £5,333 |

(To reflect reclassification of the asset.)

**11.11**  Similar accounting applies to reclassify held-to-maturity investments as available for sale if the portfolio becomes 'tainted' and the held-to-maturity classification is no longer permitted (see **Chapter 5**).

**11.12**  The held to-maturity category does not require designation on initial recognition. Therefore, a company may decide that a financial asset that was previously being accounted for as 'available for sale' is now to be classified as held to maturity. In addition, when the 'two preceding financial years' under which a company is precluded from using the held-to-maturity category as a result of 'tainting' have expired, a company may choose to reclassify financial assets as held to maturity. In these circumstances, the fair value carrying amount of the financial asset at the reclassification date becomes its new amortised cost.

**11.13**  It is necessary in these circumstances to determine how to account for any remaining balance in equity. In common with most reclassifications, the balance is dealt with on a prospective basis by amortising it to profit or loss over the remaining life of the held-to-maturity investment using the effective interest method. Any difference between the new amortised cost and the maturity amount is amortised in the same manner that a premium or discount would be amortised. Any impairment loss is recognised immediately in profit or loss.

**EXAMPLE 11.3**

Company C has an asset in the available-for-sale category with a fair value of £9,900 that it decides it will now hold to maturity. The asset was originally acquired for £9,500. Therefore, a gain of £400 has been recognised in equity. The asset matures at £10,000 in one year.

At the date of reclassification the following journal entry is made:

| Debit: | Held-to-maturity investment | £9,900 |
| Credit: | Available-for-sale investment | £9,900 |

(To reclassify the asset.)

Over the next year the following journal entries are made:

| Debit: | Held-to-maturity investment | £100 |
| Credit: | Profit and loss | £100 |

(To amortise the held-to-maturity investment.)

| Debit: | Equity | £400 |
| Credit: | Profit and loss | £400 |

(To amortise the gain remaining in equity.)

## LOANS AND RECEIVABLES

**11.14**   A financial asset classified as a loan or receivable may also meet the definition of a held-to-maturity investment if it meets the relevant criteria. However, since both are measured on the same basis, reclassification is not an issue.

**11.15**   A financial asset that otherwise meets the criteria for classification as a loan or receivable, but is required to be classified as held for trading or is designated on initial recognition as accounted for at fair value through profit, would not be capable of reclassification into loans and receivables because of the preclusion on re-classification in or out of the 'fair value through profit or loss' category.

**11.16**   A loan or receivable may be designated as an available-for-sale financial asset on initial recognition. However, once this designation has been made it cannot be reclassified as a loan and receivable – it is excluded from meeting the definition of loans and receivables once it is designated as an available for-sale financial asset.

**11.17**   The only circumstance in which reclassification would seem to be possible for a loan or receivable is when the holder may not recover substantially all of its initial net investment, other than because of credit deterioration, in which case it must be classified as available for sale. In these circumstances, the accounting is the same as for a held-to-maturity investment reclassified as 'available for sale'.

## AVAILABLE-FOR-SALE FINANCIAL ASSETS

**11.18**   The circumstances in which a financial asset may be re-classified between available-for-sale financial assets and held-to-maturity investments have been considered in the previous paragraphs. A financial asset classified as an available-for-sale financial asset cannot be reclassified in or out of the fair value through profit or loss category or back into the loans and receivables category.

## CHANGE IN ABILITY TO RELIABLY DETERMINE FAIR VALUE

**11.19**   There are two additional situations when the accounting on a reclassification needs to be considered. These are when a financial asset is classified as available for sale but is accounted for at cost because no reliable measure of fair value is available and subsequently a reliable fair value becomes available, and when a financial asset is classified as available for sale, or is a derivative with an underlying based on a non-quoted equity instrument, and is accounted for at fair value but a reliable measure of fair value is no longer available so that cost measurement becomes appropriate. The accounting in these situations is as follows:

(a)  Reliable fair value becomes available: The asset is re-measured at fair value and the difference between its carrying amount and fair value is accounted for in the same manner as explained above for a reclassification from held to maturity to available for sale[1].

(b)  Reliable fair value no longer available: The fair value of the asset at the last time that a reliable fair value was available becomes the deemed cost. Any previous gain or loss on the asset that had been recognised directly in equity is either accounted for in the same manner as explained in paragraph **11.13** for a reclassification from available for sale to held to maturity, or, if the asset has no fixed maturity, the gain or loss remains in equity until the financial asset is sold or otherwise disposed of, at which time it is recognised in profit or loss (unless it is previously impaired). This necessitates tracking that gain or loss, even though the asset is no longer accounted for on that basis[2].

[1]  Note that the same may occur for a derivative based on an underlying for which a fair value is not reliably determinable. In this case the gain or loss is accounted for in profit or loss.

[2]  This would also apply for a derivative based on an underlying for which a fair value is no longer reliably determinable.

SUMMARY

**11.20**  The following table summarises the circumstances in which reclassifications may arise and the relevant accounting.

**Figure 11.1: Reclassifications**

| Reclassification | Circumstances | Accounting |
| --- | --- | --- |
| Reclassification out of 'fair value through profit or loss' | Prohibited (except when reliably determinable fair value becomes unavailable for derivatives that are linked to and must be settled by delivery of equity instruments that do not have a quoted market price in an active market and whose fair value cannot be reliably determined (see below)). | Not applicable. |

| Reclassification | Circumstances | Accounting |
|---|---|---|
| Reclassification into 'fair value through profit or loss' | Prohibited (except when reliably determinable fair value becomes available for derivatives that are linked to and must be settled by delivery of equity instruments that do not have a quoted market price in an active market and whose fair value cannot be reliably determined (see below)). | Not applicable. |
| Reclassification out of 'held to maturity' | Reclassify as 'available for sale' | Difference between carrying amount and fair value recognised directly in equity, through the statement of changes in equity, except for impairment losses and foreign exchange gains and losses. |
| Reclassification into 'held to maturity' | Reclassify from 'available for sale' when intention or ability changes or two preceding years under tainting rules expire. | Fair value at reclassification date becomes new amortised cost to be amortised over remaining life of asset using effective interest method. Any previous gain or loss in equity is amortised to profit and loss over the remaining life of the held-to-maturity investment using the effective interest method. |

| Reclassification | Circumstances | Accounting |
|---|---|---|
| Reclassification out of 'available for sale' | Reclassify as 'held to maturity' when intention or ability changes or two preceding years under tainting rules expire. | Fair value at reclassification date becomes new amortised cost to be amortised over remaining life of asset using effective interest method. Any previous gain or loss in equity is amortised to profit and loss over the remaining life of the held-to-maturity investment using the effective interest method. If the financial asset is subsequently impaired any relevant gain or loss is recognised in profit and loss. |
| Reclassification into 'available for sale' | From 'held to maturity' or from loans and receivables. | Difference between carrying amount and fair value recognised directly in equity, through the statement of changes in equity, except for impairment losses and foreign exchange gains and losses. |
| Reliably determinable fair value becomes available | Investments in equity instruments that do not have a quoted market price in an active market and whose fair value cannot be reliably determined and derivatives that are linked to and must be settled by delivery of such unquoted equity instruments. | Difference between cost and fair value recognised directly in equity, through the statement of changes in equity, except for impairment losses and foreign exchange gains and losses, if the instrument is 'available for sale' or in profit or loss if it is a derivative. |

| Reclassification | Circumstances | Accounting |
|---|---|---|
| Reliably determinable fair value becomes unavailable | Investments in equity instruments that previously had a quoted market price in an active market or whose fair value could be reliably determined and derivatives that are linked to and must be settled by delivery of such equity instruments. | Fair value at reclassification date becomes new cost or amortised cost to be amortised over remaining life of asset using effective interest method. Any previous gain or loss in equity is amortised to profit and loss over the remaining life of the investment using the effective interest method if it has a fixed maturity, otherwise the gain or loss remains in equity until the financial asset is sold or otherwise disposed of, when it is recognised in profit and loss. If the financial asset is subsequently impaired any relevant gain or loss is recognised in profit and loss. |

GAAP COMPARISON

**11.21**   The material on reclassifications in IAS 39 is consistent with that in FASB Statement 115.

Chapter 12

# Hedge accounting

---

Principal IFRS references:

- IAS 21, paragraphs 15, 32–33.
- IAS 32, paragraphs 58–59.
- IAS 39, paragraphs 9, 71–102, AG94–AG113.

---

## INTRODUCTION

**12.1**   Hedge accounting is optional. Many companies may choose not to adopt hedge accounting and, hence, will not need to read this chapter. Others may elect to adopt hedge accounting for only a limited number of relationships. However, a decision whether or not to adopt hedge accounting in particular situations needs to be carefully considered and a clear accounting policy adopted. Except in a very straightforward situation, that decision can probably not be taken without at least understanding the inconsistencies that hedge accounting attempts to address and the basics of how it addresses them.

**12.2**   Hedge accounting is not synonymous with the economic practice of hedging risk. A company may hedge risk exposures but elect not to apply hedge accounting. There may also be circumstances in which perfectly valid risk management strategies do not require hedge accounting, or are not permitted to be accounted for in a special manner. This in no way suggests that there is anything wrong with the risk management strategy: decisions about whether to manage particular risks are independent of decisions to apply hedge accounting to the risk management relationship.

**12.3**   Once a company elects to adopt hedge accounting, all of the designation, documentation and accounting requirements must be followed. Because hedge accounting is an exception to the basic method of accounting in IAS 39 and is elective, it is essential that it is clear whether hedge accounting is being applied to a particular relationship from the outset. Accordingly, all decisions to apply hedge accounting must be taken before entering into particular relationships.

**12.4**   A company that has not documented and designated hedges at their inception is precluded from applying hedge accounting to those relationships. Thus, hedge accounting requires careful advance planning. A company should review all existing hedging relationships to determine whether they qualify for hedge accounting in accordance with IAS 39 and, if so, to ensure that all of the other necessary requirements (such as documentation and methods for effectiveness testing) are in place as soon as possible. In some circumstances a company may wish to amend hedging strategies that do not qualify.

**12.5**   This chapter discusses the reasons for hedge accounting, the three types of hedge accounting (fair value hedges, cash flows hedges and hedges of a net investment in a foreign operation), the exposures that qualify for hedge accounting and the requirements for designation, documentation and effectiveness testing.

## REASONS FOR HEDGE ACCOUNTING

**12.6**   There are two main situations in which companies often desire hedge accounting:

(a)   To correct for accounting recognition and measurement inconsistencies, since accounting does not always recognise and measure assets and liabilities that may be managed together on the same basis. In such circumstances, without hedge accounting, gains and losses on assets and liabilities that are managed together may be recognised in profit or loss in different periods.

(b)   To reflect management of risks associated with future transactions, since future transactions are not reflected in the balance sheet or profit and loss account of current periods. Therefore, when financial instruments entered into in current periods manage risks associated with future transactions, there is a desire to match the current profit and loss account effects arising from the financial instrument managing the risk with the future profit and loss account effects of the future transactions.

### Accounting recognition and measurement inconsistencies

**12.7**   Two types of accounting inconsistency may give rise to a desire for hedge accounting – recognition inconsistencies and measurement inconsistencies.

**12.8**   Recognition inconsistencies arise when assets and liabilities that are subject to financial risks are recognised on the balance sheet while others are not and, thus, gains and losses on those assets and liabilities are recognised in different periods.

### EXAMPLE 12.1

Company A enters into a foreign currency forward contract to manage foreign exchange risk related to a committed, but not yet completed, transaction. The forward contract is recognised when Company A becomes a party to the transaction, and any gains or losses thereon are recognised in profit or loss. However, the committed purchase may not be recognised until the next accounting period. Foreign exchange gains or losses on the purchase would, thus, be recognised in profit or loss in a later accounting period than corresponding gains or losses on the forward contract.

In this situation, a company desires a mechanism to recognise the gains and losses in the profit and loss account in the same accounting period.

**12.9**  Measurement inconsistencies arise when assets and liabilities that are subject to financial risks are measured on different bases and, thus, gains and losses on those assets and liabilities are recognised in profit or loss on different bases.

### EXAMPLE 12.2

Company B enters into a fixed-to-floating interest rate swap to manage interest rate risk in a fixed-rate borrowing. If the swap is measured at fair value and the debt is measured at amortised cost, a measurement inconsistency arises. Changes in market rates of interest in the period will give rise to gains or losses on the interest rate swap that will be recognised immediately in profit or loss. However, losses or gains on the debt are recognised on a different basis, since it is accounted for at amortised cost. The gains and losses on the interest rate swap are included in profit or loss at a different time from corresponding losses and gains on the debt.

In this situation, a company desires a mechanism to recognise the gains and losses in profit or loss on the same basis, in the same accounting period.

**Risks associated with future transactions**

**12.10**  There is no basis for recognising a future transaction, such as future sales or future purchases, in the current accounting period. However, companies commonly manage risks associated with those transactions by entering into financial instruments in the current period.

### EXAMPLE 12.3

Company C enters into a forward commodity contract to manage commodity price risk related to expected, but not yet committed, purchases of sugar cane for physical delivery in six months. The forward commodity contract is capable of being settled net. Therefore, it is accounted for at fair value with gains and losses recognised in profit or loss in the periods in which they arise. However, there is no basis for recognising the future purchase of sugar cane until it occurs in six months. Any gain or loss on the price paid for the sugar cane would not, therefore, be recognised until a future period.

In this situation, a company desires a mechanism to recognise gains and losses in the same accounting period.

**12.11** An intention to undertake a future transaction does not provide any basis for recognising expected value changes as current effects in profit or loss, so the only way to correct for this anomaly is to, somehow, delay the recognition of the gains or losses on the hedging instrument. Furthermore, the basic principle that only those items that meet the definitions of assets and liabilities should be recognised as such on the balance sheet (see **Chapter 1**) means that any means of delaying such recognition cannot involve deferring gains as liabilities or deferring losses as assets.

**The decision whether to apply hedge accounting**

**12.12** A company needs to assess whether it is worried by any of the above situations and, if so, how much effort it wishes to exert to mitigate any undesirable effects on net profit or loss from not applying hedge accounting. Some companies may choose not to apply hedge accounting at all, considering that any benefit from its application is outweighed by the costs of documentation, monitoring and accounting. Other companies may choose to apply hedge accounting in only limited circumstances – perhaps to mitigate the expected largest undesirable effects on net profit or loss, but not for all transactions. Such a strategy requires careful consideration and planning from the outset to ensure that the circumstances in which hedge accounting is to be applied are carefully identified and documented from inception. Some companies may choose to adopt complex hedge accounting strategies to manage all profit or loss effects of certain risks or transactions, involving numerous hedging relationships. Such strategies are likely to be limited to the largest, most sophisticated companies.

**12.13** Making the decisions as to the circumstances in which hedge accounting is to be applied requires a thorough understanding of the risks facing the company and the potential risk-mitigating activities – both those that may be actively entered into and those that naturally exist within the company. Decisions will also, probably, require a company to assess what the impact on the company of particular strategies may be – particularly how others would view the effects of decisions to apply hedge accounting or not to apply hedge accounting. This may include considering what other companies are doing, what the penalties would be for volatility in net profit and loss, and the level of sophistication of the users of the company's financial statements (ie will they understand hedging strategies with or without hedge accounting?). A company should also bear in mind that, in some circumstances, hedge accounting may introduce volatility in equity rather than in profit or loss.

**12.14** A clear distinction should be made between the decisions whether to hedge a particular risk and whether to apply hedge accounting. Each is, essentially, a separate decision. There are many economic reasons why a company may choose to hedge or not hedge a particular risk position, depending on the particular risks to which it is prepared to remain exposed. The same reasons do not necessarily apply to decisions whether to apply hedge accounting. This chapter does not deal with when an economic position should be hedged. It deals with how hedge accounting applies.

**12.15**  Once a company has decided what its economic hedging strategy should be, it then needs, separately, to consider which of those economic hedges it should apply hedge accounting to. In many cases the company may choose to apply hedge accounting to only some economic positions. In a few cases, a company may be precluded from applying hedge accounting to a relationship that it views as a legitimate economic hedge. The important point here is that economic hedging and hedge accounting are not the same thing.

**12.16**  A company will need to clearly explain in its financial statements its policy for hedge accounting (see **Chapter 16** for further information). For example, a company that states that it does not 'speculate' might want to make it clear that just because it has not designated certain relationships for hedge accounting purposes, this does not mean that it is speculating. A company might also wish to explain that there are certain economic hedges that are effective in offsetting a significant amount of underlying risks that are consistent with the risk management objectives of the company, but which are not sufficiently effective for hedge accounting to apply.

## HEDGE ACCOUNTING – HOW IT WORKS

**12.17**  Hedge accounting modifies the basic recognition and measurement requirements, discussed previously. Accordingly, hedge accounting may only be used when certain conditions are met. These are outlined in detail in paragraphs **12.50–12.109**. However, first it is useful to understand what hedge accounting accomplishes.

**12.18**  IAS 39 introduces hedge accounting for two main types of hedge – exposures to changes in fair values and exposures to changes in cash flows. Each of these is discussed in detail in paragraphs **12.25–12.47**. A company may also achieve the same effect as hedge accounting in some circumstances by using the option to designate financial instruments to be measured at fair value through profit or loss, described in **Chapter 5**. This is discussed in more detail in paragraphs **12.21–12.24**. A third type of hedge accounting is specified for a hedge of a net investment in a foreign operation (see paragraphs **12.28–12.29**).

**12.19**  The economic result a company may desire from hedging may vary considerably. A company may, for example, wish to 'fix' or 'lock in' the fair values or cash flows of a hedged item – perhaps by using a forward foreign exchange contract to create cash flows from the combination of the hedged item and the forward foreign exchange contract that are 'locked in' to a future foreign exchange rate. Alternatively, a company may wish to eliminate downside risk but retain the upside potential for gain from a particular risk exposure – perhaps by using an option contract that is exercisable if interest rates move in an unfavourable manner – or it may wish to hedge the risk of variability in fair values or cash flows outside a particular range – perhaps by using a combination of option contracts that can be exercised if foreign exchange rates move above or below certain levels. Each of these strategies would, of course, require the use of different hedging instruments, but each may qualify for special accounting in accordance with IAS 39.

**12.20**   Some common hedging strategies are summarised in the table below:

**Figure 12.1: Common hedging strategies**

| **Foreign currency hedges** |
| --- |
| 1.    A company expecting to sell goods or services denominated in a foreign currency enters into a forward foreign exchange contract as a cash flow hedge of the risk of changes in the domestic currency amount of the sales due to changes in foreign exchange rates. |
| 2.    A company expecting to sell goods or services denominated in a foreign currency enters into an option contract giving it the right to sell foreign currency at a specified rate as a cash flow hedge of the risk that the domestic currency amount of the sales will fall due to declines in foreign exchange rates. |
| 3.    A company with fixed-rate debt denominated in a foreign currency enters into a cross-currency swap as a cash flow hedge of the risk that debt payments in the domestic currency will change due to fluctuations in foreign exchange rates. |
| 4.    A company with fixed-rate debt denominated in a foreign currency enters into a cross-currency swap as a fair value hedge of the risk that the domestic currency fair value of the debt will change due to changes in foreign exchange rates. |
| **Interest rate hedges** |
| 1.    A company with fixed-rate debt enters into an interest rate swap as a fair value hedge of the risk of changes in the fair value of the debt due to changes in interest rates. |
| 2.    A company with floating-rate debt enters into an interest rate swap as a cash flow hedge of the risk of variability in interest payments due to changes in interest rates. |
| 3.    A company that intends to issue fixed-rate debt in the future at the interest rate at that time enters into a derivative as a cash flow hedge of changes in interest rates that may occur before the debt is issued. |
| 4.    A company that intends to issue fixed-rate debt in the future at the currently prevailing interest rate enters into a derivative as a cash flow hedge of changes in interest rates that may occur before the debt is issued. |

| **Foreign currency and interest rate hedges** | |
|---|---|
| 1. | A company with fixed-rate debt denominated in a foreign currency enters into a cross-currency interest rate swap as a fair value hedge of the risk that the domestic currency fair value of the debt will change due to changes in interest and foreign currency exchange rates. |
| 2. | A company with floating-rate debt denominated in a foreign currency enters into a cross-currency interest rate swap as a cash flow hedge of the risk that debt payments in the domestic currency will change due to changes in interest and foreign currency exchange rates. |
| 3. | A company with floating-rate debt denominated in a foreign currency enters into a cross-currency interest rate swap as a fair value hedge of the risk that the domestic currency fair value of the debt will change due to changes in foreign currency exchange rates. |
| **Hedge of net investment in a foreign operation** | |
| 1. | A company with a net investment in a foreign operation issues foreign currency debt or enters into a forward foreign currency exchange contract to hedge the risk of foreign currency exchange gains and losses on the net investment. |
| **Commodity hedges** | |
| 1. | A company with commodity inventories enters into a commodity futures contract as a fair value hedge of the risk of changes in the overall fair value of its inventory. |
| 2. | A company with a firm commitment to sell or purchase a commodity at a fixed price in the future enters into a futures contract as a fair value hedge of the risk of changes in the overall fair value of the firm commitment. |
| 3. | A company that anticipates selling commodities in the future at the price at that time enters into a futures contract as a cash flow hedge of the risk of variability in the cash to be received on the sales due to changes in the market price of the goods. |
| 4. | A company that anticipates selling commodities in the future at the price at that time enters into an option to sell the commodities at a fixed price as a cash flow hedge of the risk of decline in the sales price of the commodities. |

**Option to measure at fair value through profit or loss**

**12.21**  Before considering hedge accounting, a company may consider whether the ability to designate a financial instrument to be measured at fair value through profit or loss will accomplish its goals. If so, that may avoid the need for extensive designation, documentation, effectiveness testing and tracking of the items involved.

**12.22**  As explained in **Chapter 5**, a company is permitted, on initial recognition, to designate any financial instrument[1] as one that will be measured at fair value with gains and losses from changes in fair value recognised in profit or loss in the periods in which they arise.

**EXAMPLE 12.4**

Company D is about to recognise an interest-sensitive financial asset on its balance sheet. The company is concerned that adverse changes in interest rates will lead to a reduction in value of its asset. Company D, therefore, enters into an interest rate derivative instrument to manage that risk. The company could designate the derivative as a hedge of exposures to interest rate risk in the interest-sensitive financial asset, document that hedge, monitor it and account for it as a fair value hedge (see paragraphs **12.25–12.32** and **12.114–12.119**). However, the company could also choose, rather than classifying the interest-sensitive asset as held to maturity or as a loan or receivable, to classify it as at fair value through profit or loss. The asset would then be measured at fair value, like the derivative. Gains and losses on both positions would be recognised in profit or loss in the periods in which they occur and any ineffectiveness would automatically be recognised in profit or loss as a net gain or loss, without the need for any designation, documentation or tracking.

[1]   At the time of writing, the IASB is considering placing some restrictions on the circumstances in which the option may be used. However, the permissible circumstances are likely to include when the exposure to changes in fair value of a financial asset or financial liability is substantially offset by the exposure to changes in fair value of another financial asset or financial liability. Thus, any restriction on the use of the fair value measurement option is unlikely to severely restrict the circumstances in which it may be used as an alternative to hedge accounting. Indeed, the IASB's objective is for the option to alleviate the need for designation and tracking of hedges in certain circumstances.

**12.23**  Of course, in the above example, the interest-sensitive asset would be measured at fair value, taking into account changes in value not only for interest rates but also for other risks affecting the value of the asset, such as credit risk. When considering whether to use the fair value measurement option as an alternative means of achieving similar results to hedge accounting, therefore, a company must carefully assess the advantages and disadvantages of measuring the entire interest-sensitive financial asset at fair value versus the burdens of designation, documentation and tracking. It should also be noted that a company may only elect to apply the fair value measurement option on initial recognition. Therefore, this strategy only works when a decision is made at the time that the financial asset or financial liability is first recognised.

**12.24**  In the following situations the fair value measurement option may be useful as a means of achieving the same effect as hedge accounting:

(a)   A financial institution has issued fixed-rate commitments to issue mortgage loans. It chooses to manage the interest rate risk associated with those commitments by using a series of debt instruments (note that non-derivative instruments are not eligible for hedge accounting except for foreign currency risk). The financial institution can achieve a similar effect to hedge accounting by measuring both the debt instruments and the mortgage commitments at fair value.

(b)   An insurance company measures its financial liabilities on a basis similar to fair value. It wishes to minimise the risk of volatility in its financial statements as a result of different measurement bases for financial assets backing the insurance liabilities from the measurement basis for the liabilities. The insurance company may elect to measure certain financial assets at fair value so that corresponding gains and losses on assets and liabilities are recognised in profit or loss in the same periods.

There are, no doubt, additional situations.

## Fair value hedges

*What is a fair value hedge?*

**12.25**   A fair value hedge is defined in IAS 39 as:

> 'a hedge of the exposure to changes in fair value of a recognised asset or liability or an unrecognised firm commitment, or an identified portion of such an asset, liability or firm commitment, that is attributable to a particular risk and could affect profit or loss.'

[IAS 39, paragraph 86(a)]

**12.26**   Breaking down this explanation, the key part is that it is a hedge of an exposure to changes in fair value. An exposure to changes in fair value may arise when a company has an asset or liability recognised on its balance sheet for which the value may change as a result of changes in market conditions. (That change in value need not be recognised in the carrying amount of the asset or liability. Thus, it can be a hedge of an exposure to an unrecognised change in fair value in an asset or liability that is measured at cost or amortised cost.) An exposure to changes in fair value may also be associated with a firm commitment to buy or sell an asset or liability in the future. Although accounting does not recognise firm commitments, the company is exposed to value changes in the asset that is the subject of the firm commitment when that firm commitment is for a specified quantity of resources at a specified price on a specified future date or dates. (If the company is committed to pay a specified price for an asset, it is exposed to the risk that by the specified date that it makes the acquisition the market price for that asset may be higher or lower than the amount it is required to pay.)

**12.27**   If a company is concerned about changes in fair value of recognised assets or liabilities, or unrecognised firm commitments, it may purchase a derivative to manage those risks (or for foreign currency risks only, a non-derivative).

### EXAMPLE 12.5

Company E has issued fixed-rate debt and is concerned that decreases in interest rates would leave the company in the unfavourable position of having to pay higher than market interest rates – the fair value of its debt would decline. To manage this risk, Company E may choose to enter into a derivative that will pay cash flows based on floating rates, and receive cash flows based on fixed rates. If interest rates decline that derivative will become more valuable, offsetting the interest rate risk in the fixed-rate debt from an economic perspective.

**12.28**   A company may not be concerned about the fair value exposure of an entire asset, liability or firm commitment, but only about the changes in fair value of a portion of that asset, liability or firm commitment. When the item to be hedged is a financial asset or financial liability, a portion may be a percentage of the changes in fair value of the entire asset, liability or firm commitment, or may be the changes in fair value of a specified part of the asset, liability or firm commitment. However, when the item to be hedged is a non-financial asset or non-financial liability, only the fair value of the entire asset, or its exposure to foreign currency risk, may be designated as hedged for accounting purposes.

### EXAMPLE 12.6

Company F, a UK company, has issued fixed-rate debt. Company F is concerned about the effects of changes in fair value due to changes in the risk-free interest rate component of the total interest rate risk exposure. Accordingly, Company F enters into a derivative to hedge the risk-free rate interest component only – perhaps using a derivative based on changes in interest rates of government bonds.

*The accounting problem*

**12.29**   From an accounting perspective, derivatives are measured at fair value through profit or loss, but changes in fair value of the hedged item may not be recognised in the same manner. For example, the carrying amount of fixed-rate debt is not adjusted for changes in interest rates in accordance with current accounting conventions. Therefore, gains and losses on changes in fair value of the derivative will be recognised in profit or loss in the periods in which they occur, but there will be no corresponding gains or losses on the fixed-rate debt.

**12.30**   Similarly, a company may have entered into a firm commitment to buy or sell an asset at a price denominated in foreign currency[1] and is concerned about adverse fluctuations in foreign exchange rates resulting in a decline in value of the asset prior to the date at which it acquires it. The company may, therefore, enter into a derivative instrument, such as a forward foreign exchange contract, to manage that risk. There is no basis in current accounting for recognising the firm commitment to buy or sell the asset until the transaction takes place. However, the derivative instrument that is managing the risk must be measured at fair value, with gains and losses recognised in profit or loss in the period in which they arise.

¹ Note that a hedge of the foreign currency risk of a firm commitment may be accounted for as either a fair value hedge or a cash flow hedge (see paragraph **12.46**).

*The accounting solution*

**12.31**    To correct for this situation, and allow the offsetting effects on net profit or loss of changes in fair values of the hedging instrument and the hedged item to be recognised in the same period, special hedge accounting is permitted, if conditions to be detailed later (see paragraphs **12.50–12.119**) are met. The basic principle that derivative financial instruments are measured at fair value with gains and losses recognised in profit or loss in the period in which they arise (see **Chapter 1**) is not violated. However, an additional accounting entry is made to adjust the hedged item (the fixed-rate debt, or the firm commitment, in the above examples) for the gain or loss on that item attributable to the hedged risk, with a corresponding entry to profit or loss. Thus, to the extent that the hedge is effective in mitigating the risk, gains and losses offset one another in profit or loss at the same time.

**EXAMPLE 12.7**

Company G has issued £100,000 of debt with a fixed interest rate. Interest payments on 30 June and 31 December of the next year are £5,000. Company G believes that interest rates are likely to decline, in which case its debt will become less valuable as it requires an above-market interest rate to be paid. Therefore, on 1 January, Company G enters into a derivative instrument which will result in it receiving £5,000 on 30 June and 31 December of the next year and paying a market rate of interest, and designates it is a fair value hedge of the interest rate risk in the fixed-rate debt.

Assume that market interest rates change such that the payments due on the derivative instrument during the next year, and the corresponding fair value of the derivative, are as follows:

|  | Interest payments | Fair value of derivative |
|---|---|---|
| 30 June | £4,500 | £12,126 |
| 31 December | £4,800 | £8,759 |

---

**Journal entries and financial statement extracts**

**Hedged item – debt**                    **Hedging instrument – derivative**

**1 January – Debt is recorded at carrying amount of £100,000[1]. Enter into hedging instrument.**

Opening balance sheet

| Assets | £ | £ | Liabilities | £ | £ |
|---|---|---|---|---|---|
| Other assets | | 150,000 | Debt | | 100,000 |
| Fair value of derivative contract | | – | Owner's equity | | 50,000 |
| TOTAL | | 150,000 | TOTAL | | 150,000 |

Journal entry

No entry[2]

(To record acquisition of derivative.)

**30 June – Record interest payments**

| Debit: Interest expense on debt | 5,000 | | | |
|---|---|---|---|---|
| Credit: Cash | | 5,000 | | |
| | | | Debit: Interest expense on derivative | 4,500 |
| | | | Credit: Cash | | 4,500 |
| | | | Debit: Cash | 5,000 |
| | | | Credit: Interest income on derivative | | 5,000 |

(To record semi-annual interest payments)

---

**Journal entries and financial statement extracts**

**Hedged item – debt**          **Hedging instrument – derivative**

**31 December – Record interest amounts and valuation changes**

Debit: Interest      5,000
expense on debt

    Credit:          5,000
    Cash

                    Debit: Interest      4,800
                    expense on
                    derivative

                        Credit: Cash          4,800

                    Debit: Cash      5,000

                        Credit: Inter-          5,000
                        est income
                        on derivative

(To record semi-annual interest payments)

                    Debit: Hedge fair   8,759
                    value

                        Credit: Gain          8,759
                        on hedge

                    (To record revaluation of derivative)

Debit: Revaluation   8,759
loss

    Credit:          8,759
    Debt

(To record hedge accounting entry)

**Balance Sheet – 31 December**

| Assets | £ | Liabilities | £ |
|---|---|---|---|
| Other assets | 140,700 | Debt | 108,759 |
| Fair value of derivative contract | 8,759 | Owner's equity | |
| | | Retained earnings | 40,700 |
| TOTAL | 149,459 | TOTAL | 149,459 |

| Journal entries and financial statement extracts | | |
|---|---|---|
| **Hedged item – debt** | | **Hedging instrument – derivative** |
| **Profit or loss – Year to 31 December** | | |
| Interest income on derivative | 10,000 | |
| Interest expense on debt | (10,000) | |
| Interest expense on derivative | (9,300) | |
| Revaluation adjustment to debt | (8,759) | |
| Revaluation gain on hedge | 8,759 | |
| NET LOSS FOR THE YEAR | (9,300) | |

1  Amortisation of the debt is ignored, for simplicity.
2  Assumed to be entered into at fair value and, for simplicity, any premium is ignored.

**12.32**   Any adjustment to the carrying amount of an asset as a result of fair value hedge accounting is taken into account for impairment testing (ie the carrying amount of the asset is adjusted first, then impairment testing is applied to that adjusted carrying amount). Therefore, it is possible that an increase in the asset carrying amount as a result of fair value hedge accounting may require reversal as a consequence of impairment testing.

## Cash flow hedges

*What is a cash flow hedge?*

**12.33**   A cash flow hedge is defined in IAS 39 as:

'a hedge of the exposure to variability in cash flows that (i) is attributable to a particular risk associated with a recognised asset or liability (such as all or some future interest payments on variable-rate debt) or a highly probable forecast transaction and (ii) could affect profit or loss.'

[IAS 39, paragraph 86(b)]

**12.34**   In this case, the exposure that a company may be concerned about is that of variability in future cash flows. An exposure to changes in cash flows may arise when a company has assets or liabilities recognised on its balance sheet from which the future cash flows will be variable, or when it anticipates entering into a highly probable transaction in the future from which the cash flows may be variable.

**12.35** If a company is concerned about changes in future cash flows from recognised assets or liabilities or highly probable forecast transactions, it may purchase a derivative to manage those risks (or for foreign currency risks only, a non-derivative).

### EXAMPLE 12.8

Company H has issued variable-rate debt and is concerned about the variations in cash flows that will arise as interest rates fluctuate. Therefore, Company H enters into a derivative instrument, such as an interest rate swap, to manage those fluctuations in cash flows. If interest rates increase, the cash outflows from interest payments on the variable-rate debt will be higher, but they will be compensated for by cash inflows from gains on the interest rate swap.

### EXAMPLE 12.9

Company I is concerned that future transactions, such as sales or pur-chases denominated in a foreign currency, may result in variable cash flows as a result of changes in foreign exchange rates. Company I enters into a derivative instrument to manage that foreign exchange risk. If foreign exchange rates move in an unfavourable manner relative to the sales or purchases, unfavourable cash flows on those transactions will be compen-sated by favourable cash flows on the derivative instrument.

**12.36** Depending on the nature of the company's concerns about cash flow risks, it may designate all or some of the future cash flows in a financial asset or financial liability as being hedged. For example, it may hedge all of the payments of both principal and interest of a variable-rate debt, or may choose to hedge only principal payments, only selected payments of either principal or interest, only selected payments of principal and interest, or a percentage of any of these cash flows.

*The accounting problem*

**12.37** In each of the examples in paragraph **12.35**, the derivative entered into to manage the cash flow risk would be measured at fair value with gains and losses from changes in fair value recognised in profit or loss in the periods in which they arise. However, the future cash flows on variable-rate debt, or future sales and purchases, do not occur until future accounting periods, and there is no basis for recognising them in the current period.

**12.38**  Rather than recognise the gains and losses on changes in fair value of the derivative instrument in profit or loss when they arise, some companies presently account for such situations by deferring such gains and losses on the balance sheet until such time as the future transactions occur (at which time they are removed from the balance sheet and recognised in profit or loss). The difficulty with this approach is that it violates the basic principle that only assets and liabilities meeting the definition of assets and liabilities should be recognised as such (see **Chapter 1**). A deferred gain recognised as a liability does not meet the definition of a liability – there is no future obligation of the company to do anything as a result of that gain. Similarly, a deferred loss recognised as an asset does not confer any future benefit on the company. Accordingly, IAS 39 does not permit deferral of gains and losses on the balance sheet as a means of solving the accounting problem.

*The accounting solution*

**12.39**  In the case of a cash flow hedge, the accounting solution is to use a separate component of equity as the temporary location in which to place certain gains and losses on a hedging instrument that is hedging cash flow risk in a future transaction. Therefore, in Example 12.8, which considers a hedge of variable-rate debt, gains and losses on changes in value of the derivative instrument that are effective as offsetting the designated risk would be recognised in equity until such time as the interest payments on the debt arise. Similarly, in Example 12.9, which considers a hedge of sales and purchases in future periods, the effective portion of the gain or loss on the derivative instrument is recognised in equity until the future sales or purchases affect profit or loss.

**12.40**  It is important to note that the intent of hedge accounting is to match profit or loss amounts. Therefore, the time when a gain or loss temporarily recorded in equity is subsequently transferred to profit or loss is the same period in which the hedged item affects profit or loss. In many cases this will be straightforward, since the hedged item will affect profit or loss as soon as, or very shortly after, the transaction occurs. For example, sales of inventory generally will affect profit or loss at the date of sale, and, therefore, the transfer from equity of gains or losses on a corresponding hedging item would also affect profit or loss at that time.

**12.41**  However, sometimes the future transaction does not immediately give rise to a profit or loss effect. For example, the future acquisition of property, plant or equipment is capitalised and only affects profit or loss as it is depreciated – perhaps over a long period of time. In this circumstance, the appropriate time to transfer gains and losses on a hedging instrument from equity to profit or loss would be at the same time as the depreciation charges are recorded in profit or loss. This is the approach that is required in accordance with FASB Statement 133 in the US, and, so as to avoid a conflict with US GAAP, is permitted in accordance with IAS 39. However, this approach results in the need to track the gains and losses, perhaps for a long period of time. Accordingly, IAS

39 permits the gain or loss previously included in equity to be included in the initial carrying amount of the asset when it is first recorded if the asset acquired is a non-financial asset.

**12.42**    While adjusting the initial carrying amount of the asset when acquired can save record-keeping in instances such as that discussed in the previous paragraph, that method of accounting can be complex in some circumstances. In particular, when the hedged item is inventory, a policy of adjusting the carrying amount of inventory to reflect gains and losses on a hedging instrument would often require significant adjustments to the normal inventory reporting system. In these circumstances, it is often easier to track the results of hedge accounting in treasury systems.

**12.43**    IAS 39 requires that a company choose between a policy of adjusting the carrying amount of the asset when acquired, and a policy of continuing to defer gains and losses on the hedging instrument in equity until the corresponding losses or gains on the hedged item affect income, for all cash flow hedges. Therefore, a company needs to carefully consider the nature of cash flow hedges it might choose to designate and what record keeping would be involved before deciding which accounting policy to adopt.

**EXAMPLE 12.10**

On 15 April 2005, Company J, a British company, contracts with an American supplier to purchase a machine priced at US$100,000. The machine will take 14 months to complete and delivery is expected in June 2006. Company J enters into a foreign exchange forward contract to purchase US$100,000 for £57,000 on 30 June 2006. It has a 31 December year-end. Company J designates the foreign currency forward contract as a hedge of foreign exchange risk in the purchase of the machine – a cash flow hedge. Company J's accounting policy is not to adjust the carrying amount of the asset acquired for gains and losses on the hedging instrument on acquisition.

---

**Journal entries and financial statement extracts**

| Hedged item – machine | Hedging instrument – forward foreign exchange contract |
|---|---|

15 April 2005 – Commit to purchase machine for US$100,000 for delivery and payment 30 June 2006. Also enter into forward foreign exchange contract committing to purchase US$100,000 for £57,000 – settlement 30 June 2006.

| | |
|---|---|
| No entry | No entry[1] |

**31 December 2005 – Six-month forward £/US$ exchange rate is £0.59/US$1**

| | £ | £ | | £ | £ |
|---|---|---|---|---|---|
| No entry | | | Debit:<br>Forward<br>foreign<br>exchange<br>contract<br>(fair<br>value) | 2,000 | |
| | | | Credit: Equity<br>gain on forward<br>foreign exchange<br>contract | | 2,000 |
| | | | (To record gain on hedging contract) | | |

**Balance sheet at 31 December 2005**

| Assets | £ | Liabilities | £ |
|---|---|---|---|
| Forward foreign<br>exchange contract<br>(fair value) | 2,000 | | |
| | | Owner's equity | |
| | | Gain on hedging<br>instrument | 2,000 |

---

**Journal entries and financial statement extracts**

| Hedged item – machine | Hedging instrument – forward foreign exchange contract |
|---|---|

**30 June 2006 – Company purchases machine and settles forward foreign exchange contract with purchase of US$100,000 for £57,000. The £/US$ spot exchange rate is £0.595/$1.**

| | £ | £ | | £ | £ |
|---|---|---|---|---|---|
| Debit: Machine | 59,500 | | Debit: Forward foreign exchange contract (fair value) | 500 | |
| Credit: Cash US$100,000 @ £0.595/$1 | | 59,500 | Credit: Equity gain on forward foreign exchange contract | | 500 |
| (To record purchase of machine) | | | (To record revaluation of hedge contract) | | |
| | | | Debit: Cash ($100,000 @ $0.595) | 59,500 | |
| | | | Credit: Forward foreign exchange contract | | 2,500 |
| | | | Credit: Cash (US$100,000 @ $0.57) | | 57,000 |
| | | | (To record settlement of hedging contract) | | |

---

**Journal entries and financial statement extracts**

Hedged item – machine        Hedging instrument – forward
                             foreign exchange contract

**31 December 2006 – Machine is to be amortised straight line over 10 years and has an estimated salvage value of £9,500**

| | | | |
|---|---|---|---|
| Debit: Amortisation expense machine | 2,500 | Debit: Gain on hedge (Equity) | 125 |
| Credit: Accumulated amortisation | 2,500 | Credit: Amortisation of hedge gain (net income) | 125 |
| (To record six months amortisation) | | (To record six months amortisation) | |

**Balance sheet – 31 December 2006**

| Assets | £ | Liabilities | £ |
|---|---|---|---|
| Machinery and equipment | 59,500 | | |
| Less: accumulated amortisation | (2,500) | Owner's equity | |
| | | Unamortised gain on cash flow hedge | 2,375 |

**Profit or loss – Year to 31 December 2006**

| | |
|---|---|
| Amortisation of hedge gain | 125 |
| Amortisation | (2,500) |
| NET LOSS | (2,375) |

---

[1] Transaction fees are ignored, for simplicity.

## EXAMPLE 12.11

The facts are the same as in Example 12.10, except Company K's accounting policy is to adjust the carrying amount of the asset acquired for gains and losses on the hedging instrument on acquisition. The accounting effects from 30 June 2006 differ as follows:

---

**Journal entries and financial statement extracts**

Hedged item – machine        Hedging instrument – forward
                             foreign exchange contract

**30 June 2006 – Company purchases machine and settles forward foreign exchange contract with purchase of $100,000 for £57,000. The £/US$ spot exchange rate is £0.595/$.**

---

### Journal entries and financial statement extracts

| Hedged item – machine | | | Hedging instrument – forward foreign exchange contract | | |
|---|---|---|---|---|---|
| | £ | £ | | £ | £ |
| Debit: Machine | 59,500 | | Debit: Forward foreign exchange contract (fair value) | 500 | |
| Credit: Cash US$100,000 @ £0.595/$1 | | 59,500 | Credit: Equity gain on forward foreign exchange contract | | 500 |
| (To record purchase of machine) | | | (To record revaluation of hedge contract) | | |
| | | | Debit: Cash £($100,000 @ $0.595) | 59,500 | |
| | | | Credit: Forward foreign exchange contract | | 2,500 |
| | | | Credit: £ cash (US$100,000 @ $0.57) | | 57,000 |
| | | | (To record settlement of hedging contract) | | |
| Credit: Machine | | 2,500 | Debit: Equity | 2,500 | |
| (To record basis adjustment on acquiring machine) | | | | | |

**31 December 2006 – Machine is to be amortised straight line over 10 years and has an estimated salvage value of £9,500**

| | | |
|---|---|---|
| Debit: Amortisation expense machine | 2,375 | No entry |
| Credit: Accumulated amortisation | 2,375 | |
| (To record six months amortisation) | | |

**Balance sheet – 31 December 2006**

| Assets | £ | Liabilities | £ |
|---|---|---|---|
| Machinery and equipment | 57,000 | | |
| Less: accumulated amortisation | (2,375) | Owner's equity | |
| | | Unamortised gain on cash flow hedge | – |

```
Journal entries and financial statement extracts

Hedged item – machine          Hedging instrument – forward
                                 foreign exchange contract


Profit or loss – year to 31 December 2006
Amortisation              (2,375)
NET LOSS                  (2,375)
```

**12.44**   Note that the accounting in both Examples 12.10 and 12.11 gives rise to the same effect on net profit or loss. However, the second alternative would result in less need to track the gains and losses temporarily recorded in equity throughout the life of the capitalised asset.

**12.45**   Any adjustment to the carrying amount of an asset as a result of cash flow hedge accounting is taken into account for impairment testing (ie the carrying amount of the asset is adjusted first, then impairment testing is applied to that adjusted carrying amount). Therefore, it is possible that an increase in asset carrying amount as a result of cash flow hedge accounting with basis adjustment may require reversal as a consequence of impairment testing.

**12.46**   IAS 39 allows a hedge of the foreign currency risk of an unrecognised firm commitment to be accounted for as either a cash flow hedge or a fair value hedge, although for other risks a hedge of a firm commitment must be accounted for as a fair value hedge. This is because foreign currency risk affects both the cash flows and the fair value of the hedged item. This also makes it more convenient for companies when hedging foreign currency risk in forecast transactions, because there is no need to re-designate a cash flow hedge of a forecast transaction as a fair value hedge when the forecast transaction becomes a firm commitment.

**12.47**   Even though cash flow hedge accounting allows a company to recognise gains and losses in equity, any gains and losses that are not expected to be recovered in the future are required to be immediately transferred to profit or loss.

**Hedge of net investment in a foreign operation**

**12.48**   In accordance with IAS 21, exchange differences arising on a monetary item that forms part of a company's net investment in a foreign operation are classified in a separate component of equity in the company's consolidated financial statements until the disposal of the net investment (see IAS 21, paragraph 32). Accordingly, if a company enters into a derivative instrument to hedge the exchange risk associated with such an investment, the company would like the exchange gain or loss on the hedging instrument to be recognised in the same place as that on the net investment – ie in the separate component of equity. This is the effect of a hedge of a net investment in a foreign operation.

**12.49** Essentially, the accounting is very similar to that applied for a cash flow hedge. The portion of the gain or loss on the hedging item that is determined to be an effective hedge is recognised directly in equity, rather than in profit or loss, until such time as the foreign operation is disposed of, at which time it is recognised in profit or loss, together with other exchange differences on monetary items that form part of the company's net investment in that foreign operation.

## QUALIFYING HEDGING RELATIONSHIPS

### Overview

**12.50** As noted previously, a company may manage a variety of hedging relationships for economic purposes. However, only certain relationships qualify for hedge accounting.

**12.51** Hedge accounting is only permitted when there is a need for it – ie when gains and losses on the hedging item and the hedged item would be recognised in profit or loss in different periods without hedge accounting (see paragraphs **12.54–12.56**).

**12.52** Furthermore, a number of items are explicitly precluded from being hedged or being designated as a hedging item for accounting purposes (see paragraphs **12.57–12.84**). Therefore, there is no need for a company to consider whether to apply hedge accounting for those items that do not qualify.

**12.53** In addition, for a hedging relationship to qualify for hedge accounting it must meet certain conditions:

(a) the hedge must be expected to be highly effective in achieving offsetting changes in fair value or cash flows attributable to the hedged risk at inception and on an ongoing basis, and that effectiveness must be reliably measurable (see paragraphs **12.85–12.113**); and

(b) there must be formal designation and documentation of the hedging relationship (see paragraphs **12.114–12.119**).

### Gains and losses must be recognised in profit or loss in different periods without hedge accounting

**12.54** Since hedge accounting is a method for recognising the gains and losses arising from items in a hedging relationship, such that those gains and losses are recognised in profit or loss in the same period when they would otherwise be recognised in different periods, it follows that hedge accounting is only neces-sary, and therefore only permitted, when gains and losses associated with items in a hedging relationship would otherwise be recognised in different periods. Thus, gains and losses on the hedged item and the hedging item must:

(a)   affect, or have the potential to affect, profit or loss; and
(b)   be recognised in profit or loss in different periods if hedge accounting were not applied.

**12.55**   It follows from the condition in the previous paragraph that it is inappropriate for either the hedging item or hedged item to be an item that is included in equity, since gains and losses on such items will not affect profit or loss.

### EXAMPLE 12.12

Company L wishes to hedge the foreign exchange risk in an anticipated dividend. This is not permitted, since any exchange fluctuations on the dividend would affect equity, rather than profit or loss, until such time as the dividend becomes payable (ie it becomes a financial liability).

### EXAMPLE 12.13

Company M wishes to hedge risks associated with financial instruments presented in equity in accordance with IAS 32, such as the equity portion of a compound instrument. This is not permitted, since gains or losses on equity instruments affect equity, rather than profit or loss.

**12.56**   It further follows from this condition that hedge accounting is not necessary and, indeed, is precluded when gains and losses affect profit or loss in the same period.

### EXAMPLE 12.14

Company N wishes to designate a derivative as a hedge of foreign currency exposure in an equity investment measured at fair value through profit or loss. This is not permitted, since both the hedged item and hedging item are measured at fair value. Hedge accounting is unnecessary in this circumstance.

### EXAMPLE 12.15

Company O, a UK company, wishes to designate a receivable due in 30 days and denominated in euros as a hedge of a payable, also due in 30 days and denominated in euros. This is not permitted, since the hedged item and hedging item are both denominated in the same foreign currency and translated at the same exchange rates. The effects of changes in foreign exchange rates on each item are reflected in profit or loss in the same period in accordance with IAS 21, without the need for hedge accounting.

## What can be hedged for accounting purposes – the hedged item?

**12.57**   The hedged item can be a single item or a group of items with similar risk characteristics, that is any of the following:

(a)   an asset or liability (except for a held-to-maturity investment with respect to interest rate risk or prepayment risk);
(b)   an unrecognised firm commitment;
(c)   a highly probable forecast transaction; or
(d)   a net investment in a foreign operation. (See IAS 39, paragraphs 78–79.)

*Assets and liabilities*

**12.58**   When the hedged item is a financial asset or financial liability, a company may designate a hedge of all or a portion of cash flows or fair value, as long as the company can reliably measure effectiveness (IAS 39, paragraph 81). Therefore, a company may hedge individual risks within a hedged item, such as interest rate risk, foreign currency risk, credit risk or commodity price risk only (**Chapter 16** discusses the types of risks that may be transferred in transactions involving financial instruments), or it may hedge individual cash flows or percentages of an asset, liability or forecast transaction.

### EXAMPLE 12.16

Examples of items that a company that has issued fixed-rate debt may hedge include:

(a)   the overall change in fair value of the debt;
(b)   the change attributable to changes in the market rate of interest;
(c)   the change attributable to changes in the risk-free interest rate (benchmark rate);
(d)   the change attributable to changes in the prime rate or some other widely quoted interest rate;
(e)   the change attributable to changes in general credit spreads;
(f)   the change attributable to changes in the credit risk of the company itself;
(g)   the change attributable to both changes in general credit spreads and the credit risk of the company;
(h)   the change attributable to payments of principal only;
(i)   the change attributable to payments of interest only;
(j)   the change attributable to the first four interest payments; or
(k)   50 per cent of the change in fair value of the debt.

**12.59**   If the hedged item is a non-financial asset or a non-financial liability, the company may hedge only foreign currency risk or the entire change in fair value of the non-financial asset or non-financial liability arising from all risks (IAS 39, paragraph 82).

### EXAMPLE 12.17

Company P, a car manufacturer, wishes to use hedge accounting for the risk of changes in the fair value of the rubber content in tyres it holds in stock. This is not permitted, since tyres are a non-financial asset. It is not possible to reliably determine the change in fair value of tyres due to changes in rubber prices separately from other factors that may affect the change in fair value of tyres.

*Firm commitments and forecast transactions*

**12.60**   A firm commitment is defined in IAS 39 as:

'a binding agreement for the exchange of a specified quantity of resources at a specified price on a specified future date or dates'

[IAS 39, paragraph 9]

It is necessary that all three of the quantity, price and future dates be specified in order for there to be a firm commitment. The agreement may be binding in law or because of disincentives for non-performance (such as a significant penalty to the company for not honouring the commitment). A forecast transaction is any 'uncommitted but anticipated future transaction' – ie an anticipated future transaction that is not a firm commitment.

**12.61**   The distinction between a firm commitment and a forecast transaction becomes important because, although a hedge of the foreign currency risk of a firm commitment can be a fair value hedge or a cash flow hedge, other hedges of risks in firm commitments are accounted for as fair value hedges while hedges of risks in anticipated transactions are accounted for as cash flow hedges.

### EXAMPLE 12.18

The following are examples of firm commitments:

(a)   A binding agreement to purchase 300kg of flour for 50p per kg on 10 June 2005.
(b)   A binding agreement to pay cash of $10 on the last day of each month in 2005.
(c)   A binding agreement to issue US$100,000 principal amount of debt on 30 June 2005, maturing in ten years, at an issue price of US$95,000.

**EXAMPLE 12.19**

The following are examples of forecast transactions that are not firm commitments:

(a)  Anticipated sales or purchases in future reporting periods for which no binding commitment exists, or for which the quantity or price has not been fixed.

(b)  Anticipated issue or purchase of debt for which no binding commitment exists.

**12.62**  A forecast transaction can be the hedged item only if it is 'highly probable'. In assessing whether a transaction is 'highly probable' a company would consider factors such as the following:

(a)  The existence of a firm commitment to undertake the transaction. When there is a firm commitment the transaction is highly probable.

(b)  The existence of similar transactions in the past. For example, generally it would not be highly probable that a company could justify levels of sales in an amount significantly greater than previous years as a forecast transaction qualifying for hedge accounting.

(c)  The financial and operational ability of the company to undertake the transaction. It would not be appropriate to apply hedge accounting for forecast purchases if the company is unlikely to have the ability to make those purchases.

(d)  The extent of the company's current commitments of resources to the business activity of which the forecast transaction is a part. It would not be appropriate to apply hedge accounting for a forecast purchase for a business that the company is discontinuing if the forecast purchase will not occur if a buyer is found for the business.

(e)  The length of time to the date the forecast transaction is expected to occur. The longer the period of time, the less probable the transaction might be.

(f)  The extent of loss or disruption to the company if it does not undertake the transaction. A forecast transaction to replace a piece of machinery that is essential to the production process would generally qualify as a highly probable forecast transaction for hedge accounting purposes.

(g)  The likelihood that another transaction might take place to achieve the same business purpose. Hedge accounting would not be appropriate for a forecast transaction to acquire inventory from one supplier when it is already clear that the entire inventory that the company needs will be acquired from an alternative supplier.

(h)  The likelihood that another party would be willing to undertake the forecast transaction with the company. It would not be appropriate to apply hedge accounting for a forecast, but uncommitted, transaction for an item that is very difficult to obtain or on terms and conditions that would be particularly onerous to another party.

(i)  The susceptibility of the transaction to changes in demand or risk of technological obsolescence of the product that is the subject of the forecast transaction.

**12.62** *Hedge accounting*

*Groups of hedged items*

**12.63** Groups of items may be hedged together only if they have similar risk characteristics. This is because, if the items in the group are dissimilar, it would not be possible to ascertain to which items any gains or losses on the hedging instrument should be allocated.

**12.64** Similarity of items means that the items share the same risk exposure that is designated as being hedged and, for a fair value hedge, the change in fair value of the items in the group is expected to be approximately proportional to the overall change in fair value attributable to the hedged risk of the group of items (for example, if the value of a portfolio of items increases by 10 per cent, each individual item increases by 8–12 per cent). Similarity of risk exposure requires not only that the items share the same risk, but also requires that the exposure moves in the same direction. Therefore, IAS 39 generally precludes hedging an overall net position, such as the net interest rate risk exposure arising from financial assets and financial liabilities with similar maturities, or from net foreign currency exposures arising from debtors and creditors – so-called 'macrohedging'.

---

**EXAMPLE 12.20**

Company Q wishes to group foreign currency purchases with foreign currency sales as a hedged item. This is not permitted, since purchases and sales do not share the same risk exposure because the risks move in opposite directions.

---

**EXAMPLE 12.21**

Company R wishes to group its accrued benefit asset and liability for employee future benefits as a hedged item. This is not permitted, since accrued benefit assets and accrued benefit liabilities comprise dissimilar asset and liabilities.

---

**12.65** In these circumstances, it may be possible to achieve the same effect as hedging the entire group by specifying the hedge in a different manner.

---

**EXAMPLE 12.22**

Company S has anticipated sales of 100,000 euros and anticipated purchases of 75,000 euros. It wishes to hedge the net foreign currency exposure, but that is not permitted. However, Company S may achieve a similar accounting result by hedging the foreign currency exposure arising from sales of 25,000 euros.

---

**12.66** The approach illustrated in Example 12.22 may be undertaken for multiple groups of hedged items, such as the net interest exposures expected during a particular period of time. However, the accounting result depends on the designation of the expected gross exposure and may not be fully representative of the desired effect if the designated gross exposure does not match the eventual net exposure from the group of items. IAS 39, paragraph AG101 provides additional examples of how this might be achieved.

**12.67** At the end of March 2004 the IASB issued a modification to IAS 39 to allow some additional hedge accounting for a portfolio hedge of interest rate risk. This is primarily applicable to financial institutions. It would allow a company to designate the gross exposure arising from interest income and interest expense expected to occur in particular time periods as the hedged item in a fair value hedge.

**12.68** A company needs to be able to identify whether a particular transaction within a group of hedged transactions is the hedged item when it occurs in order to apply the appropriate accounting and to assess whether the hedge is effective. Therefore, a company cannot identify the last £600,000 of sales as being a hedged item, since when a particular transaction occurs it is not possible to know whether it is the hedged item.

**12.69** A company may be able to carefully select groups of similar items that are more likely to qualify for hedge accounting. For example, a company might be able to disaggregate portfolios into smaller, more homogeneous groups, or exclude from the designated portfolio single items that individually are more volatile than others.

*Net investment in a foreign operation*

**12.70** Hedge accounting is possible only for foreign currency risk related to the net investment in a foreign operation.

**What doesn't qualify as a hedged item for accounting purposes?**

**12.71** It follows from the above analysis of what qualifies as a hedged item for accounting purposes that the following do not qualify.

(a)   Derivative instruments. Since all derivatives are classified as held for trading and must be measured at fair value through profit or loss, there is no need for hedge accounting. (There is an exception for a purchased option when hedged by a written option in a fair value hedge, since the written option may reduce the profit or loss exposure to changes in fair value that could otherwise arise from the purchased option alone.)

(b)   Transactions that do not affect profit or loss. For example forecast transactions when the hedging item is itself a forecast transaction, since profit or loss will not be affected whether or not hedge accounting is applied.

(c)   Interest rate or prepayment risk in held-to-maturity investments. Actively managing such risks is considered to be incompatible with the intent to hold such investments to maturity regardless of changes in conditions. (Hedge accounting is permitted for foreign currency and credit risk in held-to-maturity investments since changes in such risks are reflected in the carrying amount of these investments.)

(d)   Investments in equity instruments that do not have a quoted market price in an active market and whose fair value cannot be reliably measured, which are measured at cost. When fair value cannot be reliably measured hedge accounting is not considered appropriate, since any ineffectiveness cannot be reliably measured.

(e)   Equity method investments (associates). The equity method does not involve periodic recognition of changes in the fair value of an investment or changes in cash flows from it. Therefore, this is inconsistent with the concepts underlying hedge accounting.

(f)   Investments in a consolidated subsidiary. Consolidation recognises the subsidiary's profit or loss rather than changes in fair value. Therefore, this is inconsistent with the concepts underlying hedge accounting.

(g)   Any instrument classified as equity of the issuer, including minority interests.

(h)   Groups of items with dissimilar risk characteristics. This includes expected net profit or loss or cash flows.

(i)   Portions of non-financial items (except foreign currency risk).

(j)   Unrecognised assets or liabilities, such as an unrecognised intangible asset.

(k)   Firm commitments to enter into business combinations, except for foreign currency risk. Risks other than foreign currency risks cannot be specifically identified and measured – they are general business risks.

(l)   Forecast transactions that are not highly probable.

## What can a company hedge with for accounting purposes – the hedging instrument?

*Overview*

**12.72**   There are far fewer restrictions on the hedging item than on the hedged item. The hedging item may be:

(a)   any derivative or proportion thereof (except some written options); or

(b)   a non-derivative financial asset or financial liability (but only for a hedge of foreign currency risk).

*Derivatives*

**12.73**   A derivative instrument is most often used as a hedging instrument. Common derivatives used include forward foreign exchange contracts, interest rate swaps, cross-currency swaps, commodity swaps and purchased options. A written option is generally precluded from being a hedging instrument since the writer has accepted risk rather than reducing risk. A written option has the potential to give rise to a loss to the writer that is significantly greater than the potential gain in value of any related hedged item, except when it hedges a purchased option. Therefore, such a derivative is precluded from being designated as a hedging item unless it hedges a purchased option.

**12.74**  Because the factors causing changes in fair value of a hedging item are co-dependent, generally the entire instrument must be designated as the hedging item. The only exceptions to this are that the intrinsic value and time value of an option may be separated (with the change in the intrinsic value being the designated hedging instrument) or the interest element and the spot price of a forward contract may be separated (with the change in the interest element (the premium) being the designated hedging instrument). In these cases the intrinsic value or premium can be measured separately.

**12.75**  A proportion of an entire hedging instrument may be designated as the hedging instrument. For example, a company may designate 50 per cent of the notional amount as the hedging item. In such cases the changes in fair value of the derivative for the proportion not designated would be recognised in profit or loss. The amount recognised in profit or loss would be the total change in fair value of the derivative multiplied by the percentage of the derivative that is not designated as a hedge.

### EXAMPLE 12.23

Company T designates 80 per cent of the change in value of a derivative instrument as a cash flow hedging instrument. During the period the derivative instrument changes in value by £20. £16 is recognised in equity and £4 is recognised in profit or loss in the period.

**12.76**  A hedging relationship may not be designated for only a portion of the time period during which the hedging item remains outstanding – thus an interest rate swap running for twelve months cannot be designated as the hedging instrument for, say, the first three months only. This may require care in selecting the appropriate hedging item.

**12.77**  A company may designate two or more derivatives in combination as a joint hedging item. The only restriction on this is that a combination of instruments that creates the effect of a net written option may not be designated as a hedging item.

### EXAMPLE 12.24

Company U is prepared to accept some volatility in foreign exchange rates related to future sales, but wishes to protect itself against changes in foreign currency rates outside a certain range. Therefore, Company U enters into two option contracts – one that can be exercised if exchange rates rise above a specified level and one that can be exercised if foreign exchange rates fall below a certain level. Company U may designate the combination of the two option contracts as a cash flow hedge of the foreign currency risk in the future sales.

*Non-derivatives*

**12.78**   Non-derivatives (or combinations thereof) are permitted to be designated as hedging items only for changes in foreign currency risk. Most non-derivatives are not measured at fair value. However, they are adjusted for changes in foreign exchange rates in accordance with IAS 21. Accordingly, the timing of recognition of foreign currency gains and losses in profit or loss may not match when, say, cash flows from a recognised non-derivative foreign currency denominated asset are used as an offset to unrecognised foreign currency commitments.

**12.79**   Although a financial asset classified as a held-to-maturity financial asset or as loans and receivables is not adjusted for changes in fair value, it is adjusted for changes in foreign currency risk. Therefore, such an instrument may be a hedging item in a hedge of foreign currency risk.

**What doesn't qualify as a hedging item for accounting purposes?**

**12.80**   The following cannot be hedging items in a hedging relationship:

(a)   Portions of derivative instruments (eg the first five years of a ten-year swap).
(b)   Inter-company derivatives (unless there is an exact external set-off – see paragraphs **12.81–12.84**).
(c)   Investments in equity instruments that do not have a quoted market price in an active market and whose fair value cannot be reliably measured, which are measured at cost. When fair value cannot be reliably measured hedge accounting is not considered appropriate, since any ineffectiveness cannot be reliably measured.
(d)   Written options, unless offsetting a purchased option.
(e)   Items classified as equity of the issuer.
(f)   Non-derivatives (except for foreign currency risks).

**Internal transactions**

**12.81**   Internal transactions generally do not qualify for hedge accounting. When such transactions are undertaken between parts of the same reporting entity they eliminate on consolidation. However, the foreign currency risk of an intra-group monetary item (such as an inter-company payable or receivable) may qualify as a hedged item if it results in a foreign exchange risk that is not fully eliminated on consolidation in accordance with IAS 21. This could be the case when the intra-group monetary item is the result of a transaction between two group companies with different functional currencies. The Guidance on Implementing IAS 39 contains several examples of how this might apply in practice (see F.1.6 and F.1.7).

**12.82** Even though internal transactions may not qualify for hedge accounting in consolidated financial statements, they may qualify for hedge accounting in the separate financial statements of group companies when the transactions are with other group companies.

**12.83** A company may achieve hedge accounting related to internal transactions when an internal contract is offset with a contract with an external party. In such circumstances the external contract may be designated as the hedging instrument.

**EXAMPLE 12.25**

Company V enters into an interest rate swap with one of its subsidiaries, Company W, that will pay fixed interest payments to Company V and variable interest payments to Company W. The purpose of the transaction is to hedge the variable interest rate exposures on Company W's long-term debt.

In the consolidated financial statements hedge accounting is not permitted. The profit and loss effects of the interest payments on the interest rate swap will eliminate on consolidation. However, if Company V were to enter into another interest rate swap with an external party to receive fixed interest payments and pay variable interest payments (offsetting the interest rate swap with Company W), that external contract may be designated as a hedge of the interest rate risk in Company W's long-term debt in the consolidated financial statements.

Company W may designate the interest rate swap as a hedging instrument of its long-term debt and, assuming all other qualifications are met, apply hedge accounting in its own separate financial statements.

**12.84** A single external transaction may be entered into to offset multiple internal transactions. However, a single external transaction may not be used to offset a net exposure.

**Hedge effectiveness**

*Overview*

**12.85** IAS 39 defines hedge effectiveness as:

'the degree to which changes in the fair value or cash flows of the hedged item that are attributable to a hedged risk are offset by changes in the fair value or cash flows of the hedging instrument.'

[IAS 39, paragraph 9]

**EXAMPLE 12.26**

Company X is hedging the risk of change in the fair value of debt, using an interest rate swap. The change in fair value of the debt during the period is £100 but the change in the fair value of the interest rate swap is £105 (the ineffectiveness for the period is £5).

**12.86** The requirement that effectiveness is measured based on the degree of offset means that hedging relationships that 'modify', rather than 'offset', risks will generally not qualify for hedge accounting. Thus, entering into a derivative to swap floating-rate cash flows for a different set of floating-rate cash flows, or to swap cash flows in one currency for cash flows in a different currency, would not generally qualify as effective hedging instruments.

**12.87** Furthermore, the qualifying conditions for hedge accounting require that:

(a) 'The hedge is expected to be highly effective ... in achieving offsetting changes in fair value or cash flows attributable to the hedged risk, consistently with the originally documented risk management strategy for that particular hedging relationship' [IAS 39, paragraph 88(b)]; and

(b) 'The hedge is assessed on an ongoing basis and determined actually to have been highly effective throughout the financial reporting periods for which the hedge was designated.' [IAS 39, paragraph 88(e)]

**12.88** If these criteria are not met, or are not maintained, then hedge accounting is not permitted (or, if previously applied, is discontinued). Thus, the ability to demonstrate effectiveness is vital to achieving hedge accounting.

**12.89** In addition, effectiveness must be reliably measurable for a relationship to qualify for hedge accounting. Therefore, if the hedged risk cannot be measured reliably – such as general business risks, risks of appropriation of property, risks of overall declines or increases in profits, or risks associated with assets or liabilities for which fair value cannot be reliably measured – the relationship does not qualify for hedge accounting.

*Prospective and retrospective assessment of effectiveness*

**12.90** The assessment of effectiveness is both prospective and retrospective. A company must assess whether it can expect changes in the fair value or cash flows of the hedged item that are attributable to the hedged risk to be offset by the changes in the fair value or cash flows of the hedging instrument in the future (prospective assessment) and whether actual changes in the fair value or cash flows of the hedged item attributable to the risk being hedged have offset sufficiently up to the assessment date (retrospective assessment).

**12.91** IAS 39 requires effectiveness to be assessed, at a minimum, at the time a company prepares its annual or interim financial statements. However, a company may wish to assess effectiveness more frequently because if the retrospective assessment identifies that the hedge has become ineffective, hedge accounting is to be discontinued from the last time at which effectiveness was proven.

### EXAMPLE 12.27

Company Y assesses effectiveness only annually. On 31 December 2005, Company Y discovers that a particular hedge is ineffective. Company Y is therefore precluded from using hedge accounting for that relationship for the entire year, since the last effectiveness assessment had been performed on 31 December 2004 – unless it can identify the event or change in circumstances that caused the ineffectiveness and demonstrate that the hedge was effective before that event or change in circumstances occurred.

**12.92** If the hedge fails the retrospective assessment at the end of the period, although hedge accounting would be precluded for the period, the company may still pass the prospective assessment and be able to apply hedge accounting in future periods. Also, if the hedge fails the prospective assessment at the beginning of a period but passes the retrospective assessment at the end of the previous period, hedge accounting is permitted for the period just ended, but precluded for the next period.

*When is a hedge highly effective?*

**12.93** IAS 39 explains that a hedge is regarded as highly effective only if:

(a) at the inception of the hedge and in subsequent periods, the hedge is expected to be highly effective in achieving offsetting changes in fair value or cash flows attributable to the hedged risk during the period for which the hedge is designated; and

(b) the actual results are within a range of 80–125 per cent.

### EXAMPLE 12.28

Company Z is hedging the risk of change in the fair value of debt using an interest rate swap. The change in fair value of the debt during the period is £100, but the change in the fair value of the interest rate swap is £105. The relative change in fair values can be measured as 100 divided by 105, which is 95.2 per cent, or 105 divided by 100, which is 105 per cent. This falls within the 80–125 per cent range. Therefore, the hedge has proved to be highly effective.

**12.94** Note that the criterion for prospective assessment is the same as that for assessing actual results ('a range of 80–125 per cent'). In some past practice, the prospective effectiveness test was considered to require that the fair value or cash flows 'almost fully offset' – often interpreted as a range of 95–105 per cent, thus preventing a company from entering into, or continuing, a hedging relationship when effectiveness is expected to be marginal on inception, or on a prospective basis. The IASB has altered this requirement in conjunction with its March 2004 amendments to IAS 39.

**12.95** The selection of the method for assessing effectiveness (see paragraphs **12.98–12.108**) and the inputs to the assessment model can be vital in establishing a hedge accounting policy. In order to meet the effectiveness requirements the hedging relationship needs to be very carefully established. Changes in fair value of any excluded components, such as time value, will be recognised in profit or loss in the period in which they arise. However, this is better than to have inappropriate components included in the hedge effectiveness test, thus increasing the likelihood of ineffectiveness resulting.

**12.96** In some circumstances, for example when the volatility of the hedged item is expected to be greater than that of the hedging item, it may be desirable to designate only a portion of the hedged item as within the hedging relationship – thus reducing the risk of ineffectiveness. However, this would be possible only for hedges of financial assets and financial liabilities, since a non-financial item may only be designated as a hedged item in its entirety or for foreign currency risk.

**12.97** Even though the hedging relationship may qualify for hedge accounting by falling within the 80–125 per cent range, ineffectiveness may exist within that range. Hedge accounting can continue, but the ineffective portion of gains and losses must be recognised in net income in the period in which they arise. The hedge effectiveness assessment model determines whether the hedge remains effective. However, the amount of any ineffectiveness to be recognised in profit or loss must be measured by comparing the ratio of changes in the hedging instrument to changes in the hedged item.

*Assessing hedge effectiveness*

**12.98** IAS 39 does not specify a method for assessing hedge effectiveness. Nor does it require that a single method be used for different types of hedge – or even for the prospective and retrospective assessments for the same hedge. However, it does require that the company identify when entering into the hedge the method that it will use to assess effectiveness. It cannot change its mind and use a different method when the designated method identifies that the hedge is ineffective. The original hedge is discontinued but a new hedge may be designated prospectively, using a different effectiveness assessment method. Paragraphs **12.99–12.107** describe two approaches that might be used:

(a)  ratio analysis; and
(b)  regression methods.

Many other methods are also possible.

**Ratio analysis**

**12.99**  This method involves a company calculating the ratio of changes in the fair value or cash flows of the hedged item relating to the risk being hedged to the offsetting changes in the fair value or cash flows of the hedging item relating to the same risk. A hedging relationship is considered highly effective, in accordance with this method, when the ratio of changes in the fair values or cash flows of the hedged item and hedging item attributable to the risk being hedged is between 0.8 and 1.25.

**12.100**  The calculations are performed each time the hedge is assessed for effectiveness. While IAS 39 does not specify a frequency for such calculations, because of the fact that a company is precluded from hedge accounting after the time that effectiveness was last proven, a company would generally make such assessments at least quarterly – and often more frequently.

**12.101**  A company may choose whether to make assessments discretely by period or cumulatively from the inception of the hedging relationship. However, once it has decided on the method it must stick with it. The two methods can give very different results, as illustrated in the following example.

**EXAMPLE 12.29**

Company AA identifies changes in the fair value of a hedged and hedging item as follows:

| | | |
|---|---|---|
| Period to 31 March 2005 | Hedged item: £100 | Hedging item: £100 |
| Period to 30 June 2005 | Hedged item: £55 | Hedging item: £57 |
| Period to 30 September 2005 | Hedged item: £20 | Hedging item: £23 |
| Period to 31 December 2005 | Hedged item: £(10) | Hedging item: £(18) |

Using the discrete method, the ratio of changes in fair value in each period is as follows:

| | |
|---|---|
| Period to 31 March 2005 | 100% |
| Period to 30 June 2005 | 96% |
| Period to 30 September 2005 | 87% |

Period to 31 December 2005                                    56%

The hedge fails the effectiveness test at 31 December 2005.

Using the cumulative method the ratio of changes in fair value in each period is as follows:

Period to 31 March 2005                                      100%
Period to 30 June 2005                                       99%
Period to 30 September 2005                                  97%
Period to 31 December 2005                                   102%

The hedge does not fail the effectiveness test.

**12.102**   Note that even though the discrete method is the one that fails the effectiveness test first in the above example, it could be the cumulative test that fails first given other fact situations – particularly if there are infrequent significant differences between the effects of changes in fair values on the hedged item and hedging item in periods that continue to be included in the cumulative record.

**12.103**   A company must also decide, and document, over what period it is going to assess the effectiveness – ie the number of prior periods it will include in an effectiveness test.

**Regression**

**12.104**   This method involves the company demonstrating that changes in the fair value or cash flows of the hedged item relating to the risk being hedged vary in a manner that is similar to changes in the fair value or cash flows of the hedging item relating to the same risk. A hedging relationship is considered highly effective, in accordance with this method, when the regression is statistically valid and statistically significant and the correlation co-efficient is 0.80 or more and the slope of the regression line (as adjusted for the hedging ratio) is between 0.80 and 1.25.

**12.105**   Similar to the ratio analysis method, this method involves collecting a series of pairs of observations of changes in price for the hedged item and the hedging item. However, rather than merely calculating the ratio of the changes in price to one another, the data is input into a statistical model to calculate their relationship to one another.

**12.106**   Because of the necessity for statistical significance of the model it is necessary to use a sufficient number of data observations. Generally, this would be based on something in the order of thirty or more observations. Any attempt to perform regression analysis with less than twelve observations is likely to result in a lack of statistical significance. A company should consider gathering the necessary historical data for retrospective testing as soon as it identifies the need.

**12.107** In order for a regression analysis to yield acceptable results one would expect a confidence level (or t-statistic) of 95 per cent or greater, a co-efficient of determination ($R^2$) of 80 per cent or greater and a regression co-efficient (or the slope of the regression line) between $-0.8$ and $-1.25$.

## Ratio analysis versus regression method

**12.108** While ratio analysis is probably the simpler method of assessing effectiveness, it is also the more sensitive to small changes in values. Some research has indicated that the dollar offset method rejects as ineffective more than 30 per cent of hedges that have a correlation co-efficient of 98 per cent or greater.

*Sources of ineffectiveness*

**12.109** Hedging relationships are rarely perfect, because the risks affecting the hedged item and the hedging instrument are rarely identical, resulting in different magnitudes of change in fair value or cash flows as a result of events. The following are examples of circumstances when potential differences between the hedging instrument and the hedged item may result:

(a) Basis differences – for example, a company might use a hedging instrument with changes based on prime rates to hedge an exposure with changes based on bankers' acceptance rates. Alternatively, a company may use a US dollar denominated financial instrument as a hedge of a foreign currency exposure that is pegged to the US dollar, but does not move in an identical pattern.

(b) Notional/principal amount differences – for example, a company might hedge the change in fair value of debt with a principal balance of £550,000 using an interest rate swap with a notional principal amount of £500,000.

(c) Maturity or re-pricing date differences – for example, a company might hedge risks associated with a forecast transaction using a derivative that settles at a slightly earlier or later date than the date of the forecast transaction. Alternatively, a company might hedge floating-rate debt with an interest rate swap when the interest re-pricing dates on the swap and the debt are different.

(d) Creditworthiness differences – for example, a company might hedge interest rate risk in a BBB-rated debt using an A-rated derivative. Alternatively, a company might hedge a forecast transaction to be undertaken with one counter-party with a hedging instrument obtained from another counter-party.

(e) Quantity, location or delivery differences – for example, a company might hedge a risk of changes in prices of Brazilian coffee beans with an instrument whose value changes based on prices of Colombian coffee beans.

**12.110** Because of these risks of ineffectiveness, a company must very carefully select the items to be included in a hedging relationship and the risks to be designated as hedged. Eliminating as many of these sources of ineffectiveness as possible is more likely to avoid the possibility that the hedging relationships will fail to qualify for hedge accounting.

---

**EXAMPLE 12.30**

Company BB wishes to hedge the overall change in the fair value of a commodity whose fair value will alter due to changes in the spot price of the commodity only. A derivative to achieve its hedging purposes probably will be exposed to other risk factors, such as the credit risk of the counter-party, that will affect its fair value. Because the company is not permitted to designate only certain risks in the derivative as being the hedging item, with limited exceptions (see paragraph **12.74**) it will need to take care that the other factors resulting in changes in fair value of the hedging instrument are not likely to lead to the hedge becoming ineffective.

---

**12.111**   While there are limits to what the company can do with the hedging instrument, there is greater scope for flexibility in designating precisely what the hedged item is, since that may be limited to particular risks.

---

**EXAMPLE 12.31**

Company CC wishes to hedge exposure to changes in the fair value of a fixed-rate debt with a receive-fixed, pay-floating bankers' acceptance interest rate swap. Company CC might identify the risk being hedged as the risk of changes in the fair value of the loan attributable to changes in the bankers' acceptance rate, thus excluding changes in fair value of the hedged item attributable to other factors from effectiveness testing.

---

**12.112**   If all critical terms of the hedging instrument and hedged item are the same, it is likely that changes in fair values or cash flows on the hedging instrument and hedged item will offset, both when the hedge is entered into and subsequently – therefore, effectiveness is likely. For example, an interest rate swap is likely to be an effective hedge if the notional and principal amounts, term, re-pricing dates, dates of interest and principal receipts and payments, and basis for measuring interest rates, are the same for the hedging instrument and the hedged item. Also, a hedge of a highly probable forecast purchase of a commodity with a forward contract is likely to be highly effective if:

(a)   the forward contract is for the purchase of the same quantity of the same commodity at the same time and location as the hedged forecast purchase;
(b)   the fair value of the forward contract at inception is zero; and
(c)   either:
    (i)   the change in the discount or premium on the forward contract is excluded from the assessment of effectiveness and recognised in profit and loss; or
    (ii)   the change in expected cash flows on the highly probable forecast transaction is based on the forward price for the commodity.

This is sometimes referred to as 'critical terms matching'. A company should regularly consider whether any of the terms have changed. In particular, it should pay attention to any change in creditworthiness of counter-parties.

**12.113**   Unlike FASB Statement 133, IAS 39 does not provide for any 'short-cut' methods of assessing hedge effectiveness when critical terms match. However, this is compensated for, in part, because IAS 39 permits hedging of portions of financial assets and financial liabilities in cases when US GAAP does not, thus enabling a company to more finely divide a hedged item to ensure that ineffectiveness does not arise. Once a company has selected the hedged item as being a portion of a financial asset or financial liability, it must conduct effectiveness testing with reference to the changes in fair value or cash flows of that portion, both prospectively and retrospectively. Thus, a company is precluded from establishing hedge effectiveness prospectively based on considering a portion of the hedged asset or liability and then assessing and measuring any ineffectiveness retrospectively based on changes in fair value or cash flow of a different portion of, or the entire, hedged item.

## Designation and documentation

**12.114**   Because hedge accounting is optional, it is important that it is clear whether a particular financial instrument is being accounted for in accordance with hedge accounting options or in accordance with the regular accounting required by IAS 39. Therefore, a company is required to document the fact that it has designated a particular relationship as a hedging relationship. That may be accomplished for each individual hedging instrument, or in a manner that makes it clear when entering into a transaction whether that transaction is part of a particular relationship.

**12.115**   IAS 39 requires formal documentation of the hedging relationship, as well as the company's risk management objective and strategy for undertaking the hedge at the inception of the hedge. The documentation should include:

(a)   identification of the hedging instrument;
(b)   identification of the hedged item;
(c)   the nature of the risk being hedged; and
(d)   how the company will assess effectiveness.

**12.116**   It is essential that the documentation for each designated hedge be consistent with overall documentation of the company's risk management and hedge accounting strategy. That strategy should, in turn, be documented in a manner that allows the company to respond to changes in the business environment. For example, a company may not want to restrict itself by establishing a policy that all fixed-rate exposure is swapped to variable-rate exposure. It would probably want to be much more precise as to the circumstances in which such exposures are swapped.

**12.117**   Documentation needs to be sufficiently specific that it can be audited and effectiveness testing should be specified in such a manner that it is clear how it is to be applied in assessing whether a hedging relationship might fail to qualify for hedge accounting. Any components of a hedged item or hedging item excluded should be explicitly documented.

**12.118**   Establishing documentation for the overall strategy, as well as individual transactions, will need to be co-ordinated with those responsible for initiating and managing risk exposures. For example, it may often be a treasury department that is responsible for managing such exposures. It might be traders that are responsible for initiating the transactions. They will need to understand the documentation requirements necessary to ensure appropriate accounting for the hedging relationship.

**12.119**   The consequences of a failure to adequately document a hedging relationship are significant – an inability to apply hedge accounting. Therefore, a company should commence gathering, and carefully review, the necessary documentation well before the inception of the hedge. A company should also put in place internal control procedures to ensure that appropriate documentation is in place before any transaction intended to be designated as a hedge for accounting purposes is initiated.

**EXAMPLE 12.32**

The following is an example of how a company might document a hedge. References quoted, such as page xx, or Swap contract number 123456, would be to specific internal company documentation.

*Risk management objective and strategy*: To offset the variability in expected cash flows attributable to changes in interest rates on floating-rate debt issued by the company, by using 'receive-floating, pay-fixed' interest rate swaps. This is consistent with the company's risk management policy as documented on page xx of the Risk Management Policy Manual.

*Hedged item*: Interest payments on a £1m non-amortising loan from X Bank plc, entered into on 1 January 2005. Interest is calculated based on three-month LIBOR plus 1.5 per cent and is paid quarterly on 31 March, 30 June, 30 September and 31 December until 31 December 2010. (See loan documents Ref. ABC/123.)

*Hedging item*: 100 per cent of Swap contract number 123456, being a five-year non-amortising receive-floating, pay-fixed interest rate swap from Y Bank plc with a notional amount of £1m. Fixed payments are based on an interest rate of 5.5 per cent and floating payments are based on three-month LIBOR plus 1.5 per cent. The interest rate resets on the floating leg of the swap quarterly, payments are due quarterly and the final payment occurs on 31 December 2010. (See swap documents Ref. XYZ/789.)

*Hedge risk exposure*: The risk of changes in expected future cash flows of the hedged item attributable to changes in three-month LIBOR.

*Term of hedging relationship*: 1 January 2005 to 31 December 2010.

*Nature of hedging relationship*: Cash flow hedge.

*Effectiveness assessment method*: [Details of both the prospective and retrospective assessment methods would be provided, including the method to be used, the frequency of testing, the data to be used as inputs, the number of data points to be used, whether the assessment is based on a period-by-period basis or cumulatively from inception, etc.]

*Effectiveness measurement method*: The measurement of ineffectiveness will be determined by the ratio analysis method on a cumulative basis.


## DISCONTINUING HEDGE ACCOUNTING

**12.120**   Hedge accounting is discontinued prospectively if any of the following events occur:

(a)   The hedging instrument no longer exists – it has matured, expired, been sold, terminated, cancelled or exercised. (An exception is when the company's documented hedging strategy allows for the replacement or rollover of one hedging instrument with another – such as the rollover of a series of 30-day bankers' acceptances in a dynamic hedging strategy.)

(b)   The hedged item no longer exists – it has matured, expired, been sold, terminated, cancelled or exercised.

(c)   The forecast transaction is no longer expected to occur. (Note that this is a lower threshold than the expectation that a forecast transaction is expected to be highly probable on inception of the hedge.)

(d)   The hedging relationship no longer meets qualifying requirements – either the hedging relationship is no longer effective or the company voluntarily chooses to terminate its designation of the hedging relationship.

**12.121**   Prospective discontinuance means that hedge accounting continues to apply up to the date of the event leading to the discontinuance, but ceases from that date. The effects of previous hedge accounting are not reversed.

**12.122**   The accounting in each of the situations in paragraph **12.120** is as follows:

(a)   The hedging instrument no longer exists – any adjustment to the carrying amount of a hedged item that is measured at amortised cost, made as a result of a fair value hedge, continues to be amortised to profit or loss. Any cumulative gains or losses related to the hedged item previously recognised in equity in a cash flow hedge are carried forward to be recognised in profit or loss when the forecast transaction occurs, at which time they are accounted for in the same manner as if the hedge had remained effective.

(b)   The hedged item no longer exists – any gains or losses related to the hedging item are recognised in profit or loss along with the related gains or losses on the hedged item.

(c)   The forecast transaction is no longer expected to occur – any cumulative gains or losses related to the forecast transaction previously recognised in equity are recognised in profit or loss.

(d)  The hedging relationship no longer meets qualifying requirements – any adjustment to the carrying amount of a hedged item that is measured at amortised cost, made as a result of a fair value hedge, continues to be amortised to profit or loss. Any cumulative gains or losses related to the hedged item previously recognised in equity in a cash flow hedge are carried forward to be recognised in profit or loss when the forecast transaction occurs, at which time they are accounted for in the same manner as if the hedge had remained effective. If the forecast transaction is no longer expected to occur, any cumulative gains or losses related to the forecast transaction previously recognised in equity are recognised in profit or loss.

**12.123**  When a company enters into a firm commitment to acquire an asset or assume a liability that is a hedged item in a fair value hedge and the company makes that acquisition, the cumulative change in the fair value of the firm commitment attributable to the hedged risk that was recognised on the balance sheet is included in the initial carrying amount of the asset or liability acquired.

DISCLOSURES

**12.124**  IAS 32 requires a company to disclose information about its risk management and hedging policies. This is considered in **Chapter 16**.

**12.125**  When a company actively undertakes hedging activities – ie it designates hedges for accounting purposes – additional disclosures are necessary to enable a user of the financial statements to understand the effect of those activities on the financial statements. In these circumstances, IAS 32 requires the following disclosures for designated fair value hedges, cash flow hedges and hedges of a net investment in a foreign operation:

(a)  a description of the hedge;
(b)  a description of the financial instruments designated as hedging instruments and their fair values at the balance sheet date; and
(c)  the nature of the risk being hedged.

**12.126**  For cash flow hedges, IAS 32 also requires disclosure of:

(a)  the periods in which the cash flows are expected to occur;
(b)  when they are expected to enter into the determination of profit or loss;
(c)  any forecast transaction for which hedge accounting had previously been used but which is no longer expected to occur;
(d)  the amount that was recognised in equity during the period;
(e)  the amount that was removed from equity and included in profit or loss during the period; and
(f)  the amount that was removed from equity during the period and included

in the initial measurement of the acquisition cost or other carrying amount of a non-financial asset or non-financial liability in a hedge highly probable forecast transaction.

**EXAMPLE 12.33**

This example illustrates disclosure for cash flow hedges.

Company DD hedges 50 per cent of its anticipated exposure to risks of variability of foreign exchange rates affecting purchases in euros for the next twelve months by entering into forward foreign exchange contracts. At 31 December 2005 the fair value of forward foreign exchange contracts was £34,200 (31 December 2004 £26,300). Company DD anticipates euro-denominated purchases of £500,000 in each of the next three quarters and £600,000 in the fourth quarter of 2005.

As a result of hedging activities during 2004, £98,400 was recognised in equity during the period. £102,300 related to gains and losses on forward foreign exchange contracts at the end of 2003 and entered into during 2004 was removed from equity during 2004 and recognised in profit or loss.

(Note that the disclosures in the second paragraph may be evident from the statement of changes in equity and might, therefore, not need separate note disclosure.)

GAAP COMPARISON

**12.127**   The basic hedge accounting model is similar to US GAAP, which specifies the same basic types of hedges – fair value hedges, cash flow hedges and hedges of net investments – and accounts for them in similar manners. Most of the differences are in the details as to what qualifies for hedge accounting. The following summarises some of the most significant differences:

(a)   Non-derivatives may be designated as hedges of any foreign currency risk in accordance with IAS 39. Non-derivatives may be designated as hedging instruments only for fair value hedges of foreign currency risk in unrecognised firm commitments and net investments in foreign operations in accordance with US GAAP.

(b)   Hedging of prepayment risk in a held-to-maturity investment is precluded in accordance with IAS 39. Hedge accounting is permitted for the overall fair value of a prepayment option in accordance with US GAAP.

(c)   A portion of a financial asset or financial liability may be designated as a hedged item in accordance with IAS 39. However, US GAAP restricts the circumstances in which the hedged item may be a portion of an asset or liability.

(d)   IAS 39 permits hedging of foreign exchange risk relating to an anticipated business combination. US GAAP does not permit hedge accounting of foreign exchange risk in these circumstances.

(e)   IAS 39 does not permit a 'short-cut' method for assuming no ineffective-ness in certain hedges of interest rate risk using interest rate swaps, which is available in accordance with US GAAP.

(f)   The definition of a firm commitment in IAS 39, while very similar to that in US GAAP, is slightly less extensive. Although the first parts of the definitions are very similar, the FASB definition adds additional criteria. Therefore, there is a possibility that a particular circumstance would qualify as a cash flow hedge in accordance with IAS 39 while qualifying as a fair value hedge in accordance with US GAAP, or vice versa.

(g)   IAS 39 does not appear to prohibit designation of an embedded derivative that is clearly and closely related to the host contract as the hedged item. FASB Statement 133 permits designating an embedded derivative as the hedged item in a fair value hedge only if it is a put option, call option, interest rate cap, or interest rate floor embedded in an existing asset or liability that is not an embedded derivative accounted for separately. If the entire asset or liability is an instrument with variable cash flows, FASB Statement 133 expressly prohibits the hedged item from being an implicit fixed-to-variable swap (or similar instrument) perceived to be embedded in a host contract with fixed cash flows. This does not create an impediment to complying with US GAAP, since a company that also wishes to comply with US GAAP could choose not to designate any such items as hedged items.

(h)   IAS 39 does not permit a company to hedge separately changes in the fair value of a recognised loan servicing right or a non-financial firm commit-ment with financial components due to interest rate risk, credit risk or foreign currency risk, because these items are non-financial in nature. US GAAP specifically permits these exposures to be hedged notwithstanding their non-financial nature.

(i)   FASB Statement 133 requires additional disclosures about hedge account-ing that are not included in IAS 39.

**12.128**   For many UK companies, detailed hedge accounting requirements will be new and may seem onerous compared to the relatively free choice of the past. Amongst the more significant changes will be:

(a)   the elimination of deferral hedge accounting – no more deferred gains and losses on the balance sheet;

(b)   the need to determine which type of hedge accounting applies to each situation;

(c)   the need to account for each part of the hedging relationship separately, rather than applying 'synthetic accounting' to the net position;

(d)   extensive documentation requirements;

(e)   prohibitions on many portfolio hedges;

(f)   prohibitions on many central treasury hedging strategies; and

(g)   the need to perform effectiveness testing and recognise ineffectiveness in profit or loss.

# Chapter 13

# Derecognition

Principal IFRS references:

● IAS 39, paragraphs 9, 15–37, 39–42, AG36–AG52, AG57–AG63.

## INTRODUCTION

**13.1**  Derecognition is the process of removing a previously recognised financial asset or financial liability from the balance sheet.

**13.2**  In many cases the decision to derecognise a financial asset or a financial liability is straightforward. If a company no longer has any contractual rights or obligations associated with the financial asset or financial liability it is derecognised.

### EXAMPLE 13.1

Company A has a financial asset on its balance sheet in the form of an account receivable from a customer. The customer has a corresponding financial liability on its balance sheet in the form of an account payable. The customer pays Company A in full so that there are no further rights or obligations between the two parties in respect of that contract. The account receivable is derecognised by Company A and the account payable is derecognised by the customer.

**13.3**  In other situations the decision as to when to derecognise a financial asset or a financial liability may be less straightforward – particularly when the entire financial asset or financial liability does not expire at once, or when new contractual rights or obligations are obtained in replacement for some or all of the original rights or obligations.

**13.4**  A company will need to analyse more complex contracts carefully to see if the underlying assets or liabilities qualify for derecognition, particularly if the transaction includes derivatives, such as forward contracts and options. On initial recognition of IAS 39 this may necessitate reviewing carefully contracts that have been in existence for some time. On an ongoing basis, an analysis by individuals familiar with accounting will probably be necessary to consider the accounting consequences of any complex transaction which may be entered into by other departments, such as those in tax or treasury functions. A company should have processes in place to ensure that the accounting consequences are taken into account before a complex transaction is undertaken.

**13.5**   This chapter considers derecognition of a financial asset, starting with the more straightforward situations. It also considers derecognition of a financial liability.

DERECOGNITION OF A FINANCIAL ASSET

**Overview**

**13.6**   The flowchart in Figure 13.1, based on that in IAS 39, summarises the decision process to be followed in determining the appropriate accounting on derecognition of a financial asset. Note that the straightforward situation described in Example 13.1 is dealt with at the beginning of the flowchart. The rights to the cash flows from all of Company A's assets have expired (Boxes 2 and 3) and hence the asset is derecognised (Box 10).

**13.7**   If the company is required to prepare consolidated financial statements, all subsidiaries and consolidated special purpose entities are consolidated before applying the derecognition requirements. This ensures that decisions as to whether to derecognise a financial asset are made taking the consolidated position into account.

**Derecognition of all or a part of a financial asset**

**13.8**   The first step in considering whether derecognition is appropriate is to determine whether the asset to be considered is all or a part of a financial asset. IAS 39 requires that the entire asset be considered unless any one of the following three conditions exists.

(a)    The part comprises only specifically identified cash flows from a financial asset.

**EXAMPLE 13.2**

Company B enters into an interest rate strip, whereby the rights to the interest cash flows from a debt instrument are transferred to another party but the principal cash flows are retained by Company B. In this situation, the interest cash flows, only, are considered for derecognition.

**Figure 13.1: Summary of decisions regarding derecognition of a financial asset**

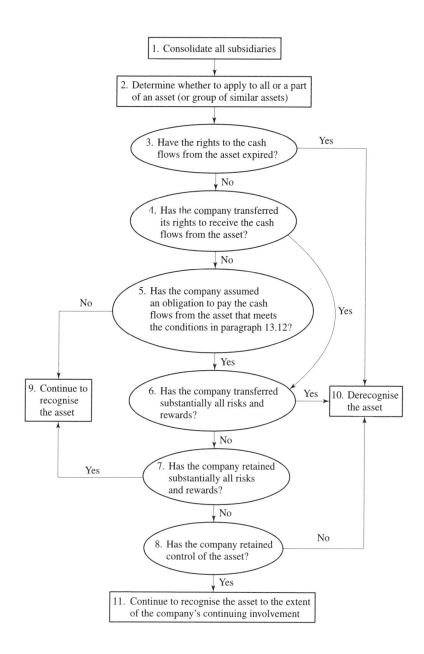

(b) The part comprises only a fully proportionate share of the cash flows from a financial asset.

### EXAMPLE 13.3

Company C transfers to another party 50 per cent of the entire cash flows from a particular financial asset. In this situation, the 50 per cent share is considered for derecognition.

Note that it is Company C that must have a fully proportionate share for this condition to exist. It would still apply if Company C were to transfer 50 per cent of the interest cash flows of a debt instrument to one party and 50 per cent of the principal cash flows to another party. Company C is still left with a 50 per cent proportionate interest in the entire cash flows of the financial asset.

(c) The part comprises only a fully proportionate share of specifically identified cash flows from a financial asset.

### EXAMPLE 13.4

Company D transfers to another party 50 per cent of the interest cash flows from a debt instrument. In this situation, 50 per cent of the interest cash flows are considered for derecognition.

If a group of financial assets, rather than a single financial asset, are being considered, these conditions are applied to the group of financial assets – as long as the financial assets in the group are similar.

**13.9** If the part transferred comprises a combination of cash flows other than those specified in paragraph **13.8**, then the entire financial asset must be considered for derecognition.

### EXAMPLE 13.5

Company E transfers to another party the first 90 per cent of the cash collections from a group of accounts receivable. These are not specifically identified cash flows since there is no certainty as to which cash flows will result in transfers to the other party. Accordingly, the entire group of accounts receivable is considered for derecognition.

**Determining whether a transfer has taken place**

**13.10** Once a company has determined whether all or a part of the financial asset is to be considered for derecognition it needs to assess what, if anything, should be derecognised. In some cases this will be straightforward, as in the situation discussed in Example 13.1. However, in other situations it may be much less clear. In these situations further considerations require assessment, including the manner in which the transfer is made.

**13.11** First, the company must consider whether it has transferred the rights to receive the cash flows from the financial assets or part of a financial asset being assessed for derecognition. If so, it then considers whether substantially all of the risks and rewards have been retained or transferred (see paragraphs **13.13–13.14**).

**13.12** Alternatively, a company may not have transferred the rights to the cash flows but, rather, assumed an obligation to pay the cash flows received to one or more other parties. In this situation, the company considers the transaction to be a transfer of the financial asset only if all of the following conditions are met:

(a)    the company has no obligation to pay amounts to the other parties unless it collects equivalent amounts from the original asset;

(b)    the company is prohibited from selling or pledging the original asset, other than as security to the parties to which cash flows must be paid; and

(c)    cash flows must be remitted without material delay, together with any interest on investment of cash from the collection date to remittance date.

If all of these conditions are met, the company considers whether substantially all of the risks and rewards have been retained or transferred (see paragraphs **13.13–13.14**). If they are not met, the asset continues to be recognised by the company – there is no transfer.

**Transfer of substantially all of the risks and rewards**

**13.13** Three scenarios are possible once it is determined that there has been a transfer:

(a)    substantially all risks and rewards have been transferred – in which case the financial asset is derecognised (and any rights or obligations created or retained in the transfer are separately recognised as assets or liabilities);

(b)    substantially all risks and rewards have been retained by the company – in which case the financial asset is not derecognised (the entire asset or part of the asset being assessed remains recognised); or

(c)    some risks and rewards have been retained, while others have been transferred, but neither constitutes substantially all of the risks and rewards – in which case consideration is given to whether the company has retained control of the asset transferred (see paragraphs **13.15–13.16**).

**13.14** The assessment as to whether substantially all risks and rewards have been transferred or retained is made by comparing the company's exposure to the variability in the present value of future net cash flows of the asset, before and after the transfer. If its exposure does not change significantly as a result of the transfer, it has retained substantially all risks and rewards and does not derecognise the asset. If its exposure to such variability is no longer significant, in relation to the total variability, it has transferred substantially all risks and rewards. If neither of these circumstances apply (ie the exposure remains significant and has changed), the company proceeds to consider whether control has been retained.

---

**EXAMPLE 13.6**

Company F sells a financial asset subject to an agreement to buy it back at a fixed price in the future (a sale and repurchase agreement). Company F remains subject to substantially all of the risks and rewards associated with the transferred asset. Therefore, it is not derecognised.

---

**EXAMPLE 13.7**

Company G sells a financial asset subject to an option to buy it back at its fair value in the future. Company G is not exposed to risks and rewards associated with changes in the fair value of the financial asset. Therefore it is derecognised.

---

## Transfer of control

**13.15** Assessment of whether there has been a transfer of control applies only when the company has neither transferred nor retained substantially all of the risks and rewards of the financial asset, or part of a financial asset, being assessed. In this case, if the company has not retained control the financial asset is derecognised (and any rights or obligations created or retained in the transfer are separately recognised as assets or liabilities). If the company has retained control, it continues to recognise the financial asset, but only to the extent of its continuing involvement in the asset (see paragraphs **13.26–13.27**).

**13.16** If the party to which the asset has been transferred (the transferee) has the practical ability to sell the asset in its entirety to a third party without needing to impose additional restrictions on the transfer – such as the need to have an option to repurchase the asset – then the transferee has control of the asset and it is derecognised by the transferor. In all other circumstances control is not transferred. The transferee has the practical ability to sell the asset in its entirety if it is traded in an active market because the transferee could immediately repurchase the asset, if necessary. In the following circumstances the transferee would not generally have the practical ability to sell the asset to a third party without imposing additional restrictions:

(a)   the transferee would have to pay a price significantly above fair value to repurchase the asset;

(b)    the delivery time to obtain the asset would be significantly longer than is needed to return it to the original transferor;
(c)    the assets are unique or held only by a limited number of other parties; or
(d)    the transferor restricts the ability to transfer the assets to only a limited number of parties.

### EXAMPLE 13.8

As part of a transfer of other financial assets, Company H transfers quoted common shares of a FTSE 100 listed company to another party, with a condition that they can be repurchased on demand. Because quoted shares of a FTSE 100 listed company are actively traded in an active market, the transferee can readily sell the shares and re-obtain them if necessary to return to the transferor. Therefore, Company H has transferred control.

### EXAMPLE 13.9

As part of a transfer of other financial assets, Company I transfers several rare banknotes to another party, with a condition that those specific banknotes can be repurchased on demand. Because the banknotes cannot be readily repurchased if necessary by the transferee, without attaching a repurchase option to an onward sale, Company I has not transferred control of the banknotes.

## Accounting for transfers that qualify for derecognition

**13.17**    When a company derecognises an entire financial asset it removes the financial asset from its balance sheet and recognises any gain or loss in profit or loss. That gain or loss is the difference between the carrying amount of the asset and the consideration received, including any new asset obtained, less any new liability assumed.

### EXAMPLE 13.10

Company J sells a financial asset previously carried at amortised cost of £100, in exchange for cash of £50 and common shares of another company with a fair value of £55. Company J removes the financial asset from its balance sheet, recognises new assets for cash (£50) and investment in common shares (£55) and a gain in profit or loss of £5.

**13.18**    When a company derecognises only a part of a financial asset, it allocates the carrying amount of the entire financial asset between the part derecognised and the remainder based on the relative fair values of the parts on the date of transfer. It then derecognises the part of the asset qualifying for derecognition and recognises a gain or loss based on the difference between the carrying amount allocated to the part of the financial asset derecognised and the consideration received for the part derecognised.

---

**EXAMPLE 13.11**

Company K transfers interest cash flows that are part of a debt instrument to another party in exchange for cash consideration of £450. At the date of the transfer the debt instrument is carried at amortised cost of £990 and has a fair value of £1,060, with £450 being attributable to the future interest flows and £610 being attributable to future principal cash flows. Company K allocates the carrying amount of the debt instrument between the part derecognised and the part retained based on the ratio of 610:450. Thus, it allocates £569.72 (990 × 610/1060) to the part retained and £420.28 (990 × 450/1060) to the part derecognised. Company K derecognises £420.28 of the debt instrument, recognises £450 cash and recognises a gain of £29.72 in profit or loss.

---

**13.19**   In determining the carrying amount for an asset, such as accounts receivable, for which an allowance for uncollectible amounts has been established but not explicitly allocated to the asset, the allocation of the allowance would be based on the relative fair values of the assets transferred as compared to the fair values of the class of accounts receivable for which the allowance has been established.

**13.20**   If the fair value of the parts cannot be reliably determined, the best estimate of the fair value of the part retained is the difference between the fair value of the entire asset and the consideration received from the transfer of the part derecognised.

**13.21**   If the asset, or part of an asset, that is derecognised was previously classified as available for sale, or was a cash flow hedging instrument, with gains and losses recognised directly in equity, the amount recognised in equity related to the asset derecognised is transferred to profit or loss at the time of derecognition. If that relates to a part of a financial asset, the amount of the gain or loss to be recognised in profit or loss is determined based on the relative fair values of the parts.

**13.22**   IAS 39 also addresses the calculation of the gain or loss on derecognition when a fee is received by the transferor in exchange for the right to service the financial assets transferred.

### Accounting for transfers that do not qualify for derecognition

**13.23**   If a transfer does not qualify for derecognition, the asset continues to be recognised on the transferor's balance sheet. However, if consideration has been received for a transfer that does not qualify for derecognition because the transferor has retained substantially all of the risks and rewards of ownership, a financial liability is recognised for the consideration received.

**13.24**  If a transfer does not qualify for derecognition because of a particular condition or restriction imposed, and that condition is removed or lapses, then the transfer may qualify for derecognition at the time that the condition is removed.

#### EXAMPLE 13.12

Company L transfers a financial asset under a sale and repurchase agreement subject to a restriction that the transferor is prohibited from pledging or exchanging the asset for the first six months after the transfer. Company L would be precluded from derecognising the financial asset until the six-month period has expired, at which time, assuming all other conditions are met, it would be able to derecognise the financial asset.

**13.25**  If the existence of a derivative such as a call option prevents a financial asset from being derecognised, that derivative is not separately recognised as a derivative asset if that would result in recognising the same rights or obligations twice – in the derivative asset and in the financial asset that is not derecognised.

### Continuing involvement

**13.26**  Continuing involvement in a financial asset is the extent to which a company continues to be exposed to changes in fair value of a transferred financial asset. Such continuing involvement might arise as a result of a guarantee or an option to repurchase the asset.

**13.27**  When a company continues to recognise an asset to the extent of its continuing involvement it also recognises an associated liability. The associated liability is measured in such a way that the net carrying amount of the transferred asset and the associated liability equals the amortised cost of the retained rights and obligations (if the transferred asset is measured at amortised cost) or the fair value of the retained rights and obligations (if the transferred asset is measured at fair value).

#### EXAMPLE 13.13

Company M transfers a financial asset to another party but guarantees that if the value of the transferred asset falls below a specified amount by a certain date Company M will make a fixed payment to the other party as compensation. Company M has continuing involvement in the financial asset transferred to the extent of the possible obligation in accordance with the guarantee. Company M continues to recognise a financial asset, measured at the maximum amount of the guarantee under which it might be required to perform – ie the lower of the amount of the asset or the consideration it could be required to repay. An associated liability is recognised, measured at amortised cost or fair value, depending on the measurement basis for the transferred asset.

## Collateral

**13.28**  IAS 39 also specifies the accounting treatment for non-cash collateral that might be provided to the transferee.

(a)  If the transferee has the right by contract or by custom to sell or re-pledge the collateral, the transferor reclassifies the collateral on its balance sheet separately from other assets.
(b)  If the transferee sells collateral pledged to it, it recognises the proceeds from the sale and a liability for the fair value of its obligation to return the collateral to the transferor.
(c)  If the transferor defaults under the terms of the contract and is no longer entitled to redeem the collateral, it derecognises the collateral and the transferee recognises the collateral as its asset.

In all other situations the transferor continues to recognise the collateral as its asset and the transferee does not recognise it.

## Application to some common fact situations

**13.29**  The Application Guidance to IAS 39 contains many examples of how the derecognition requirements would apply to particular fact situations. Some of the more common conclusions would be as follows.

**13.30**  The following would generally qualify for derecognition of a financial asset:

(a)  an unconditional sale;
(b)  a sale, together with an option to repurchase at the fair value of the asset at the time of repurchase;
(c)  a sale, together with a put or call option that is so far out of the money that it is highly unlikely to become in the money before expiry;
(d)  a sale of a readily obtainable asset, together with a call option that is neither deeply in the money nor deeply out of the money; and
(e)  a loan participation, as long as significant constraints are not placed on the transferee's ability to pledge or exchange its participating part of the loan.

**13.31**  The following would generally not qualify for derecognition of a financial asset:

(a)  a sale and repurchase agreement to repurchase the same or substantially the same asset at a fixed price;
(b)  a securities lending agreement;

(c)   a sale, together with a swap that transfers the risk exposure from the asset back to the company;

(d)   a sale, together with a put or call option that is so far in the money that it is highly unlikely to become out of the money before expiry; and

(e)   a sale of receivables, for which the transferor guarantees to compensate the transferee for all credit losses that may occur.

**13.32**   Other, more complex, situations must be evaluated in accordance with the principles outlined above.

## GAAP comparison

**13.33**   It is unclear at present whether the new requirements in IAS 39 will result in substantial differences from conclusions that may be reached on derecognition in accordance with US GAAP or UK GAAP. Many of the principles included in IAS 39 are similar to those in US GAAP or UK GAAP. However, the combination of applying those principles to specific fact situations, particularly more complex situations, will sometimes result in different conclusions being reached. One potentially significant difference between US GAAP and IAS 39 is that, unlike IAS 39, FASB Statement 140, 'Accounting for Transfers and Servicing of Financial Assets and Extinguishments of Liabilities' relies on legal isolation as a requirement for derecognition. It is also likely that certain sale and repurchase agreements and securities lending transactions will be accounted for differently in accordance with IAS 39 from the manner in which they would be accounted for in accordance with US GAAP. US GAAP also does not consider whether substantially all risks and rewards have been transferred or retained. The concept of 'linked presentation' in UK GAAP, in accordance with FRS 5, 'Reporting the Substance of Transactions', does not exist in IAS 39.

## DERECOGNITION OF A FINANCIAL LIABILITY

### Overview

**13.34**   The requirements for derecognition of a financial liability are more straightforward. The only circumstance in which a company has fulfilled a contractual obligation, and thus should derecognise the financial liability reflecting that obligation, is when the company has been released from primary responsibility for that obligation. This may be achieved by settling the obligation, by paying the creditor, or by discharging the obligation by accommodation with the creditor or by process of law. Such a discharge includes the expiry of the term of an obligation.

**13.35**   If a company exchanges its obligation for a different obligation with substantially different terms, or the terms of an obligation are substantially modified, the original liability, or part of it, is derecognised and a new liability recognised in place. A modification of terms may include such changes as a reduction of the stated interest rate, extension of maturity dates at a rate of interest differing from current market interest rates, reduction of the principal amount of the debt or forgiveness of accrued interest.

**13.36** Terms are considered to be substantially different if the discounted present cash flows under the new terms are at least 10 per cent different from the discounted present values of the remaining cash flows of the original financial liability (US GAAP provides additional guidance on this calculation – see EITF 96–19, 'Debtor's Accounting for a Substantive Modification and Exchange of Debt Instruments'). Any fees incurred are included in the present value calculation using the original effective interest rate and are recognised as part of any gain or loss on extinguishment.

**13.37** On derecognition of a financial liability, any difference between the carrying amount of the liability and the consideration paid, including any assets or liabilities received in exchange, is recognised in profit or loss. Any costs or fees incurred are recognised as part of the gain or loss on extinguishment. (Note that this differs from US GAAP, which requires that any costs or fees are considered to relate to the new debt instrument and, thus, are amortised over the term of the new instrument.)

**13.38** When a part of a financial liability is derecognised, the company allocates the previous carrying amount of the financial liability between the parts retained and derecognised based on the relative fair values of the parts at the transaction date.

**13.39** Derecognition of a financial liability is not appropriate in an 'in-substance defeasance' of debt. Under this practice the debtor transfers essentially risk-free assets to an irrevocable defeasance trust and the cash flows from those assets, which are used to meet obligations to the creditor, closely approximate the scheduled interest and principal payments of the liability. In those circumstances, the debtor is not released from the primary obligation under the debt agreement. If the assets in the trust prove to be insufficient (for example, because default by the debtor accelerates its debt repayment), the debtor must make up the difference. The rights of the creditor, who may not know of the defeasance arrangements, are not limited to the cash flows from the assets in the trust.

**GAAP comparison**

**13.40** The requirements for derecognition of a financial liability are essentially the same as those in US GAAP.

Chapter 14

# Offsetting

Principal IFRS references:

- IAS 32, paragraphs 42–50, AG38–AG39.

## INTRODUCTION

**14.1**   Generally, financial statement users are best served by a separate presentation of financial assets and financial liabilities – particularly when those financial assets and financial liabilities may be subject to different risks. Therefore, offsetting of financial assets and financial liabilities on the balance sheet is permitted in only very limited circumstances. Offsetting is required when, and only when, two criteria are met:

(a)   the company has both a legally enforceable right to set off the financial asset and the financial liability; and

(b)   the company intends to settle the financial asset and financial liability on a net basis, or to realise the financial asset and settle the financial liability simultaneously.

If both criteria are met, the relevant financial assets and financial liabilities are presented net, rather than as separate financial instruments.

**14.2**   A company will need to consider not only the legal relationships between financial assets and financial liabilities but also its intentions, as demonstrated by past practice and management representations, in determining whether offsetting is required. Of course, if there is no legal right to set off a financial asset and financial liability, the company's intentions are irrelevant.

**14.3**   This chapter considers what is offsetting, the circumstances when offsetting is required and when offsetting is prohibited, as well as the primary differences from current US and UK GAAP.

## WHAT IS OFFSETTING?

**14.4** Offsetting is the presentation of financial assets and financial liabilities that are recognised on the balance sheet as if they were a single net financial asset or financial liability.

---

### EXAMPLE 14.1

If offsetting criteria are met, a debtor of £100,000 and a creditor of £75,000 may be presented as a net debtor of £25,000.

---

**14.5** Offsetting differs from derecognition. Derecognition deals with the question of when a financial instrument should be removed from the balance sheet. In the example in the previous paragraph, neither the debtor of £100,000 nor the creditor of £75,000 is removed from the balance sheet. They are merely presented in a manner that shows their net exposure (net presentation). Derecognition may result in gain or loss recognition, whereas offsetting does not result in gain or loss recognition – it addresses presentation only.

## CIRCUMSTANCES IN WHICH OFFSETTING IS REQUIRED

### Overview

**14.6** IAS 32 states that the only circumstance in which offsetting of a financial asset and a financial liability is appropriate is when a company both:

'(a)  currently has a legally enforceable right to set off the recognised amounts; and
(b)  intends either to settle on a net basis, or to realise the asset and settle the liability simultaneously.'

[IAS 32, paragraph 42]

If this circumstance is present, then the financial asset and financial liability must be presented net.

### A legally enforceable right of set-off

**14.7** IAS 32 explains that a legally enforceable right of set-off is a debtor's legal right, often established in the financial instrument contract – though not necessarily – to settle or otherwise eliminate all, or a portion, of an amount due to a creditor by applying against that amount another amount due from the creditor. Occasionally, a company may have a legal right to apply an amount due from a third party against the amount due from the creditor, but offsetting of these amounts is permitted only when there is an agreement among the three parties that clearly establishes the right of set-off.

## Intent to settle net or realise simultaneously

**14.8** IAS 32 requires not only the existence of a legally enforceable right to set off, but also the intention to settle net or to realise the asset and settle the liability simultaneously if offsetting is to be permitted. Without such intention, there is no certainty that the amount and timing of the cash flows will occur on a net basis. A company's intention is demonstrated from the perspective of the reporting company – there is no requirement to consider the counter-party's intention. A company's intention would generally be consistent with its risk management policy and would be demonstrated by management representations as well as past actions. The requirements of financial markets or other circumstances may limit a company's ability to exercise its intention, in which case offsetting is not permitted.

**14.9** Simultaneous settlement of an asset and liability requires that the settlement take place at the same moment. It is not sufficient that the two instruments are settled by receiving and paying separate amounts if the company becomes exposed to credit risk or liquidity risk for even a brief period of time as a result of having settled one amount but not the other.

### EXAMPLE 14.2

Company A has a financial asset and a financial liability that otherwise qualify for offsetting. However, the financial asset is subject to a prior claim, such that a third party may obtain the funds from disposition of that financial asset in preference to the settlement of the financial liability. In this example, there is a risk that the funds from realising the asset will not be available to settle the financial liability. Therefore, offsetting is not appropriate.

### EXAMPLE 14.3

Company B has a financial asset and a financial liability otherwise qualifying for offsetting. Company B fully intends to use the proceeds from selling the financial asset to settle the financial liability, but there remains a risk that when Company B goes to realise the financial asset there could be a difficulty with the counter-party, resulting in the funds not being available. In such circumstances offsetting is not appropriate.

**14.10** Following from this, it is the settlement of cash flows that is important. When one company has an obligation to another company, which in turn has an obligation to the first company (for which there is a legal right of set-off), but the timing of settlement of the obligations differs, there is no intent to settle net for those cash flows that occur on different dates. There is a risk that the other party will not be able to settle the corresponding cash flow.

## CIRCUMSTANCES IN WHICH OFFSETTING IS PROHIBITED

**14.11** Perhaps one of the most significant circumstances in which offsetting is not appropriate is in the case of a so-called 'synthetic instrument'.

**EXAMPLE 14.4**

Company C enters into fixed rate debt and a fixed-to-floating interest rate swap, both with the same counter-party, as a means of creating essentially the same risk exposures as floating rate debt. It would be unlikely that these instruments would qualify for offsetting unless additional arrangements had been entered into by the parties to the contract. Each instrument could be settled separately and is exposed to different risks. The interest rate swap would be presented as a derivative financial instrument measured at fair value, separately from the fixed rate debt instrument. The company would, however, explain its risk management strategy in the notes to the financial statements, which may include an explanation of the nature of the relationship between the instruments when that is significant to the company's activities – ie the fact that interest rate risk is managed by entering into interest rate swaps to manage the interest rate risk associated with fixed rate debt.

**14.12** Other circumstances in which offsetting is generally not appropriate include:

(a) Financial assets and financial liabilities with different counter-parties.

**EXAMPLE 14.5**

Company D has a portfolio of interest rate swaps with the same exposure to interest rate risk, but with different counter-parties. The interest rate swaps do not share the same credit risks and do not qualify for offsetting. However, offsetting may be possible if a three-party netting agreement has been entered into, whereby more than one counter-party legally agrees that net settlement would be appropriate. Such circumstances would probably be highly unusual.

(b) Financial or other assets pledged as collateral against financial liabilities. Usually the company has no intention to settle the liability with the collateral – that is a last resort for the counter-party should the company be unable to pay the liability.
(c) Financial assets set aside in a trust by a debtor for the purpose of discharging an obligation, unless the creditor has legally accepted the assets in the trust in settlement of the obligation.
(d) Obligations incurred as a result of events giving rise to losses, such as repairs as a result of fire or flood, would not be offset against related insurance claims since the counter-parties involved in the transactions are different. This would be the case even if the creditor looks to the insurance company as the primary source of settlement.

**14.13** Financial institutions may enter into master-netting agreements whereby they agree that single net settlement of all instruments with a particular counter-party is provided for in the event of termination or default on any one contract with that party. Such an agreement only meets the offsetting requirements in IAS 32 if both the legally enforceable right to set off and the intent to settle net, or to realise the assets and liabilities simultaneously, are met. Commonly, the latter requirement would not be met until there is some event of default or termination. Accordingly, such agreements generally do not provide a basis for offsetting.

## GAAP COMPARISON

**14.14**   US GAAP addresses offsetting in FASB Interpretation No 39, 'Offsetting of Amounts Related to Certain Contracts'. This differs in two main aspects from IAS 32:

(a)   US GAAP requires that the right of set-off exists between two parties. Thus, three-party netting agreements without specific agreement between each party would not qualify for offsetting under US GAAP.

### EXAMPLE 14.6

If Company E meets offsetting criteria with regard to instruments entered into with Company F and with Company G, but there is no agreement between Company F and Company G, there would be no ability for Company E to offset in accordance with US GAAP.

(b)   US GAAP provides an exception for master-netting agreements, which is not available in accordance with IAS 32.

**14.15**   The approach to offsetting in IAS 32 differs in some respects from that in FRS 5, with the result that some situations qualifying for offset in accordance with FRS 5 will no longer qualify, and vice versa. In particular, FRS 5 requires offsetting when there is a right to net settlement that will survive the insolvency of the other party. This requires consideration only of the ability to offset an asset and liability. It does not require consideration of the intention to settle the asset and liability net.

Chapter 15

# Presentation

Principal IFRS references:

- IAS 1, paragraphs 51–75.
- IAS 21, paragraph 52.
- IAS 30, paragraphs 9–25.
- IAS 32, paragraphs 15–41, 94, AG25–AG37.

## INTRODUCTION

**15.1** The presentation of financial instruments is largely determined by the definitions of a financial asset, a financial liability and an equity instrument (see **Chapter 3**). An entity is required to classify a financial instrument according to these definitions, as well as in accordance with the substance of the contract. In some circumstances, this will require separating a financial instrument into its component parts.

**15.2** A financial instrument that is a debit balance is classified as a financial asset. However, a financial instrument with a credit balance may need to be classified as a financial liability or as an equity instrument. It is this distinction that is the subject of most of the discussion in this chapter. Presentation of financial instruments as financial liabilities or equity may have significant consequences for debt covenants – particularly when these depend on maintaining certain debt-to-equity ratios or other factors based on the amounts classified as debt versus equity.

**15.3** Some other IFRS contain requirements for the presentation of financial instruments. These requirements are considered in paragraphs **15.25–15.29** at the end of this chapter.

## BALANCE SHEET PRESENTATION

### Liabilities and equity

*Overview*

**15.4** The most important presentation requirements for financial instruments are those in IAS 32, which relate to classification of financial liabilities versus equity instruments. These apply to the issuer of a financial instrument only. (However, the embedded derivative requirements in IAS 39 (see **Chapter 6**) might require separation of debt and equity components in a financial asset when they are not closely related and the financial asset is not measured at fair value through profit or loss.) The requirements are based on the economic substance of the financial instrument rather than its legal form.

**15.5**   The legal description of a financial instrument as equity or debt may be inconsistent with its economic substance. However, if the legal form were to be the basis of the accounting, it would open up greater possibilities for structuring transactions to meet a particular accounting presentation objective, rather than reflecting the substance of the transaction itself.

### EXAMPLE 15.1

Company A issues 'term preferred shares' with a fixed redemption date. Even though they are termed 'shares', the fixed redemption date makes their economic substance more like debt than equity capital.

### EXAMPLE 15.2

Company B issues debt that is required to be converted into common shares at a date in the future, with no ability for the debt to be retracted by the issuer. Even though the financial instrument is termed 'debt' its economic substance is more like equity than debt.

**15.6**   A financial instrument might also contain a combination of 'debt-like' and 'equity-like' features. In such circumstances the instrument is required to be separated into its liability and equity parts, with each part accounted for in accordance with its respective characteristics.

### EXAMPLE 15.3

Company C issues debt that is convertible into Company C's common shares at the option of the holder. From Company C's perspective, this instrument contains two parts:

(a)   a contractual obligation to pay cash – a financial liability; and
(b)   a call option granting the holder the right to convert into common shares of Company C – an equity instrument of Company C.

*Distinguishing between financial liabilities and equity*

**15.7**   The main difference between a financial liability and an equity instrument is that a financial liability involves a contractual obligation either to deliver cash or another financial asset, or to exchange financial assets or financial liabilities, under conditions that are potentially unfavourable to the issuer. An instrument that does not give rise to such a contractual obligation is an equity instrument – unless it is a contract that will or may be settled in the issuer's own equity instruments and is:

(a)  a non-derivative for which the issuer has a contractual obligation to deliver, or may be required to deliver, a variable number of its own equity instruments; or

(b)  a derivative that will be or may be settled other than by exchanging a fixed amount of cash or another financial asset for a fixed number of its own equity instruments.

**Figure 15.1: Financial liabilities versus equity instruments**

|  | Financial liability | Equity instrument |
|---|:---:|:---:|
| Contractual obligation to deliver cash or another financial asset, to exchange financial assets or financial liabilities, under conditions that are potentially unfavourable to the issuer | ✓ | |
| Non-derivative contract to deliver, or be required to deliver, a variable number of own equity instruments | ✓ | |
| Derivative that will or may be settled other than by issuing a fixed number of own equity instruments | ✓ | |
| Derivative that will or may be settled by issuing a fixed number of own equity instruments | | ✓ |
| Non-derivative contract to deliver, or be required to deliver, a fixed number of own equity instruments | | ✓ |

**EXAMPLE 15.4**

Company D issues shares that entitle the holder to a pro rata share of any dividends or distributions of equity that Company D may make. Because the holder cannot compel Company D to make any payments, there is no contractual obligation and hence Company D classifies the contract as an equity instrument. This applies whether the instrument is described as common shares or preferred shares. It does not depend on the history of paying dividends in the past or the likelihood of paying dividends in the future. Nor does it depend on whether dividends are cumulative or non-cumulative.

**EXAMPLE 15.5**

Company E issues preferred shares that pay a fixed-rate dividend and are mandatorily redeemable at a future date. The issuer has a contractual obligation to make payments and therefore it presents such a financial instrument as a financial liability.

**EXAMPLE 15.6**

Company F issues a financial instrument that gives the holder the right to a residual interest in the assets of the issuer, as well as a right to put the instrument back to the issuer for cash or another financial asset. This contract imposes a contractual obligation on the issuer to make a payment to the holder if the holder exercises the put option. Therefore, Company F presents such a contract as a financial liability.

**15.8** Example 15.6 is a common structure of a contract establishing an investment in a unit trust, partnership or open-ended mutual fund, as well as investments in some co-operatives. Typically, the investor (the holder) has the right to redeem their investments for cash equal to their proportionate share of the net asset value of the issuer. This put option means that the issuer classifies such a financial instrument as a financial liability. This may be of concern to many, since it may appear that the unit trust, partnership, mutual fund or co-operative has little or no equity. IAS 32 notes that there is no requirement to describe such instruments as financial liabilities and provides two examples of how 'net asset value attributable to unit holders' may be presented (see IAS 32, paragraphs IE32–IE33). The following is an additional example.

**EXAMPLE 15.7**

|  | 2005 £000 | 2004 £000 |
|---|---|---|
| **Assets** | | |
| Investments at market value | 5,032 | 5,402 |
| Accrued interest and dividends receivable | 16 | 16 |
| Receivables for securities sold | 20 | – |
| | 5,068 | 5,418 |
| **Liabilities** | | |
| Payables for securities purchased | 1 | – |
| Redemptions payable | 5 | 5 |
| Operating expenses payable | 2 | 2 |
| | 8 | 7 |
| Net asset value attributable to unit-holders | 5,060 | 5,411 |

**15.9**   A contractual obligation to deliver cash or another financial asset may be established explicitly or indirectly through the terms and conditions of a contract.

**EXAMPLE 15.8**

Company G, a grocery retailer, issues a financial instrument that specifies that if Company G does not pay dividends in any year, it must provide groceries to a certain value in lieu of dividends. Even though Company G can avoid the contractual obligation to pay cash or another financial instrument, it must provide equivalent value. Accordingly, Company G presents the instrument as a financial liability.

**15.10**   Similar to the situation in Example 15.8, a company might issue a contract that requires it to settle a contractual obligation using its own shares in an amount that equals the contractual obligation. Just because the contract is settled in the company's own shares does not make it an equity instrument. This contract is no different from that in Example 15.8 and is classified as a financial liability.

**15.11**   In contrast, if the contract in the previous paragraph were to be settled by delivering a fixed number of the company's own shares it would be classified as an equity instrument. When the number of shares to be delivered is unaffected by changes in market conditions, then the contract is classified as an equity instrument.

**15.12**   A contingent settlement provision does not give the issuer any discretion to avoid the contractual obligation if the contingency comes to fruition. Therefore, such a contract is a financial liability of the issuer unless the contingent settlement provision is not genuine (ie there is no realistic possibility that the contingency would ever arise) or the contingency depends on the liquidation of the issuer.

**EXAMPLE 15.9**

Company H issues a financial instrument that requires it to make a dividend payment of 5p per share if a specified benchmark interest rate falls below 2.5 per cent. The issuer has no discretion to avoid payment if the benchmark interest rate falls below the specified threshold. Therefore, Company H presents the contract as a financial liability.

**15.13**   When the holder of a derivative financial instrument has the option to settle in different manners, the instrument is classified as a financial liability unless all of the options result in it being an equity instrument. If there is any option under which the holder can compel payment in cash or another financial asset, the instrument is a financial liability.

**15.14**   Sometimes a company may reacquire its own equity instruments. If so, these 'treasury shares' are deducted from equity, rather than being presented as a financial asset, recognised at the amount of consideration paid. However, any contractual obligation to reacquire a company's own equity instruments for cash or another financial asset at a fixed or determinable date or on demand is presented as a financial liability until the reacquisition takes place. The financial liability is measured at the present value of the redemption amount.

*Compound instruments*

**15.15** When financial instruments contain both a liability component and an equity component (as in Example 15.3), IAS 32 requires that the component parts be presented separately according to their substance.

**15.16** IAS 32 specifies that in determining the amount to allocate to each of the liability and equity components, the liability component is to be valued first, with the difference between that component and the fair value of the entire instrument assigned to the residual equity component. This results in the equity component being allocated the residual amount – consistent with the definition of equity as a residual.

**EXAMPLE 15.10**

Company I issues 2,000 convertible bonds on 1 January 2005. The bonds have a three-year term and are issued at par with a face value of £1,000 per bond, giving total proceeds of £2,000,000. Interest is payable annually in arrears at 6.5 per cent per annum. The bonds are convertible, at the option of the holder, at any time until maturity at a rate of 250 common shares for each £1,000 bond. The prevailing market rate of similar debt without conversion options at 1 January 2005 is 9 per cent per annum, and the market price of one common share of Company I at that date is £3.

The values of the liability and equity components are calculated as follows:

| | | |
|---|---|---|
| Present value of principal payable at the end of three years (£2,000,000 discounted at 9 per cent for three years) | = | £1,544,367 |
| Present value of interest payable annually in arrears for three years (£120,000 discounted at 9 per cent for each of one year, two years and three years) | = | £303,755 |
| Total liability component | = | £1,848,122 |
| Proceeds of bond issue | = | £2,000,000 |
| Residual – equity component | = | £151,878 |

**15.17** A company makes its decision as to the classification of an instrument at the time the instrument is initially recognised. The classification is not changed subsequently if circumstances change, such as if the likelihood that an option will be exercised becomes more or less probable.

**EXAMPLE 15.11**

Company J issues redeemable preferred shares that require it to pay to the holders a fixed amount of cash if the quoted market price of its common shares falls below a specified amount. At the time of issuing the shares it is not probable that the quoted market price of its common shares will fall below the specified amount. However, several years later the quoted market price of its common shares declines such that it becomes probable that it will fall below the specified amount.

Company J classifies the shares on initial recognition as equity, since it is not probable that a cash payment will be required. However, when the cash payment becomes probable, Company J does not reclassify the instrument as debt. It continues to classify the instrument as equity until such time as its market value actually falls below the specified amount, at which time it accounts for the payment of the cash, with any gain or loss as an equity transaction.

**15.18** On conversion of a convertible instrument, the company derecognises the liability component and recognises it as equity. On modification of the terms of a convertible instrument to induce early conversion, the difference between the fair value of the consideration the holder of the conversion option would receive in accordance with the new terms versus that in accordance with the original terms is recognised in profit or loss at the date that the terms are modified.

**15.19** When a derivative is involved, in addition to a liability and equity component, the company considers the embedded derivatives requirements of IAS 39 to determine whether there is an embedded derivative that requires separate accounting (see **Chapter 6**).

**Interest, dividends, gains and losses**

**15.20** Recognition and measurement of interest and dividends associated with financial liabilities, equity instruments and compound instruments follows the classification of the underlying component. Interest, dividends, gains and losses relating to an instrument classified as a financial liability are reported in profit or loss. Although there is no requirement to disclose interest expenses and dividends classified as expenses separately, it may often be desirable to do so. Distributions to holders of a financial instrument classified as equity are charged directly against equity.

**EXAMPLE 15.12**

The 'dividends' paid on the mandatorily redeemable preferred shares issued by Company D in Example 15.4, are accrued on an effective interest basis and treated as expenses in profit or loss, since the shares are presented as a financial liability.

**15.21**  *Presentation*

**15.21**  Gains or losses on refinancing or redemption of a financial instrument would also be classified as income or equity according to the debt or equity classification of the instrument.

**15.22**  Transaction costs incurred on issuing or acquiring an entity's own equity instruments are equity transactions and are deducted from equity. Transaction costs incurred on issuing a compound instrument are allocated to the liability and equity components in proportion to the allocation of proceeds.

*Consolidated financial statements*

**15.23**  A company considers all terms and conditions agreed between members of the consolidated group and outside parties in presenting a financial instrument in the consolidated financial statements. Thus, if a parent company agrees additional terms with an outside party in addition to those agreed to by another group member, all of the terms are considered in presenting the consolidated financial statements of the group. The group member may present the instrument differently in its separate financial statements, since it does not consider the additional terms agreed to by the parent company. An example of such a situation is when the parent company provides a guarantee of distributions by a subsidiary. The subsidiary may present the instrument as an equity instrument, but from the consolidated group perspective there is a contractual obligation and, thus, the combined effect is a financial liability.

*Financial statement presentation of convertible debt*

**15.24**  The following comprises extracts from financial statements illustrating the balance sheet, statement of profit or loss and note disclosure for a company that has issued convertible debt.

**EXAMPLE 15.13**

| Balance sheet disclosure (£m) | | |
| --- | --- | --- |
| As at 31 December | 2005 | 2004 |
| Liabilities | – | – |
| Debt component of convertible debentures (Note 11) | 28.1 | 33.4 |
| Owners' equity | – | – |
| Equity component of convertible debentures (Note 11) | 124.8 | 117.0 |

| Profit or loss disclosure (£m) For the years ended 31 December | 2005 | 2004 |
|---|---|---|
| Other profit and loss items | (22.0) | (111.2) |
| Interest on convertible debentures (Note 11) | (6.9) | (7.1) |
| Loss before taxes | (28.9) | (118.3) |
| Provision for taxes | (2.9) | (0.9) |
| Net loss for the year | (31.8) | (119.2) |
| Increase in equity component of convertible debentures (Note 11) | (7.8) | (7.2) |
| Net loss for the year attributable to owners | £(39.6) | £(126.4) |

*Note 11: Convertible debentures*

On 5 December 2000, the company issued unsecured subordinated convertible debentures in the aggregate principal amount of £146m. The debentures bear interest at 5.5 per cent per annum, mature on 5 December 2010 and, at the holders' option, are convertible into common shares of the company at a conversion price of £13.35 per share, being a rate of 74.906 common shares per £1,000 principal amount of debentures. Interest is payable in cash; however, the company has the right to settle the principal amount by the issuance of common shares. The debentures were redeemable after 30 June 2004 and until 31 December 2005 at par plus accrued and unpaid interest under certain conditions relating to the price of the common stock. On or after 31 December 2005 the debentures are redeemable at par plus accrued and unpaid interest. No debentures were redeemed in either 2004 or 2005. The company may, at its option, elect to satisfy its obligation to pay the principal amount of the debentures upon redemption or at maturity by issuing and delivering to the holders, for each £1,000 principal amount of debentures, that number of common shares obtained by dividing such amount by 95 per cent of the weighted average trading price of the common shares on the New York Stock Exchange for the 20 consecutive trading days ending on the fifth trading day prior to the date that the requisite notice of such election is given.

The debentures are being accounted for in accordance with their substance and are presented in the financial statements in their component parts, measured at their respective fair values at the time of issue. The debt component has been calculated as the present value of the required interest payments discounted at a rate approximating the interest rate that would have been applicable to non-convertible debt at the time the debentures were issued. Interest expense is determined on the debt component, such component being reduced by the required semi-annual interest payments. The difference between the debt component and the face value of the debentures is classified as equity, net of issue costs adjusted for taxes. The equity component of the debentures, net of the value ascribed to the holders' option, is increased over the term to the full face value by charges to retained earnings (deficit).

During 2004, the company bought back £0.15m principal amount of the debentures for £0.07m. None were bought back in 2005.

As at 31 December 2005, the outstanding principal amount of the debentures was £122.8m (31 December 2004 – £130.4m).

**Other balance sheet presentation requirements**

**15.25**  IAS 1 requires that the face of the balance sheet include separate line items for the following financial instruments, with additional sub-classifications depending on the size, nature or function of the amounts involved:

(a)  investments accounted for using the equity method;
(b)  trade and other receivables[1];
(c)  cash and cash equivalents;
(d)  all other financial assets;
(e)  trade and other payables; and
(f)  all other financial liabilities.

[1]  The notes to the financial statements are required to disaggregate trade receivables, related party receivables, prepayments and other amounts.

**15.26**  IAS 1 also specifies other requirements that will be applicable to financial instruments, including the presentation of current and non-current assets and liabilities.

PROFIT OR LOSS PRESENTATION

**15.27**  There are few specific presentation requirements related to financial instruments for the statement of profit or loss. IAS 21 requires that the amount of foreign exchange differences recognised in profit or loss for the period be separately presented, except for those arising on financial instruments measured at fair value through profit or loss in accordance with IAS 39. IAS 21 also requires separate presentation of foreign exchange differences classified in a separate component of equity and a reconciliation of such differences at the beginning and end of the period[1].

[1]  Other aspects of the presentation of the statement of changes in equity are discussed in **Chapter 10**.

**15.28**  IAS 32 requires separate presentation or disclosure of material items of income, expense, gains or losses resulting from financial assets and financial liabilities, whether included in profit or loss or equity, including at least:

(a)  total interest income and interest expense for financial assets and financial liabilities other than those measured at fair value through profit or loss;
(b)  the amounts of any gains or losses recognised directly in equity during the period and removed from equity during the period relating to available-for-sale financial assets; and
(c)  the nature and amount of any impairment loss recognised in profit or loss,

separately for each class of financial asset, and the amount of interest income accrued on impaired financial assets.

## BANKS AND SIMILAR FINANCIAL INSTITUTIONS

**15.29**   Additional presentation requirements apply to banks and similar financial institutions, in accordance with IAS 30. These include requirements to separately present additional balance sheet line items, including loans and advances and deposits, as well as requirements to present line items such as interest income, interest expense, and net gains and losses from selling different types of financial instrument, in profit or loss. The IASB is currently undertaking a project to improve IAS 30, addressing financial risk and other amendments to financial instruments disclosures, which would be applicable to disclosures about financial risk for all companies – not only banks and financial institutions. An exposure draft is expected in the second quarter of 2004.

## GAAP COMPARISON

**15.30**   It is likely that a number of financial instruments will be presented differently in accordance with IAS 32 from the manner in which they are currently presented in accordance with either UK or US GAAP. The FASB in the US is presently undertaking a project on liabilities and equity, the general direction of which is likely to bring US GAAP more in line with the presentation requirements of IAS 32. Parts of this project were completed with the issue of FASB Statement of Financial Accounting Standards No 150, 'Accounting for Certain Financial Instruments with Characteristics of both Liabilities and Equity' in May 2003. A further exposure draft addressing the remaining aspects of this project is expected by the end of 2004.

**15.31**   UK GAAP presently looks more to the predominant characteristics of a financial instrument, such as convertible debt or preference shares, to determine their classification rather than considering the substance of debt and equity, and does not require separation of the debt and equity components in a compound instrument.

Chapter 16

# Disclosure

Principal IFRS references:

- IAS 1, paragraphs 108–124.
- IAS 30, paragraphs 26–58.
- IAS 32, paragraphs 51–95, AG40.

## INTRODUCTION

**16.1** Most of the disclosure requirements for financial instruments are contained in IAS 32. However, additional disclosures for banks and similar financial institutions are contained in IAS 30 and limited disclosures regarding foreign currency risks are contained in IAS 21.

**16.2** This chapter identifies the disclosures required and, where appropriate, provides examples of some of those disclosures. There are many ways in which a company can provide disclosures. However, the overall objective should be to provide information in a manner that is useful to users of the financial statements. When understanding will be enhanced, it will be useful to relate disclosures to one another. As a minimum, information is provided to enable disclosures to be reconciled with relevant line items on the balance sheet. It may also be necessary to provide additional disclosures – particularly to provide context for the disclosures required by the standards.

**16.3** The level of detail to be provided will depend on the significance of financial instruments to the company. When financial instruments have similar characteristics and no individual instrument is material, disclosures would be provided by classes of similar financial instrument. However, if an individual instrument is, or has the possibility of being, material to the company, then disclosures about that instrument would be provided separately. Classes of financial instruments would generally include only instruments measured on the same basis, so that instruments measured at fair value would not be included in the same class as those measured at amortised cost. Financial instruments excluded from the scope of IAS 32 would be included in separate classes from those falling within the scope.

## RISK MANAGEMENT AND HEDGING POLICIES

**16.4**  The manner in which a company has managed risk during the accounting period is of vital importance to understanding the financial position and results of the company. IAS 32 requires various disclosures about financial risk management policies and hedging activities undertaken to manage those risks. However, before considering those disclosures it is necessary to understand how IAS 32 defines financial risks.

**16.5**  IAS 32 deals only with financial risks. Other risks, such as the risk that raw material prices will change, raw materials will be in short supply or major customers may change to a new supplier, may be equally, or more, significant than financial risks for some companies. However, IAS 32's focus is only financial instruments and, hence, financial risks.

**16.6**  IAS 32 defines the risks that may be transferred in transactions involving financial instruments as follows:

'(a)  "Market risk" includes three types of risk:
  (i)  "currency risk" – the risk that the value of a financial instrument will fluctuate because of changes in foreign exchange rates.
  (ii)  "fair value interest rate risk" – the risk that the value of a financial instrument will fluctuate because of changes in market interest rates.
  (iii)  "price risk" – the risk that the value of a financial instrument will fluctuate because of changes in market prices. ...
(b)  "Credit risk" – the risk that one party to a financial instrument will fail to discharge an obligation and cause the other party to incur a financial loss;
(c)  "Liquidity risk" ... – the risk that an entity will encounter difficulty in raising funds to meet commitments associated with financial instruments. ...
(d)  "Cash flow interest rate risk" – the risk that the future cash flows of a financial instrument will fluctuate because of changes in market interest rates. ... '

[IAS 32, paragraph 52]

**16.7**  IAS 32 requires a company to:

'describe its financial risk management objectives and policies, including its policy for hedging each main type of forecast transaction for which hedge accounting is used.'

[IAS 32, paragraph 56]

It goes on to explain that this would include a discussion of the extent to which financial instruments are used, the associated risks and the business purposes served, and should include policies on matters such as hedging of risk exposures, avoidance of undue concentrations of risk and requirements for collateral to mitigate risk.

**16.8**  In providing such disclosures a company may consider each of the risks in paragraph **16.6**, as well as the financial instrument contracts that it has entered into. If financial instrument contracts have been entered into other than for the ordinary business activities of the company, then it is likely that some disclosure about the risk management objectives of using those instruments is necessary. For example, the incurrence of accounts receivable created in the normal course of trade sales probably does not require any special disclosure unless the accounts receivable are unusually large. However, active management of interest rate risk arising from long-term debt using interest rate swaps would require some disclosure.

**16.9** It would be reasonable for a user of the financial statements to assume that a company does not actively manage financial risks in the absence of any disclosure. This may be reasonable in the case of a small company with unsophisticated transactions. However, it may not seem reasonable to a user of financial statements for a complex company with large financial risk exposures. A company should consider whether it wishes to accept the possible implication that it does not actively manage financial risks, if it is silent in note disclosures.

**16.10** It is interesting to note that the policy for hedge accounting is limited to forecast transactions. Typically, information about other hedge accounting policies would also be provided. (See **Chapter 12**, paragraphs **12.125–12.126** for more on. disclosures about active hedging activities that a company has undertaken.)

### EXAMPLE 16.1

This example illustrates disclosure of risk management policies related to particular financial risks.

*Credit risk*

Company A grants credit to its customers in the normal course of business. Credit valuations are performed on a regular basis and the financial statements take into account an allowance for bad debts. The company does not have any credit risk concentration.

*Interest rate risk*

Short-term bank credit facilities and long-term bank loans bear interest at fluctuating rates. The company occasionally enters into interest swap contracts to hedge against exposures to increases in interest rates.

*Currency risk*

In the normal course of operations, the company enters into certain foreign currency transactions. The company manages its currency risks by occasionally entering into forward foreign exchange contracts.

The majority of the company's operations are carried out in the United States. The cash flows from US operations constitute a natural hedge against the exchange risk related to debt expressed in US dollars.

## ACCOUNTING POLICIES

**16.11**  General requirements to disclose all significant accounting polices are contained in IAS 1. Specific requirements relating to financial instruments include disclosure of:

(a)    criteria for recognition and derecognition;
(b)    the basis of measurement (cost, amortised cost or fair value) applied on initial recognition and subsequently, by asset category;
(c)    the basis on which income and expenses are recognised and measured; and
(d)    whether regular-way purchases and sales are accounted for at trade date or settlement date.

**16.12**  It is particularly important to disclose accounting policies when a choice is available. When no choice is available, companies reporting in an international environment may still wish to disclose their significant policies as a means of informing foreign users of the financial statements of the main policies adopted.

**16.13**  IAS 1 also requires disclosure of the judgments management has made in the process of applying accounting policies. In the case of financial instruments, this might include:

(a)    whether financial assets qualify to be classified as held to maturity;
(b)    whether fair value of an available-for-sale financial asset is reliably measurable;
(c)    whether an embedded derivative is capable of separation and separate reliable measurement; or
(d)    when substantially all risk and rewards of ownership of a financial asset are transferred.

**16.14**  In addition, IAS 1 requires disclosure of major sources of measurement uncertainty at the balance sheet date. This would almost certainly include information about assumptions made in valuing financial instruments, including the nature of the uncertainties and the balance sheet carrying amount of the financial instruments affected by the uncertainty. However, it is not necessary to disclose the fact that the fair value of financial instruments may fluctuate subsequent to the balance sheet date. It is the estimation uncertainty that requires disclosure rather than the fact that the estimated value might, itself, fluctuate.

## TERMS AND CONDITIONS

**16.15**  For each class of financial asset, financial liability and equity instrument a company is required to disclose:

'information about the extent and nature of the financial instruments, including significant terms and conditions that may affect the amount, timing, and certainty of future cash flows.'

[IAS 32, paragraph 60(a)]

IAS 32 also specifies that when financial instruments held or issued, either individually or as a class, create a potentially significant exposure to the risks described in paragraph **16.6**, the following warrant disclosure:

'(a)  the principal, stated, face or other similar amount, which, for some derivative instruments, such as interest rate swaps, might be the amount (referred to as the notional amount) on which future payments are based;

(b)  the date of maturity, expiry or execution;

(c)  early settlement options held by either party to the instrument, including the period in which, or date at which, the options can be exercised and the exercise price or range of prices;

(d)  options held by either party to the instrument to convert the instrument into, or exchange it for, another financial instrument or some other asset or liability, including the period in which, or date at which, the options can be exercised and the conversion or exchange ratio(s);

(e)  the amount and timing of scheduled future cash receipts or payments of the principal amount of the instrument, including instalment repayments and any sinking fund or similar requirements;

(f)  stated rate or amount of interest, dividend or other periodic return on principal and the timing of payments;

(g)  collateral held, in the case of a financial asset, or pledged, in the case of a financial liability;

(h)  in the case of an instrument for which cash flows are denominated in a currency other than the company's functional currency, the currency in which receipts or payments are required;

(i)  in the case of an instrument that provides for an exchange, information described in items (a)–(h) for the instrument to be acquired in the exchange;

(j)  any condition of the instrument or an associated covenant that, if contravened, would significantly alter any of the other terms (for example, a maximum debt-to-equity ratio in a bond covenant that, if contravened, would make the full principal amount of the bond due and payable immediately); and

(k)  information on an instrument's legal form when it differs from its presentation form.'

[IAS 32, paragraph 63]

**16.16**  Generally, disclosures about terms and conditions will be included with other disclosures relating to those same financial instruments. The following example provides an extract from financial statements providing disclosures about terms and conditions of certain financial instruments, as well as other disclosures required by IAS 32.

**EXAMPLE 16.2**

*Note 13: Financial instruments*

The purpose of this Note is to disclose Company B's exposure related to financial instruments.

Company B enters into interest rate swap contracts with approved credit-worthy counter-parties to manage the company's current and anticipated exposure to interest rate risks. The company also enters into foreign exchange contracts, primarily in US dollars, to hedge future purchases of foreign-denominated goods and services with an emphasis on those that are expected to be completed within a four- to six-month period.

As at 31 December 2004, outstanding financial instruments of the company are summarised as follows:

| Notional amounts maturing in: | | | | | | |
|---|---|---|---|---|---|---|
| (Numbers in £000) | < 1 year | 1–5 years | 5–10 years | > 10 years | Total 2004 | Total 2003 |
| Interest rate swap contracts | – | 675,000 | – | 100,000 | 775,000 | 650,000 |
| Foreign exchange contracts | 1,496,378 | – | – | – | 1,496,378 | 762,496 |

For the year ended 31 December 2004, interest expense included a net receipt of approximately £3,821,000 (2003 – net payment of £358,000) relating to interest rate swaps. Any unsettled interest differentials outstanding at year-end were accrued for and included in accounts payable and other.

The estimated fair values of financial instruments as at 31 December 2004 and 31 December 2003 are based on relevant market prices and information available at that time. For financial instruments which are short-term in nature, carrying value approximates fair value. The fair values of other financial instruments are as follows:

| (Numbers in £000) | 2004 | | 2003 | |
|---|---|---|---|---|
| | Book value | Fair value | Book value | Fair value |
| Loans and mortgages receivables | 9,718 | 10,294 | 12,632 | 12,734 |
| Long-term debt (excluding current portion) | (1,310,000) | (1,314,733) | (1,115,027) | (1,093,587) |
| Interest rate swap contracts | 15,128 | 15,128 | 5,531 | 5,531 |
| Foreign exchange contracts | 7,998 | 7,998 | 592 | 592 |

The fair values of loans and mortgages receivable, long-term debt and interest rate swap contracts were estimated based on quoted market prices (when available) or discounted cash flows, using discount rates based on market interest rates and the company's credit rating. The foreign exchange contracts were valued based on the differential between contract rates and year-end spot rates. For interest rate swap and foreign exchange contracts, the fair values reflect the estimated amounts that the company would receive or pay if it were to unwind the contracts at the reporting date.

## FOREIGN CURRENCY RISK

**16.17** IAS 21 contains a brief reference to the requirements to disclose a company's foreign currency risk management policy. However, it contains little additional disclosure requirements regarding foreign currency risk exposures. IAS 32 does not contain additional disclosure requirements regarding foreign currency risk.

## INTEREST RATE RISK

**16.18** A company is required to disclose the following regarding its exposures to interest rate risk, for each class of financial asset and financial liability:

(a) contractual repricing or maturity dates, whichever dates are earlier (information about expected repricing or maturity dates when these differ significantly from contractual dates is also desirable, in which case disclosure is also made that it is management expectation and an explanation of how the assumptions differ from the contractual dates);
(b) effective interest rates, when applicable (ie when there is a cost reflecting the time value of money. This does not apply to equity instruments or derivatives that do not bear a determinable effective interest rate);
(c) financial assets and liabilities that are exposed to:
  (i) fair value interest rate risk (such as those with a fixed interest rate);
  (ii) cash flow interest rate risk (such as those with a floating interest rate); and
  (iii) no interest rate risk; and
(d) the effect on its interest rate risk exposure of hedging transactions.

### EXAMPLE 16.3

The following provides an example of interest rate risk disclosure for the same company as in Example 16.2.

*Interest rate risk*

The following table identifies Company B's financial assets and liabilities which are sensitive to interest rate movements and those which are non-interest rate sensitive as they are either non-interest bearing or bear interest at fixed rates.

| (Numbers in £000) | 2004 Interest sensitive | 2004 Non-interest sensitive | 2003 Interest sensitive | 2003 Non-interest sensitive |
|---|---|---|---|---|
| Cash and cash equivalents | 578,759 | – | 130,999 | – |
| Credit card receivables | – | 525,317 | – | 453,412 |
| Loans and mortgages receivable | – | 9,718 | – | 12,632 |
| Commercial paper | – | – | (234,025) | – |
| Long-term debt (including current portion) | (65,000) | (1,275,027) | (65,000) | (1,050,342) |
| Total | £513,759 | £(739,992) | £65,999 | £(584,298) |

Company B enters into interest rate swap contracts to manage its exposure to interest rate risk. As at 31 December 2004, the company had entered into contracts that exchanged a net notional amount of £175m from fixed to floating rate debt (2003 – £50m exchanged from fixed to floating). These contracts hedge the company's net balance sheet interest rate sensitivity position. A 1 per cent change in interest rates would not materially affect the company's earnings, cash flow or financial position.

**16.19**   Interest rate risk exposure may arise from transactions that do not give rise to recognised financial assets and financial liabilities. For example, fixed-rate loan commitments result in interest rate risk exposure. In such circumstances a company would disclose the stated principal, interest rate and term to maturity of the amount to be lent, as well as any other significant terms of the transaction.

**16.20**   IAS 32, paragraph 74 provides examples of several suggested formats for disclosing interest rate risk, including tabular or narrative descriptions based on maturity time bands, fixed- and floating-rate exposures, interest rate sensitivity analysis and through the use of weighted average rates or ranges of rates.

## CREDIT RISK

**16.21**   IAS 32 requires disclosure of the following about its exposure to credit risk for each class of financial asset and other credit exposures:

(a)   maximum credit risk exposure at the balance sheet date, without taking account of the fair value of any collateral; and

(b)   significant concentrations of credit risk, including a description of the shared characteristic that identifies each concentration (such as nature of activities undertaken by debtors, industry in which they operate, geographical area in which activities are undertaken or level of creditworthiness of groups of borrowers) and amount of maximum credit risk exposure associated with all financial assets sharing that characteristic.

**16.22**   In many cases, the balance sheet carrying amounts of assets will represent the amount exposed to credit risk, as with an account receivable.

However, in other instances, such as with certain option contracts, the maximum amount exposed may differ considerably from the balance sheet carrying amount.

**16.23** When rights of set-off or master-netting agreements exist, but the financial assets and financial liabilities involved are not offset for accounting purposes (see **Chapter 14**), information about these agreements is provided to give users information about the extent that credit risk may be reduced.

**16.24** Credit risk may arise as a result of transactions that do not result in recognition of financial assets or financial liabilities. Examples include certain financial guarantees or credit derivatives. Disclosures about credit risk arising from such transactions are provided in the same way as for recognised financial assets and financial liabilities.

### EXAMPLE 16.4

*Credit risk disclosure for a manufacturing company*

Company C is exposed to credit-related losses in the event of non-performance by counter-parties to derivative financial instruments but does not expect any counter-parties to fail to meet their obligations. The company deals with only highly-rated counter-parties, normally major financial institutions. The company is exposed to credit risk when there is a positive fair value of derivative financial instruments at a reporting date. The maximum amount that would be at risk if the counter-parties failed completely to perform under the contracts was £4.8 million at 31 December 2004 (2003 – £1.2 million).

**16.25** Disclosures about concentrations of credit risk are likely to be new for UK companies. The following provides an example of how such disclosure might be presented.

### EXAMPLE 16.5

*Concentration of credit risk*

Loans receivable of £300,000 includes £275,000 from two oil production companies. There is a risk that a significant decline in oil prices could jeopardise the viability of those companies and, hence, the repayment of the full amount of the loans receivable.

## FAIR VALUE

**16.26** Fair value is required to be disclosed for all financial instruments, including those measured at amortised cost in accordance with IAS 39. The disclosure is to be presented in a manner that permits it to be compared with the corresponding balance sheet carrying amount. When carrying amount is a reasonable approximation of fair value, such as for short-term trade receivables and trade payables, no separate disclosure of fair values is necessary.

**16.27**  For purposes of fair value disclosures, fair value is to be determined in the same manner as in IAS 39. Of course, for those financial instruments measured at fair value on the balance sheet, additional disclosure of the fair value will not be necessary, but the following disclosures about the methods of determining fair values are required.

**16.28**  For all fair values, whether recognised on the balance sheet or disclosed, disclosure is required to include:

(a)  the methods and significant assumptions applied in determining fair values for each significant class of financial assets and financial liabilities;

(b)  whether fair values are determined directly, in full or in part, by reference to published price quotations in an active market or are estimated using a valuation technique;

(c)  whether valuation techniques include assumptions that are not supported by observable market prices or rates and information about the sensitivity of the fair value to changes in the assumption to a reasonably possible alternative; and

(d)  the total amount of change in fair value estimated using a valuation technique that is included in profit or loss for the period.

**16.29**  For investments in unquoted equity instruments or derivatives linked to such instruments, measured at cost in accordance with IAS 39, the fact that fair value cannot be determined, the characteristics of the financial instruments and, if possible, a range of estimates within which fair value is highly likely to lie is disclosed. Any gains or losses on sale of such financial instruments are also disclosed.

**16.30**  A company is also required to disclose separately the carrying amounts of financial assets and financial liabilities that were designated on initial recognition as financial assets and financial liabilities at fair value through profit or loss. It would not be appropriate to imply that such instruments are held for trading when they are not. In addition, users need to know which financial instruments are accounted for in this manner because they must be and which instruments the entity had some discretion over the accounting for. In presenting and disclosing information, a company should use a descriptor other than held for trading for financial instruments that have been designated in this way.

**16.31**  The fair value of a liability designated as at fair value through profit or loss may differ significantly from the settlement amount, in particular for financial liabilities with a long duration where a company has experienced a significant deterioration in creditworthiness since the issue of those liabilities. Therefore, for financial liabilities at fair value through profit or loss, the amount of changes in fair value of financial liabilities that is not attributable to changes in a benchmark interest rate, such as LIBOR, as well as any difference between the carrying amount of the financial liability and the amount the company would be contractually required to pay at maturity to the holder of the obligation, are required to be disclosed.

**EXAMPLE 16.6**

This example illustrates fair value disclosures.

*Note 15: Fair value disclosures*

The carrying value and fair value of financial instruments are as follows:

|  | 2004 | | 2003 | |
|---|---|---|---|---|
|  | Carrying value | Fair value | Carrying value | Fair value |
| Long-term debt | £(399,444) | £(392,000) | £(399,204) | £(395,000) |
| Derivative financial instruments: |  |  |  |  |
| Forward exchange contracts | £(84,453) | £(84,453) | £(100,055) | £(100,055) |
| Foreign currency options | £– | £– | £108 | £108 |

The fair value of Company D's long-term debt is estimated by reference to current market prices for other debt securities with similar terms and characteristics. The fair value of the company's forward exchange contracts and currency options is determined based on quoted market prices received from counter-parties. Until settled, the fair value of the derivative financial instruments will fluctuate based on changes in foreign exchange rates. The gains and losses on these financial instruments are included directly in equity and included in the measurement of the related hedged transaction on its initial recognition.

The carrying values of cash and cash equivalents, trade receivables, accounts payable and accrued liabilities, and other long-term liabilities meeting the definition of a financial instrument approximate their fair value.

## RECLASSIFICATION

**16.32**   If a company has reclassified a financial asset as being measured at cost or amortised cost rather than at fair value, the reason for that reclassification is required to be disclosed.

## DERECOGNITION

**16.33** When a transfer of a financial asset does not qualify for derecognition or results in a company having continuing involvement in the asset transferred (see **Chapter 13**), the company is required to disclose:

(a) the nature of the asset;
(b) the nature of the risks and rewards of ownership to which the company remains exposed;
(c) the carrying amounts of the asset and the associated liability (when all of the asset continues to be recognised); and
(d) the total amount of the asset, the amount of the asset the company continues to recognise and the carrying amount of the associated liability (when the asset continues to be recognised to the extent of the company's continuing involvement).

## COLLATERAL

**16.34** When a company has pledged financial assets as collateral for liabilities or contingent liabilities it is required to disclose separately the carrying amount of assets pledged for liabilities and contingent liabilities, as well as any material terms and conditions relating to assets pledged as collateral that may affect the amount, timing and certainty of future cash flows.

**16.35** When a company has accepted collateral that it is permitted to sell or repledge it is required to disclose:

(a) the fair value of the collateral accepted;
(b) the fair value of any such collateral sold or repledged and whether the company has an obligation to return it; and
(c) any material terms and conditions associated with its use of this collateral that may affect the amount, timing and certainty of future cash flows.

## DEFAULTS AND BREACHES

**16.36** A company is required to disclose details of any defaults of principal, interest, sinking fund or redemption provisions that can permit a lender to demand repayment, unless those breaches are remedied on or before the balance sheet date. This would include any breaches of debt covenants. In such circumstances, the company also discloses the balance sheet carrying amount of the loans payable on which breaches have occurred and whether the default has been remedied before the date the financial statements are authorised for issue.

## COMPOUND FINANCIAL INSTRUMENTS WITH MULTIPLE EMBEDDED DERIVATIVES

**16.37**   Disclosures relating to compound financial instruments with multiple embedded derivatives include the existence of interdependent features and the effective interest on the liability component (see **Chapter 15**, paragraph **15.19** for information on the accounting for such instruments).

## GAAP COMPARISON

**16.38**   FASB Statement 107, 'Disclosures about the Fair Values of Financial Instruments' requires information about fair values of financial instruments commensurate with the requirements of IAS 32. Other FASB standards dealing with financial instruments, including FASB Statement 115 and FASB Statement 133, require additional disclosures, in particular about derivatives. US GAAP does not require as extensive disclosures about financial risks or judgments and estimates in applying accounting polices as IAS 32 (although some such disclosures are required by the Securities and Exchange Commission for listed companies). Disclosures about non-derivative financial instruments, in particular financial liabilities, may be more extensive in IFRS than in accordance with US GAAP.

**16.39**   FRS 13 is the primary UK standard addressing disclosures about financial instruments. However, this applies only to companies with a capital instrument that is publicly listed, as well as banks and other financial institutions. The disclosures required in accordance with IFRS will not only apply to more companies, but will also be more extensive – particularly regarding judgments and estimates in applying accounting policies, financial liabilities, and significant terms and conditions of financial instruments.

Chapter 17

# Transitional provisions

Principal IFRS references:

- IAS 32, paragraph 97.
- IAS 39, paragraphs 104–108.
- IFRS 1, paragraphs 13, 23, 27–30, 36A, 47A, IG35–IG36, IG52–IG60B.

## INTRODUCTION

**17.1** The transition to applying IFRS for financial instruments depends on whether a company is adopting IFRS for the first time or whether the company has previously been applying IFRS, including the versions of IAS 32 and IAS 39 previously in place. Since the vast majority of companies will be applying IFRS for the first time, this chapter considers the transition provisions for those companies applying IFRS for the first time before moving on to the transition provisions for companies already applying IAS 32 and IAS 39. Before either consideration, however, some planning points in preparing for the transition are examined.

## PLANNING FOR TRANSITION

**17.2** Whether adopting IFRS for the first time, or considering the transition to the revised standards, it is vital to plan ahead. Decisions regarding such matters as designating hedges and classifying financial assets need to be made before the relevant transition date. The consequences of not planning for transition may be significant undesirable effects on the financial statements, including additional volatility in profit or loss, or in equity.

**17.3** A company adopting IFRS for the first time needs to identify all of its financial instruments, including embedded derivatives, consider the manner in which to classify those instruments and the extent to which it wishes to adopt hedge accounting. It may also need to review contracts to determine whether transactions previously entered into, including asset securitisation and similar transactions, continue to have the same financial statement impacts under the new standards.

**17.4**  For those items requiring designation or documentation relevant decisions must be made on or before the date of transition. These are not decisions that can be made on the spur of the moment immediately before adoption – a company needs to understand the financial risk exposures which it faces, the manner in which those exposures are being managed and the consequences of different accounting choices. The company then needs to establish the relevant documentation to support the elections adopted.

**17.5**  For a large company, a transition team will generally need to be established. This team should either include, or have direct links to, personnel other than those in the department responsible for financial reporting. The impact on the financial statements and users of those financial statements of different choices about, say, the extent to which to adopt hedge accounting, or the option to measure financial assets or financial liabilities at fair value through profit or loss, needs to be clearly understood. For example, a company may need to make an assessment as to whether investors will tolerate certain degrees of volatility in profit or loss, or in equity, or whether particular strategies will result in the company breaching debt covenants or unwelcome tax consequences.

**17.6**  A company should also consider educating those that will be affected by the changes. This will include not only those inside the company, such as senior management, investor relations and treasury personnel, but also external users of the company's financial statements. The education needs of each of these groups may vary considerably, with some needing only a high-level overview of the possible impacts of the standards, while others require more in-depth knowledge in order to make key decisions.

**17.7**  A company should also consider whether additional expertise is necessary to help implement the standards. That expertise is likely to be scarce as a large number of companies will implement IAS 32 and IAS 39 at the same time. The earlier that accounting and, possibly, valuation expertise is enlisted the better.

EFFECTIVE DATE

**17.8**  Whether or not a company is applying IAS 32 and IAS 39 for the first time, the effective date of application is the same – for annual periods beginning on or after 1 January 2005. This means that for companies with calendar year reporting periods the new requirements will be effective for the year ending 31 December 2005. For companies with reporting periods ending on other than 31 December the new requirements will be effective somewhat later. For example, a company with a 31 March year-end must apply the new requirements in its year ending 31 March 2006.

**17.9**  Companies should bear in mind that, even though the new requirements will not be effective until years ending 31 December 2005 or later, many of the requirements, such as those related to designation of financial assets as at fair value through profit or loss, or designation of hedges, must be in place before the financial year commences. Accordingly, a company should plan early so as to make relevant designations and have all documentation in place by 1 January 2005.

**17.10** A company preparing interim financial reports would be expected to apply the new requirements in interim financial periods falling within the first annual period beginning on or after 1 January 2005. Thus, a company with a calendar year-end preparing quarterly interim reports would apply the new requirements to the first quarter ending 31 March 2005.

**17.11** Early adoption is permitted. If a company chooses to adopt the new requirements before the mandatory effective date, it should adopt all of the requirements of both IAS 32 and IAS 39 and should disclose that it has done so. The requirement in IAS 34, 'Interim Financial Reporting' that the same accounting policies be used for interim and annual financial statements effectively means that early adoption must be at the beginning of an annual period and not at the beginning of an interim period. Thus, a company with a 31 December year-end is not permitted to adopt the new requirements at 1 July 2004, although a company with a 30 June year-end could choose to do so.

## FIRST-TIME ADOPTION OF IFRS

**17.12** The requirements for first-time adoption are set out in IFRS 1, 'First-time Adoption of IFRS', as amended on the publication of IAS 32 and IAS 39.

### Comparative information

**17.13** Perhaps one of the most significant accommodations to companies adopting IFRS for the first time is the exemption that allows a company adopting IFRS before 1 January 2006 not to comply with IAS 32 and IAS 39 in comparative information. Therefore, a company adopting IFRS for the first time in its year ending 31 December 2005 need not apply IAS 32 and IAS 39 in its comparative financial statements for the year ended 31 December 2004. The same would apply for a company with a 30 September year-end, which, in preparing financial statements for the year ending 30 September 2006, would not need to apply IAS 32 and IAS 39 in its comparative information for the year ending 30 September 2005.

**17.14** A company that chooses to avail itself of the option not to prepare comparative information in accordance with IAS 32 and IAS 39 should apply its previous GAAP to items falling within the scope of IAS 32 and IAS 39 in the comparative information. The company is also required to disclose the fact that it has used this option, together with the basis used to prepare the comparative information, and to disclose the nature (but not the amount) of the main adjustments that would be necessary to comply with IAS 32 and IAS 39. When the company first adopts IAS 32 and IAS 39 it treats any adjustment between the comparative information and the first period information in accordance with IFRS in the same manner as a change in accounting policy.

**17.15** Since the revised text of IAS 32 and IAS 39 was available only just before the end of 2003, it is anticipated that many companies will elect to apply this option because they will have had insufficient time to adequately plan for the designations, etc, necessary to be in place before the commencement of the comparative accounting period to deal with such matters as classification of financial assets and hedge accounting. The US Securities and Exchange Commission has also agreed to allow companies switching to IFRS for the first time for any financial year beginning no later than 1 January 2007, in their first year of reporting in accordance with IFRS, to include only two years of audited financial statements, with appropriate disclosure, instead of the normal three years.

### Classification of financial instruments

**17.16** Another significant accommodation in IFRS 1 is the ability to start afresh with designation at the beginning of the first period in which IFRS is adopted. Thus, in spite of the requirements in IAS 39 to designate any classification of financial instruments as at fair value through profit or loss, or as available for sale, on initial recognition of the relevant financial instruments, a company may make this designation at the date of transition to IFRS. A company using this option is required to disclose the fair value of any financial assets or financial liabilities designated into each category at the date of transition and the previous classification and carrying amount.

**17.17** This accommodation provides a valuable, one-time planning opportunity for a company. However, given the restriction on reclassifications, particularly in or out of the 'fair value through profit or loss' category, designations need to be carefully considered – including the longer-term consequences.

### Embedded derivatives

**17.18** Embedded derivatives are separated from host contracts when necessary (see **Chapter 6**), based on the carrying amount of the embedded derivative and the host contract at the date when the instrument initially satisfies the recognition criteria in IAS 39. Accordingly, this may require a company to retroactively identify the components in an existing contract when it was first recognised. Generally, this should be possible by reviewing the original contractual documentation. However, a company may need to go to some effort to retrieve and study that documentation. If the initial carrying amounts of the host contract and the embedded derivative are not reliably measurable, the entire contract is measured at fair value with gains and losses in profit or loss (unless it meets the exception in IAS 39 for certain instruments whose fair value is based on changes in fair value of equity that is not quoted in an active market and for which fair value is not reliably measurable).

**Recognition**

**17.19** A company recognises all financial assets and financial liabilities in its opening IFRS balance sheet in accordance with the recognition requirements of IAS 39, except as specified elsewhere in the remainder of this paragraph, and eliminates any gains or losses deferred as assets or liabilities in accordance with previous accounting requirements. However, non-derivative financial assets and non-derivative financial liabilities derecognised under previous GAAP in a financial year before 1 January 2004 are not recognised once more, unless the company chooses to apply the derecognition requirements retrospectively from a date of its choosing before 1 January 2004 and the information needed to apply IAS 39 to financial assets and financial liabilities derecognised as a result of past transactions was obtained at the time of initially accounting for those transactions. Thus, a company with, say, a single transaction resulting in a transfer of financial assets entered into in July 2003, which qualified for derecognition in accordance with previous accounting but not in accordance with IAS 39 and for which all information is readily obtainable, might choose to apply the derecognition criteria retrospectively to that date and reinstate the financial assets previously derecognised on its balance sheet.

**Measurement**

**17.20** A company measures all financial assets and financial liabilities in its opening IFRS balance sheet in accordance with the measurement requirements of IAS 39. Transition adjustments arising on re-measurement of financial assets and financial liabilities are recognised in the opening balance of retained earnings at the date of transition to IFRS. This provides a one-time opportunity for gains and losses on re-measurement to be recognised in equity rather than profit or loss. However, care needs to be taken to ensure that the measurement options chosen on transition are consistent with the company's longer-term desires – particularly for financial instruments that may be held for a long period of time.

**Gains and losses**

**17.21** Any gains or losses deferred on the balance sheet in accordance with previous accounting are transferred to the opening balance of retained earnings at the date of transition to IFRS. If a company previously recognised gains and losses on changes in fair value of financial assets directly in equity, the balance attributable to these gains and losses is reclassified to retained earnings or a separate component of equity depending on the classification of the asset after adoption of IFRS.

**Hedge accounting**

**17.22** No particular accommodation is provided for hedge accounting. If a hedge does not meet the requirements for hedge accounting at the transition date to IFRS the company discontinues previous hedge accounting in accordance with the requirements of IAS 39. Transactions entered into before the date of transition to IFRS are not permitted to be retrospectively designated as hedges. Thus, if a company wishes to use hedge accounting after the transition to IFRS for transactions entered into before the transition date, it should ensure that those transactions comply fully with the requirements for hedge accounting in IAS 39, including designation and documentation, when they are first entered into.

**17.23** If a company had designated a net position as a hedged item in accordance with previous GAAP it may designate an individual item within that net position as the hedged item, provided it does so no later than the date of transition to IFRS. Like many of the other first-time adoption requirements, this requires advance planning to consider whether to re-designate such hedges.

**Derecognition**

**17.24** A company is required to apply the derecognition requirements in IAS 39 prospectively for financial years beginning on or after 1 January 2004. However, a company may apply the derecognition requirements retrospectively to an earlier date of its choosing if information was available at the time of initially derecognising financial assets and financial liabilities under previous GAAP.

**17.25** A company will need to carefully review structured transactions, such as securitisation transactions, to determine whether assets or liabilities previously derecognised may need to be recognised, or whether assets or liabilities previously recognised may need to be derecognised if the transaction was after 1 January 2004.

**Presentation**

**17.26** A company is required to classify financial instruments as liabilities or equity (see **Chapter 15**) at the date of transition to IFRS, in accordance with the version of IAS 32 effective at the reporting date for its first IFRS financial statements. For most companies this will be the revised version of IAS 32. This classification is in accordance with the substance of the contractual arrangement when the instrument first satisfied the recognition criteria in IAS 32. Therefore, this may require reviewing records relating to when the instrument was first recognised.

**17.27** IFRS 1 allows a company not to separately present components of a compound instrument when those components are both in equity because the liability component is no longer outstanding – for example, it has been converted to equity. Such presentation would result in a reclassification between retained earnings and equity only.

## TRANSITION FOR COMPANIES PREVIOUSLY APPLYING IAS 32 AND IAS 39

**17.28**   The transitional rules for companies previously applying IAS 32 and IAS 39 require retrospective application except in the circumstances outlined in the following paragraphs. This means that the opening retained earnings for the earliest period presented, and all other comparative amounts, must be adjusted as if IAS 39 had always been in place – unless that is impracticable. If that is impracticable a company is required to state that fact and indicate the extent to which the information was restated.

**17.29**   To relieve the burden of restating comparative information The Committee of European Securities Regulators (CESR) has recently recommended to the European Commission that debt issuers need restate only one year of comparative figures in accordance with IAS 32 and IAS 39 for purposes of filing a prospectus in European capital markets, and that no issuer should be required to produce IFRS figures in a prospectus for any period earlier than 1 January 2004 (see press release from CESR, 8 January 2004).

**17.30**   Like the first-time adoption transition, IAS 39 provides a one-off option for companies to designate a financial asset or financial liability as available for sale or at fair value through profit or loss on transition, even though this would normally be permitted only on initial recognition. For financial assets designated as available for sale, all cumulative changes in fair value are recognised in a separate component of equity. In each case, the financial asset or financial liability is restated to fair value and the fair value and previous classification and carrying amounts are disclosed. This provides an opportunity for a company to re-designate its classifications. However, such re-designation must be done on or before the date the new version of IAS 39 is applied.

**17.31**   Also like the first-time adoption transition, the derecognition requirements of IAS 39 are applied prospectively. That is, financial assets derecognised in accordance with the previous version of IAS 39 as a result of a transaction occurring before 1 January 2004 are not recognised once again. However, a company may choose to apply the derecognition requirements retrospectively from a date of the company's choosing if the information needed to apply IAS 39 to assets and liabilities derecognised as a result of past transactions was obtained at the time of initially accounting for those transactions.

**17.32**   If the carrying amount of non-financial assets or non-financial liabilities at the date of applying IAS 39 includes gains and losses related to cash flow hedges as a result of adjusting the carrying amount of those assets or liabilities on initial recognition, these amounts are not adjusted.

**17.33**   Any amount included in equity for a hedge of a firm commitment accounted for as a cash flow hedge in accordance with previous accounting, but accounted for as a fair value hedge in accordance with the revised IAS 39, is reclassified as an asset or liability.

**17.34** There are no special transition requirements for IAS 32. It is applied retrospectively, so that liabilities and equity are classified in accordance with the new requirements and offsetting rules are applied in the period of adoption of the new requirements and comparative information, unless impractical.


GAAP COMPARISON


**17.35** Transitional provisions are specific to the timing and method of adoption of IAS 32 and IAS 39. While many of the provisions are similar to those the FASB put in place for companies adopting FASB Statement 133, it is unlikely that a company would be implementing both standards at the same time, A comparison is, therefore, not meaningful.

Chapter 18

# Future outlook

## INTRODUCTION

**18.1**   As noted in **Chapter 1**, IFRS for financial instruments are complex. Some of that complexity is a result of the mixed-measurement model applied. However, other aspects of the complexity derive from the complexity of financial instruments themselves.

**18.2**   Some are already unhappy with aspects of the standards and are calling for amendments. In particular, European financial institutions are concerned about the application of IAS 39 to their 'banking books', including the inability of the hedge accounting requirements to mirror the manner in which they manage certain financial risks. They are also concerned that the requirements do not allow them to hedge core deposit intangibles and that their profit or loss and equity will become more volatile as a result of the recognition of gains and losses from changes in fair values. Some insurance companies are also concerned about a possible mis-match between the accounting treatment for their financial assets and that of insurance liabilities. Others are concerned about the ability to reliably determine fair values in many instances. As large numbers of companies apply the requirements for the first time, in Europe and beyond, it is inevitable that both the companies and the IASB will learn from the experience and that new implementation questions will arise. Additional implementation guidance or Interpretations may become necessary. The standards will probably be modified, or significantly changed, at some time in the future. However, for now, they represent the state-of-the-art in financial reporting for financial instruments, and are significantly better than nothing.

**18.3**   This chapter briefly reviews what is likely to happen in the near, and possibly not so near, future as the standards are applied and are, perhaps, further improved.

## IMPLEMENTATION

**18.4**   The improved IAS 32 and IAS 39 were issued shortly before the end of 2003. However, the text is not complete. The IASB has made several amendments to the text of IAS 32 and IAS 39 resulting from consequential amendments on the issue of new standards, such as IFRS 2, 'Share-based Payment', IFRS 3, 'Business Combinations' and IFRS 4, 'Insurance Contracts'. At the end of March 2004, the IASB issued changes to IAS 39 based on its exposure draft on Fair Value Hedge Accounting for a Portfolio Hedge of Interest Rate Risk. While these changes do not fundamentally alter the text of IAS 39 as issued in December 2003, the changes are of great significance to banks and other financial institutions, in particular. As a result of these re-deliberations, certain other modifications, in particular to clarify aspects of hedge effectiveness testing, were also made. These changes will have more wide-ranging effects. As a result of constituent requests, the IASB is also considering whether to explain the circumstances in which adoption of the option to measure any financial asset or financial liability at fair value through profit or loss on initial recognition would be appropriate. An exposure draft proposing changes to this aspect of the standards is expected in the second quarter of 2004. An exposure draft clarifying the interaction of IFRS 4 and IAS 39 as they apply to financial guarantee contracts is also expected in the second quarter of 2004[1].

[1] The possible effects of changes arising from these two exposure drafts are included by footnote reference in the text of the book.

**18.5** Once these re-deliberations are complete, the IASB has promised that it will enter a 'period of calm'. It will not make any further amendments to its standards that would be mandatory before 2006. Accordingly, the text of IAS 32 and IAS 39 should remain unchanged. However, consultations continue with certain financial institutions to explore the possibility of additional amendments to the circumstances in which hedge accounting for interest rate margins is permitted.

**18.6** In Europe, there remains a further hurdle to be overcome: before the requirements of IAS 32 and IAS 39 become mandatory for European public companies they require endorsement by the European Union. That endorsement is not a formality, with significant concerns about certain aspects of the standards having been raised by some, as discussed in paragraph **18.2**. The formal process of considering the standards for endorsement cannot commence until the March 2004 amendments referred to in paragraph **18.4** are complete. It is possible that they may even be delayed until any further amendments are complete (see also paragraph **18.4**). However, it is expected that the European Union will make a decision on endorsement in the second half of 2004.

**18.7** Because of the complexity of IAS 32 and IAS 39, and the need to make many choices about such aspects of the standards as classification of financial assets and hedge accounting before implementation in 2005, a company cannot afford to stand back and wait for the European Union's decision. It needs to plan early for implementation.

**18.8** Any work undertaken to plan for implementation will be time well invested. Credible accounting for financial instruments is important, whether or not IAS 32 and IAS 39 are endorsed by the European Union. Planning to understand the requirements, to identify a company's financial instruments, to document hedging relationships and to make choices about classifying financial instruments would be prudent regardless of the outcome of the European Union endorsement. Furthermore, it seems unlikely that the European Union would prevent a company from adopting IAS 32 and IAS 39.

**18.9**   For large companies, the implementation process will probably be a major project in itself – and, for many companies, one linked with the process for adopting IFRS for the first time. For smaller companies, an early consideration of whether the company has instruments that will require changes in accounting or new systems to gather information for that accounting will be a worthwhile investment to identify probable problem areas and save a last minute scramble.

**18.10**   A key part of implementation at an early stage will be ensuring that all personnel required to be knowledgeable about IAS 32 and IAS 39, or aspects of their implementation, are appropriately educated in the requirements. This may include not only those within the accounting department, but key personnel outside the accounting department who will be required to provide information to the accounting department.

**18.11**   Once implementation by a large number of companies is underway, issues will inevitably arise. Companies should consider consulting with their auditors and perhaps with their colleagues in other companies to assist in resolving issues. If significant issues arise, they may require referral to the IASB's International Financial Reporting Interpretations Committee (IFRIC) for consideration. It is thus possible that new IFRIC interpretations, or other guidance, will be issued to supplement IAS 32 and IAS 39[1].

[1]   Indeed, there are already indications that IFRIC may consider additional issues relating to what may constitute a 'portion' of a hedged item.

**18.12**   Companies may also need to consider whether it is necessary to get implementation perfect the first time around. In some cases it may be appropriate to ensure that all major matters are attended to within the bounds of financial statement materiality, while leaving refinements of the process to a later stage of implementation. In particular, a company might choose to implement hedge accounting for only some of its most significant hedging relationships, refining that strategy as necessary in future periods.

OTHER IASB ACTIVITIES

**18.13**   Two current IASB projects are likely to have an effect on accounting for financial instruments in the near future:

(a)   reporting comprehensive income; and
(b)   financial risk disclosures.

**18.14**   The IASB project on reporting comprehensive income is expected to result in a discussion paper, or perhaps an exposure draft on some aspects, in the second half of 2004. The IASB is considering an approach, in conjunction with the UK Accounting Standards Board, that would recognise all gains and losses in a single statement of comprehensive income. If the proposals were to be implemented as presently contemplated, the ability to recognise gains and losses on available-for-sale financial assets and on cash flow hedges in a separate component of equity would no longer be available) Instead, such gains and losses would be presented separately within the single statement of comprehensive income. The US FASB is also conducting a project on the same topic, which is being co-ordinated with the IASB/UK Accounting Standards Board project.

**18.15** (The IASB project on financial risk disclosure is expected to result in an exposure draft in the second quarter of 2004. This project is being undertaken with significant input from the banking community and is intended to result in a replacement of IAS 30, as well as changes to the disclosure requirements of IAS 32.)However, unlike IAS 30, the resulting standard would apply not only to banks and similar financial institutions, but would address disclosures of financial risks more broadly for all companies and is likely to result in amendments to aspects of the disclosures required by IAS 32, in addition to replacing IAS 30. This project is unlikely to change any aspects of recognition or measurement of financial instruments.

ACTIVITIES OF OTHER STANDARD-SETTERS

**18.16**   In the US, the FASB is undertaking a project to accumulate guidance on determining fair values, whether for financial instruments or for other balance sheet items, in one place on a consistent basis. The FASB expects to issue an exposure draft in the second quarter of 2004. This material will probably provide additional useful information to those seeking to determine fair values.

**18.17**   The FASB also has on its agenda a short-term convergence project, an aspect of which is to consider the improvements made to IAS 32 and IAS 39 and whether similar improvements should be made to US GAAP. Work on this aspect of the project has yet to commence and it is unclear when further information might be available. However, once it gets underway, there is the possibility both that greater convergence between IFRS and US GAAP will be possible, and that additional refinements may be identified that, ultimately, will find their way into IFRS.

**18.18**   As noted in **Chapter 15**, the FASB also has a project underway to consider liability and equity classification, which is likely to reach conclusions similar, but not identical, to IAS 32.

**18.19**   In the UK, the Accounting Standards Board issued FRED 23, 'Financial Instruments: Hedge Accounting' in May 2002 and FRED 30, 'Financial Instruments: Disclosure and Presentation, Recognition and Measurement' in June 2002, proposing changes to UK GAAP for financial instruments. It also issued a supplement to FRED 30, 'Fair Value Hedge Accounting for a Portfolio Hedge of Interest Rate Risk'. In many cases the proposals would move UK GAAP closer to the requirements of IAS 32 and IAS 39. However, these proposals would exclude many of the requirements of IAS 39, such as more detailed restrictions on qualifying hedging relationships, how hedge accounting is to be applied, recycling of gains and losses on available-for-sale financial assets, cash flow hedges and hedges of a net investment in a foreign operation, and the derecognition requirements. It is unclear at the present time what will happen to these exposure drafts. The UK ASB plans to issue a consultation paper in the second quarter of 2004 to consider how it should proceed with these proposals. However, to the extent that they are implemented they would apply to UK companies not adopting IFRS.

## UK COMPANIES ACT LEGISLATION

**18.20**   UK companies should bear in mind that there are additional requirements of the Companies Acts that would need to be considered in addition to the requirements of IFRS. Work has been undertaken to remove any conflicts between these requirements and IFRS.

## THE LONGER TERM

**18.21**  The IASB continues to have on its research agenda a project to consider more comprehensive changes to IAS 39 – perhaps to replace aspects of the mixed-measurement model. Such an approach was explored by the Financial Instruments Joint Working Group of Standard-Setters and issued in December 2000 in the form of a draft standard and basis for conclusions, 'Financial Instruments and Similar Items'. It was clear from consultations on those proposals that there were many unresolved problems to be addressed in implementing such an approach. However, it is likely that the IASB and other national standard-setters will, at some time in the future, explore further whether some of these problems can be overcome. It does not seem likely, however, that any significant changes to IFRS for financial instruments resulting from such considerations would be capable of implementation for at least five years, and probably longer.

Appendix 1

# Chapter cross-references to IAS 32 and IAS 39

This appendix lists the main parts of IAS 32 and IAS 39 (December 2003), including the Application Guidance, providing cross-references to the chapters of this book dealing with those aspects of IAS 32 and IAS 39.

| References to Standards and Application Guidance | Chapter references |
|---|---|
| **IAS 32, 'Financial Instruments: Disclosure and Presentation'** | |
| Scope – paragraphs 4–10 | 4 |
| Definitions – paragraphs 11–14 | 3, 4, 9 |
| Liabilities and equity – paragraphs 15–27 | 15 |
| Compound financial instruments – paragraphs 28–32 | 15 |
| Treasury shares – paragraphs 33–34 | 15 |
| Interest, dividends, losses and gains – paragraphs 35–41 | 15 |
| Offsetting a financial asset and a financial liability – paragraphs 42–50 | 14 |
| Disclosure – paragraphs 51–95 | 12, 16 |
| Effective date – paragraphs 96–97 | 1, 17 |
| *Application Guidance* | |
| Definitions – paragraphs AG3–AG24 | 3 |
| Liabilities and equity – paragraphs AG25–AG29 | 15 |
| Compound financial instruments – paragraphs AG30–AG35 | 15 |
| Treasury shares – paragraph AG36 | 15 |
| Interest, dividends, losses and gains – paragraph AG37 | 15 |
| Offsetting a financial asset and a financial liability – paragraphs AG38–AG39 | 14 |
| Disclosure – paragraph AG40 | 16 |
| **IAS 39, 'Financial Instruments: Recognition and Measurement'** | |
| Scope – paragraphs 2–7 | 3, 4, 8 |
| Definition of a derivative – paragraph 9 | 3 |
| Definitions of four categories of financial instruments – paragraph 9 | 5 |
| Definitions relating to recognition and measurement – paragraph 9 | 7, 8, 9, 13 |
| Definitions relating to hedge accounting – paragraph 9 | 12 |

# Abbreviations and frequently-used terms

This appendix lists abbreviations and terms frequently used throughout the book, together with an explanation of the abbreviations and references to the main locations of where the terms are explained.

| | |
|---|---|
| Available-for-sale financial assets | Non-derivative financial assets that are designated as available for sale or are not classified as:<br>(a)  loans and receivables;<br>(b)  held-to-maturity investments; or<br>(c)  financial assets at fair value through profit or loss.<br>See **Chapter 5**, paragraph **5.42**. |
| Cash flow hedge | A hedge of the exposure to variability in cash flows that:<br>(a)  is attributable to a particular risk associated with a recognised asset or liability (such as all or some future interest payments on variable rate debt) or a highly probable forecast transaction; and<br>(b)  could affect profit or loss.<br>See **Chapter 12**, paragraph **12.33**. |
| Derecognition | The process of removing a previously recognised financial asset or financial liability from the balance sheet.<br>See **Chapter 13**, paragraph **13.1**. |
| Derivative | A financial instrument or other contract within the scope of [IAS 39] ... with all three of the following characteristics: |

|                      | (a) | its value changes in response to the change in a specified interest rate, financial instrument price, commodity price, foreign exchange rate, index of prices or rates, credit rating or credit index, or other variable, provided in the case of a non-financial variable that the variable is not specific to a party to the contract (sometimes called the 'underlying'); |
|----------------------|-----|---|

(b) it requires no initial net investment or an initial net investment that is smaller than would be required for other types of contracts that would be expected to have a similar response to changes in market factors; and

(c) it is settled at a future date.

See **Chapter 3**, paragraph **3.14**.

| Embedded derivative | A component of a hybrid instrument that also includes a non-derivative host contract, with the effect that some of the cash flows of the hybrid instrument vary in a way similar to a stand-alone derivative. See **Chapter 6**, paragraph **6.6**. |
|---|---|
| Equity instrument | Any contract that evidences a residual interest in the assets of an entity after deducting all of its liabilities. See **Chapter 3**, paragraph **3.10**. |
| EITF | Emerging Issues Task Force (the interpretations committee of the FASB). |
| Fair value | The amount for which an asset could be exchanged or a liability settled between knowledgeable, willing parties in an arm's length transaction. See **Chapter 9**, paragraph **9.3**. |
| Fair value hedge | A hedge of the exposure to changes in fair value of a recognised asset or liability, or unrecognised firm commitment (or an identified portion of such an asset, liability or firm commitment) that is attributable to a particular risk and could affect profit or loss. See **Chapter 12**, paragraph **12.25**. |
| FASB | Financial Accounting Standards Board (the US accounting standard-setter). |
| FASB Statement 115 | FASB Statement of Financial Accounting Standards No 115, 'Accounting for Certain Investments in Debt and Equity Securities'. |

| | |
|---|---|
| FASB Statement 133 | FASB Statement of Financial Accounting Standards No 133 (as amended by FASB Statement of Financial Accounting Standards No 138), 'Accounting for Derivative Instruments and Hedging Activities'. |
| Financial asset | Any asset that is: |

(a)  cash;

(b)  an equity instrument of another entity;

(c)  a contractual right:

    (i)    to receive cash or another financial asset from another entity; or

    (ii)   to exchange financial assets or financial liabilities with another entity under conditions that are potentially favourable to the entity; or

(d)  a contract that will or may be settled in the entity's own equity instruments and is:

    (i)    a non-derivative for which the entity is or may be obliged to receive a variable number of the entity's own equity instruments; or

    (ii)   a derivative that will or may be settled other than by the exchange of a fixed amount of cash or another financial asset for a fixed number of the entity's own equity instruments. For this purpose the entity's own equity instruments do not include instruments that are themselves contracts for the future receipt or delivery of the entity's own equity instruments.

See **Chapter 3**, paragraph **3.4**.

**Financial asset or financial liability at fair value through profit or loss**  A financial asset or financial liability that meets either of the following conditions:

(a)  it is classified as held for trading. A financial asset or financial liability is classified as held for trading if it is:

    (i)    acquired or incurred principally for the purpose of selling or repurchasing it in the near term;

(ii) part of a portfolio of identified financial instruments that are managed together and for which there is evidence of a recent actual pattern of short-term profit-taking; or

(iii) a derivative (except for a derivative that is a designated and effective hedging instrument).

(b) Upon initial recognition it is designated by the entity as at fair value through profit or loss.

See **Chapter 5**, paragraphs **5.6** and **5.12**.

Financial instrument

Any contract that gives rise to a financial asset of one entity and a financial liability or equity instrument of another entity.

See **Chapter 3**, paragraph **3.4**.

Financial liability

Any liability that is:

(a) a contractual obligation:

(i) to deliver cash or another financial asset to another entity; or

(ii) to exchange financial assets or financial liabilities with another entity under conditions that are potentially unfavourable to the entity; or

(b) a contract that will or may be settled in the entity's own equity instruments and is:

(i) a non-derivative for which the entity is or may be obliged to deliver a variable number of the entity's own equity instruments; or

| | |
|---|---|
| | (ii) a derivative that will or may be settled other than by the exchange of a fixed amount of cash or another financial asset for a fixed number of the entity's own equity instruments. For this purpose the entity's own equity instruments do not include instruments that are themselves contracts for the future receipt or delivery of the entity's own equity instruments.<br>See **Chapter 3**, paragraph **3.4**. |
| Firm commitment | A binding agreement for the exchange of a specified quantity of resources at a specified price on a specified future date or dates.<br>See **Chapter 12**, paragraph **12.60**. |
| Forecast transaction | An uncommitted but anticipated future transaction.<br>See **Chapter 12**, paragraph **12.60**. |
| Forward (or futures) contract | A contract that gives the parties an obligation to buy or sell an underlying instrument or commodity at a predetermined price at a future date.<br>See **Chapter 3**, paragraph **3.26**. |
| FRS 4 | UK Accounting Standards Board Financial Reporting Standard No 4, 'Capital Instruments'. |
| FRS 5 | UK Accounting Standards Board Financial Reporting Standard No 5, 'Reporting the Substance of Transactions'. |
| FRS 13 | UK Accounting Standards Board Financial Reporting Standard No 13, 'Derivatives and Other Financial Instruments: Disclosures'. |
| GAAP | Generally Accepted Accounting Principles. |
| Hedge effectiveness | The degree to which changes in the fair value or cash flows of the hedged item that are attributable to a hedged risk are offset by changes in the fair value or cash flows of the hedging instrument.<br>See **Chapter 12**, paragraph **12.85**. |
| Hedged item | An asset, liability, firm commitment, highly probably forecast transaction or net investment in a foreign operation that: |

|                          |                                                                                                                                                                                                                                                          |
|--------------------------|----------------------------------------------------------------------------------------------------------------------------------------------------------------------------------------------------------------------------------------------------------|
|                          | (a)  exposes the entity to risk of changes in fair value or future cash flows; and                                                                                                                                                                        |
|                          | (b)  is designated as being hedged.                                                                                                                                                                                                                       |
|                          | See **Chapter 12**, paragraph **12.57**.                                                                                                                                                                                                                   |
| Hedging instrument       | A designated derivative or (for a hedge of the risk of changes in foreign currency exchange rates only) a designated non-derivative financial asset or non-derivative financial liability whose fair value or cash flows are expected to offset changes in the fair value or cash flows of a designated hedged item. |
|                          | See **Chapter 12**, paragraph **12.72**.                                                                                                                                                                                                                   |
| Hedging relationship     | A relationship established by an entity's management between a hedged item and a hedging item.                                                                                                                                                            |
|                          | See **Chapter 12**, paragraph **12.50**.                                                                                                                                                                                                                   |
| Held-to-maturity investments | Non-derivative financial assets with fixed or determinable payments and fixed maturity that an entity has the positive intention and ability to hold to maturity ... other than:                                                                    |
|                          | (a)  those that the entity upon initial recognition designates as at fair value through profit or loss;                                                                                                                                                   |
|                          | (b)  those that the entity designates as available for sale; and                                                                                                                                                                                          |
|                          | (c)  those that meet the definition of loans and receivables.                                                                                                                                                                                             |
|                          | See **Chapter 5**, paragraph **5.17**.                                                                                                                                                                                                                     |
| IAS                      | International Accounting Standard.                                                                                                                                                                                                                        |
| IAS 1                    | International Accounting Standard No 1, 'Presentation of Financial Statements'.                                                                                                                                                                           |
| IAS 21                   | International Accounting Standard No 21, 'The Effects of Changes in Foreign Exchange Rates'.                                                                                                                                                              |
| IAS 30                   | International Accounting Standard No 30, 'Disclosures in the Financial Statements of Banks and Similar Financial Institutions'.                                                                                                                           |
| IAS 32                   | International Accounting Standard No 32, 'Financial Instruments: Disclosure and Presentation'.                                                                                                                                                            |
| IAS 39                   | International Accounting Standard No 39, 'Financial Instruments: Recognition and Measurement'.                                                                                                                                                            |
| IASB                     | International Accounting Standards Board.                                                                                                                                                                                                                 |

| IASC | International Accounting Standards Committee. |
|------|----------------------------------------------|
| IFRIC | International Financial Reporting Interpretations Committee (the interpretations committee of the IASB). |
| IFRS | International Financial Reporting Standards. A generic term incorporating both the standards originally issued by the IASC (IAS 1, 2, etc) and those issued by the IASB (IFRS 1, 2, etc). |
| IFRS 1 | International Financial Reporting Standard 1, 'First-time Adoption of International Financial Reporting Standards'. |
| Loans and receivables | Non-derivative financial assets with fixed or determinable payments that are not quoted in an active market, other than: |

(a) those that the entity intends to sell immediately or in the near term, which shall be classified as held for trading, and those that the entity upon initial recognition designates as at fair value through profit or loss;

(b) those that the entity upon initial recognition designates as available for sale; or

(c) those for which the holder may not recover substantially all of its initial investment, other than because of credit deterioration, which shall be classified as available for sale.

See **Chapter 5**, paragraph **5.33**.

| Option contract | A contract that provides the right, but not the obligation, to buy or sell an underlying instrument or commodity at a predetermined price. See **Chapter 3**, paragraph **3.20**. |
|------|------|
| Swap contract | A contract in which the parties agree to exchange future cash flows calculated by reference to different underlying instruments or commodities. See **Chapter 3**, paragraph **3.28**. |
| UK GAAP | Generally accepted accounting principles in the United Kingdom. |
| US GAAP | Generally accepted accounting principles in the United States. |

# Index